THE EUROPEAN

GAME

THE SECRETS OF
EUROPEAN FOOTBALL SUCCESS

DANIEL FIELDSEND

First published in 2017 by

ARENA SPORT
An imprint of Birlinn Limited
West Newington House
10 Newington Road
Edinburgh
EH9 1QS

www.arenasportbooks.co.uk

ISBN: 9781909715486
eBook ISBN: 9780857903464

British Library Cataloguing-in-Publication Data
A catalogue record for this book is available on request from the British Library.

Designed and typeset by Polaris Publishing, Edinburgh

Printed and bound by MBM Print SCS Ltd, Glasgow

MIX
Paper from
responsible sources
FSC
www.fsc.org   FSC® C117931

For Mum and Dad

'A Golden Sky'

Order of
Contents

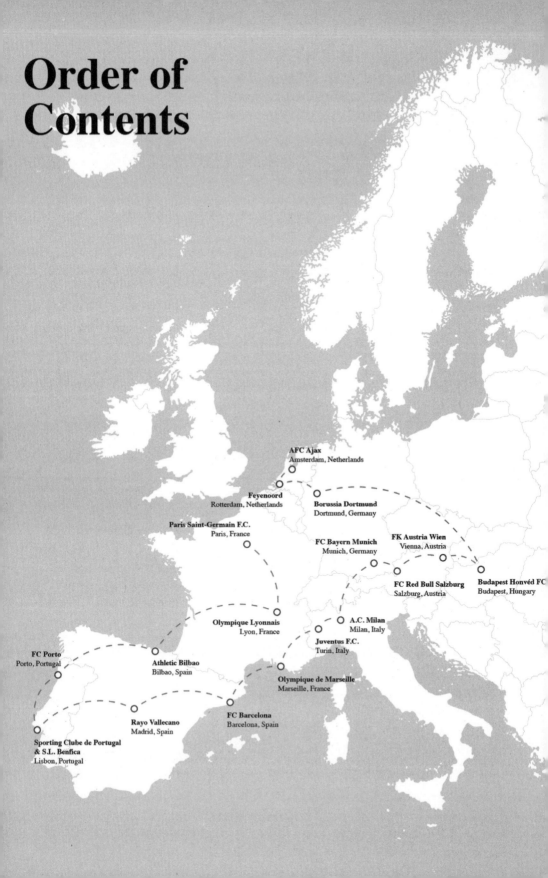

AFC Ajax
Amsterdam, Netherlands

Feyenoord
Rotterdam, Netherlands

Borussia Dortmund
Dortmund, Germany

Paris Saint-Germain F.C.
Paris, France

FC Bayern Munich
Munich, Germany

FK Austria Wien
Vienna, Austria

FC Red Bull Salzburg
Salzburg, Austria

Budapest Honvéd FC
Budapest, Hungary

Olympique Lyonnais
Lyon, France

A.C. Milan
Milan, Italy

Juventus F.C.
Turin, Italy

FC Porto
Porto, Portugal

Athletic Bilbao
Bilbao, Spain

Olympique de Marseille
Marseille, France

Rayo Vallecano
Madrid, Spain

FC Barcelona
Barcelona, Spain

Sporting Clube de Portugal
& S.L. Benfica
Lisbon, Portugal

CONTENTS

AUTHOR'S NOTE

There was a time when football in Europe retained a degree of mystery. Sunny days of *Calcio*, when Edgar Davids at Juventus and Ronaldo at Inter Milan could enchant a generation of potential Europhiles. To watch them was enthralling, made so by the elusiveness of regular footage. That aura would be punctured over time in a globalised age, as society binged on visual consumption, stripping naked the once alluring football enigma. My generation saw the sun set on mystery, leaving an enduring nostalgia for football on the continent, for names like Barcelona, Bayern Munich and Ajax and what they used to represent.

As I later came to work in football, I was able to carve myself an opportunity to visit those clubs (and others), sending hundreds of emails over the course of many months, plotting a route through the continent based on the replies received. My intention was to discover whether or not such clubs retained the cultural uniqueness that brought them fame, or had an age of hyper-communication merged them all into a sad amalgamation of sameness?

I didn't intend to write a book on the matter, but thought only of having an adventure – a personal indulgence. Yet because of the standard and abundance of my findings, I asked staff if they minded me compiling their methods officially. They did not, and in fact seemed quite favourable toward the idea. I had, whilst there, asked them questions that I was personally interested in. Upon returning and reading back through transcripts it became apparent that *The European Game* could be divided into three areas.

Firstly, the book explores the roles of staff in football, from owners and managers to scouts and agents. Staff working in such capacities, secondly, explain the methods used that make them, and indeed their clubs, successful. Thirdly, it is a profile of the clubs I visited and the components that make them special. The reader is able to flick between chapters in whatever order he or she wishes, from Milan to Amsterdam, but I recommend following the journey in sequence. In covering three specific areas I hope that the diversity of the project makes it unique. Laced within each chapter are mini segments of findings: about travel, about society, about identity and attachment. I have written on fandom, tactics, coaching, scouting, politics, finance, leadership and everyday European life.

On a train somewhere in the middle of France, I began reading a coffee-stained free magazine stuffed into the pouch of the chair in front. Most of it was in French, of course, but I persisted to scan through the pretty pictures and strange advertisements to fight the clutches of boredom. In amongst the alien words, strangely, was an English language article. It was about a woman's experiences travelling and how the places she visited, the actual environments, shaped the belief system of the people there, and vice versa. Psychogeography was the term she referenced, 'the study of mutual influences between people and place'. I liked the idea and retained it, later redefining it to suit a football perspective. It features in most chapters, as I found there to be an obvious relationship between the success of a club and its association with the environment around it. In Bilbao, as you will read, Athletic teach youngsters about the oppressed history of the region in school to inspire pride. At Feyenoord, they align players with the grit of local Rotterdammers, training them in rain and hail. All clubs should look inwards to their local environment and find what makes them culturally unique, harnessing this to retain identity.

Finally, let me explain my method. To meet and spend time at clubs was essential for a studied insight. I could have written parts of this book from home once I decided upon my intentions, but to quote da Vinci, 'Experience has been the mistress of whoever has written well.' Only through having been there am I able to describe everything in full.

You must also allow me to indulge in the romantics of my chosen form of travel. To fly from place to place would have been to cheat. Only rail travel – past mountains and countryside – offers aesthetic pleasure for hours on end. Beyond the lazy vineyards of Bordeaux, the gritty terrain of northern Spain and the reflected blue Mediterranean was inspiration. I tried to capture that when possible. Flying takes you from one generic glass and metal complex to another – everything in between is missed. On the train, I saw great countries change.

I hope you enjoy this book. There is a passion for football compounded in these pages that I know you share. Thank you for being a part of this project.

Dan Fieldsend, February 2017

Postscript: The notion of a European Game book far predates Brexit. Not including British clubs isn't a political statement, it's a niche.

Footnote: Throughout the book I have referred to clubs as 'them' rather than 'it'. I believe that a club is a society of people, rather than an institution, and therefore deserves the warmth of personification. For example, 'Juventus are magnificent' instead of 'Juventus is magnificent'.

Disclaimer: Views expressed in chapters from staff members are, for the most part, personal theories, opinions, ideas and ways of working that, while contributing to the effectiveness and success of a club, are not representative of that institution on the whole. For example, some staff members have since moved on to new clubs and take their beliefs with them. Nevertheless, the clubs in each chapter offer themselves as a fantastic backdrop for us to explore ways in which the modern game works.

ONE

CREATING A SUPER-CLUB: SOCCERNOMICS IN PARIS

After a day spent at each end of the Eurostar, the similarities between London and Paris become apparent. There are, it seems, two faces to each city. There's one that tourists see, with cathedrals, landmarks and museums, and then there's the cultured yet economically deprived periphery where most people live. Those well-dressed, well-spoken people inside, who create the hustle of both capitals, caught up in that fiercely competitive quest for prosperity, differ little in their mien. They are quiet and well-mannered, softly courteous. On the metro inside Paris' Périphérique, much like London's underground, conversation is recherché. Yet what is exceptional about Paris as a city is its insistence upon presenting new arrangements of fine architecture at the exit of every station. There can be nowhere in the world that decorates itself as thoughtfully. The invisible constant that Lawrence Durrell speaks of as 'a tenderness of good living' can be felt in the sights and sounds. It is the only city sensitive enough to treasure art's many forms, with ambitious young men determined to see their street paintings one day hanging in the Louvre. At long last, thankfully, for this fine metropolis, there is a football team romancing locals with worthy displays.

It has not always been like this, though. At one time the Paris Saint-Germain emblem was too shameful, without a weight of sophistication, undeserving of the gift shops of Paris. The club began to tilt in the favour of Parisian society when the world-famous Swede Ibrahimović (the footballer is known as 'Ibra', the caricature as 'Zlatan') arrived from Milan. Wearing a crystal white shirt, smiling in front of the Eiffel Tower, PSG jersey in hand, surrounded by an adoring public, this was the standout image of a football club reborn. 'It is a dream come true,' he said at the time, before admitting: 'I don't know much about the French league.'

Nor should he. When Ibra was presented at Camp Nou in front of 55,000 hopeful Barcelona fans back in 2009, the French first division (Ligue 1) was in a state of decline. That season, PSG averaged 33,266 fans, Lyon 34,767 and AS Monaco, with its seemingly uninterested fanbase, 7,894. Fast forward eight seasons and Ibrahimović came to France, brought commercial investors, upped levels of curiosity and departed. He left in his wake a great rippling of interest. In 2016, PSG averaged 44,433 fans (a 33.5% increase brought on by five league title wins), Lyon 38,113 (a 9.6% increase that would be higher were it not for the location of their new stadium outside city boundaries) and AS Monaco 9,752 (a 23.5% increase, impressive for the champagne south-coasters).

PSG and Ligue 1's rise was mostly thanks to money from the Persian Gulf, which coincided with a gentrification of image and spectators. Throughout much of its history, the state of Qatar, a desert country in the Arabian Peninsula, relied on pearl hunting and the exportation of gems for a steady economy. The country regarded later as a financial power had its genesis in 1971 when the world's largest natural gas field, the North Dome Gas-Condensate, was discovered off its coast. Yet for all Qatar's economic potential, the ruling Sheikh Khalifa bin Hamad Al Thani was unable to capitalise. He was dislodged from his rule in a bloodless *coup d'état* by his son, Hamad bin Khalifa Al Thani, and other members of the family in 1995 whilst out of the country in Geneva.

Sheikh Hamad (for short) transformed Qatar between 1995 and 2013, from naturally blessed yet underachieving desert land, into the largest financial exporters of oil and gas post-millennium. No longer would they rely on pearl fishing. One of his first moves was to fast-track the development of the North Dome field. The country's GDP skyrocketed and Qatar amassed a sovereign wealth of $170 billion. Smartly, Sheikh

Hamad treated income from natural resources as a hedge fund of sorts. He founded the Qatar Investment Authority in 2003 and purchased Western institutions like Harrods, Porsche and Volkswagen. If the well were to dry, so to speak, the money would be safe.

His son, Sheikh Tamim, was educated at Harrow School in England. Whilst there, the young sheikh witnessed the influence of football on Western culture and grew to admire the sport. Qatar Investment Authority set up a sporting branch in 2005, Qatar Sports Investments (QSi), to be managed by Sheikh Tamim's close friend Nasser Al-Khelaifi. In 2011, coherent to their strategy of permeating Western consciousness, QSi spent €70 million to buy the young but troubled football club Paris Saint-Germain.

At the time of the purchase, PSG were in a raging inferno. 'Fans' faux pas ensures that PSG lose even when they manage to win' was a *Guardian* headline as early as 2008, as the club sat 19th in Ligue 1.[1] Supporters had unfurled a derogatory banner against Lens in the French League Cup final, calling the northern *Ch'tis* inbred paedophiles, inciting national outrage. But there's a reason why, during a lunch meeting in 2011 with Michel Platini and President Sarkozy, Qatari representatives decided to invest in PSG. They were the only major club in a city of 12 million inhabitants. What did it matter that the fans had a violent element and attendances were declining? This was Paris, the elegant, spiritual capital of Europe. Home of the bourgeois; art, fashion, food and good living. Its centrality and famous landmarks drew more tourists than anywhere else in the world. Plus, this was modern football; local fan dependency was no longer a thing. The Qatari government had a business plan to monopolise Western institutes and, as PSG-supporting Sarkozy most likely pitched, owning the Paris club would be a continuation of that. Sheikh Tamim and Nasser Al-Khelaifi liked the project – PSG in many ways were similar to the Qatar they grew up in during the 1980s – a miniature sleeping giant – and decided they would fund PSG to make them a 'super-club' no matter the cost. 'Revenues generated from ventures are to be reinvested into Qatar,' the QSi website rationalised. [ii]

---

1. Andrews, M (2015). 'Being Special: The Rise of Super Clubs in European Football.' *Working Papers – Harvard*. 229 (1), 2–43.

Super-club Domination

A Harvard University paper by Matt Andrews written in 2015 likened super-clubs to multinational or transnational corporations. It defined them as having, 'Much higher revenues than average clubs, [potential to] win many more games and titles, and greater likelihood to contribute positively to their economies.' The current super-clubs are (excluding English examples): Real Madrid (with €620.1m revenue in 2016 – *Deloitte*), Barcelona (€620.2m), Bayern Munich (€592m), Paris Saint-Germain (€520.9m), and Juventus (€341.1m). They are defined as such because of their mass revenue and ability to monopolise wealth domestically. Juventus, for example, earned €159m more than second-placed Napoli in 2016, and Bayern Munich some €194m more than Dortmund.

The most ominous aspect of super-club rule is their grip on success, strengthened with every passing season. 'Successful clubs earn more from TV revenue which, in turn, allows them to acquire and retain better players and that enables them to continue to be successful,'[iii] wrote Gab Marcotti for ESPN on the perpetual cycle. PSG and Bayern won four consecutive league titles in France and Germany respectively from 2012 to 2016, and Juventus five consecutive titles in Italy. In Spain's La Liga, having overtaken Italy's Serie A as the home of superstar footballers, Barcelona and Real Madrid shared 25 of the 30 league titles won between 1986 and 2016.

Historically, as the Harvard paper explained, super-clubs built up a brand over many years. Their success came from identifying investors and offering them new products through advertisement and media campaigns. As society evolved, super-clubs recognised the shift from local dependency and ticket sales towards internationalisation, much earlier than their rivals did. Manchester United, for example, noticed commercialisation in football, or at least capitalised on it, before Liverpool. As did Bayern Munich before Dortmund and Real Madrid before Valencia. New forms of finance were available and they pushed their history to attract sponsors, television deals and new fans.[iv]

But that crop of super-clubs (Bayern, Juventus, Real Madrid and Barcelona) all had a history to push. Their status was founded on years of success. Take Bayern Munich. Following the Second World War and the creation of communist East Germany, big businesses like Siemens moved to Munich.

Before the Bundesliga came to be in 1963, Audi and BMW had moved to the city and its population swelled. Such companies chose to invest in FC Bayern and not city rivals 1860 München because of the domestic successes achieved in the 1970s. In a parallel universe, 1860 could be a super-club rather than Bayern, had they convinced Gerd Müller (from TSV Nördlingen) and Franz Beckenbauer (from Giesing) to join them instead of their city rivals (Beckenbauer was slapped in the face when playing against 1860 as a boy and thus chose to play for Bayern when he was old enough to do so).

Bayern moved into the 70,000-capacity Olympic Stadium in 1972 and were represented by the German company Adidas in 1974. They have, since, maintained their position as the richest club in Germany, later joining a band of equally ambitious super-clubs on the continent. Similarly, the Harvard paper acknowledged how success coupled with early internationalisation at Real Madrid and Barcelona provided foundations for their brand promotion and subsequent super-club status, citing Alfredo di Stéfano's arrival from Colombia in 1953 and Johan Cruyff's from the Netherlands in 1973 as examples. 'Real Madrid is legendary for building on similar blends of historical legacy and brand identity, dating back to the nationalist identity with Franco's Spain,' it writes.

Joining the Party

However, thanks to developments in globalisation and instant degrees of communication, a club does not necessarily need a rich history of domestic success to become 'super'. PSG are living proof of that. 'The world is now instantaneous, digital. It took 50 years to make Real Madrid into a great world club. Now it can be done in five years,' club *directeur général* Jean-Claude Blanc told Simon Kuper of the *Financial Times.* [v]

During my visit to Paris, PSG showed me a report presented usually to potential commercial investors. It is subtle, yet between the rather boastful paragraphs praising recent successes, one can analyse where PSG and QSi felt key areas of investment were. By that I mean areas they chose to focus on in order to propel the club from incompetence to super-club significance. From eternally underwhelming capital club, the coming together of Paris FC and Stade Saint-Germain in 1970, with a hooligan problem and no money, to becoming one of the richest and most sponsored teams in world football, PSG have evolved like no club before. They have done so, according to the report, by: developing club facilities; prioritising academy development; creating a favourable style of play; harnessing the power of media; and investing in famous players.

Step 1: Facilities

At one time, Parisian socialites wouldn't dream of being seen at *le football.* But with the gentrification of traditional, often unruly, fans and the increased presence of celebrities (Kendall Jenner, Gigi Hadid, Rihanna, Jay Z and Beyonce), Parc des Princes stadium replaced Théâtre de la Ville as vogue. 'Dream Bigger' read the sign outside the player entrance on the afternoon of my arrival, written in perfect English, the consumerist tongue. Below it, where fans at one time mingled, ran a red carpet and velvet rope. PSG, by all appearances, had made their dreams reality.

Cédric is a student from Paris and a lifelong PSG supporter. We met outside Parc des Princes, a grey cinderblock structure built over highway A13, on an overcast February day. Construction workers circled the complex in yellow hard hats, their conversations inaudible over drilling noise. 'They're beautifying the stadium for the European Championships!' Cédric shouted.

A stadium is the face a club wishes to present of itself. Parc des Princes stands between the two Parises; close enough to the 2 million well-to-do living inside the ring road, and the 10 million less-well-off people on the outskirts. Photos of 'club legends' (depending on perception) were screwed into the stadium, much to the annoyance of Cédric. 'There are more pictures of Beckham than of real legends like Raï or Pauleta.' There were in actuality four images of David Beckham, taken during his five-month stint at PSG (in which time he made ten league appearances), in contrast to two of Pauleta, PSG's one-time record goalscorer, and one of Raï.

What Cédric deplored was, he felt, an attempt by the club to forget their history. Beckham's presence enticed celebrities, businessmen, clients and wealthy socialites to Parc des Princes, which in turn transformed to accommodate them. 'Paris Saint-Germain's hospitality programme has also attracted a considerable number of corporate clients,' their report confirmed. 'They have been drawn to the exceptional collection of fourteen luxury suites at the Parc des Princes and the range of premium services on offer.' Revenue from the hospitality programme increased six-fold between 2011 and 2016, reaching Euros 24.6 million.

'Thanks to an increased amount of VIP seating, the reorganisation of the Parc, the improvement of refreshment areas and the creation of new products, Paris Saint-Germain has put in place one of the most competitive ticketing policies in world football,' they wrote. Competitive pricing at PSG, however, became more adherent to theatre rates than football, Cédric moaned. Average season ticket costs rose from €460 in 2011 to €938 in 2015, hence the gentrification of fans and the subsequent attractiveness of the club to the middle classes. 'Paris Saint-Germain now possesses a stadium which measures up to its ambitions,' the report concludes.

Harvard University wrote that super-clubs would create new products to retain their status as elite. PSG, in accordance to that rule, created a concierge service with American Express. 'This partnership is in line with our strategy, initiated three years ago, to reposition the club as a premium brand,' said commercial director Frédéric Longuépée. Clients are chauffeured around *le Gai Paree*, taken to a Champions League game and then invited to party with the players afterwards. 'We represent Paris, France and Qatar,' Ibrahimović explained – the boy from a ghetto in Malmö.

Step 2: Academy
Barcelona and Bayern Munich won Champions Leagues in 2013 and 2015 with a clear vision of how to play the game, allowing for young footballers to transition into their squads with greater ease. Barcelona had seven home-grown players in their full squad, while Bayern started four. A historic allegation attached to Paris Saint-Germain is that they were always blind to the local talent under their nose. 'The best player who came through has been [Mamadou] Sakho. He was our captain at 18 and could have been our [Paolo] Maldini, but we sold him,' Cédric later told me on our train journey to Lyon. PSG were playing OL that weekend and we had tickets.

'We have been blasé with local players; our academy never used to be good but it is getting better now.' In 2015, the winner of the Golden Boy award – a trophy given to European football's best under-21-year-old player – was Anthony Martial, a striker raised in Paris but signed by Lyon. Kingsley Coman, another Parisian talent allowed to leave PSG, was the runner-up.

Other such stars from a wider Paris region who PSG overlooked are: Riyad Mahrez, Lassana Diarra, N'Golo Kanté, Abou Diaby, Patrice Evra, Hatem Ben Arfa and the world's most expensive footballer, Paul Pogba. Even Didier Drogba spent his formative years living in the city but was not signed by PSG.

Whilst it can be argued that some talent is quiet, requiring years to announce itself, as was the case with Drogba, Kanté and Mahrez who needed time to slowly develop, other talent screams from an early age. Thierry Henry and David Trezeguet were examples of that. By 20, they were World Cup winners with France, and European Championship winners at 22. Both were overlooked by PSG as youth players despite living in the suburbs of the city.

Trezeguet was born in France but raised in Buenos Aires. When he moved to Paris in 1995 he went on trial with PSG and asked for an apartment for his family to move in to. The club refused. Consequently, he joined AS Monaco, where he would form a partnership with fellow exile, Henry. 'My dream was Paris! During the test training, Luis Fernandez told me, "David, you're going to stay here." The only thing I wanted in the contract was an apartment for my family. It was supposedly agreed, but ultimately my requests were not accepted. Two days later, I was forced to leave Paris.' [vi]

The outskirts of which are a hotbed. Whilst PSG may have historically failed to recognise this, other clubs have not. Around 25% of French professional footballers come from the suburbs. An amateur club in western Paris, CO Les Unis, tends to capitalise on the negligence of PSG, despite being in the sixth tier of French football. They attracted and developed Patrice Evra, Yaya Sanogo and Thierry Henry before professional academies took them elsewhere. Anthony Martial was also at Les Unis and the club received £270,000 when he joined Manchester United.

'Paris Saint-Germain were complacent with their academy in the past and allowed Anelka to leave, whilst Henry and Evra slipped through the net,' said Jonathan Johnson of ESPN and beIN over dinner. 'Trezeguet was also desperate to sign for PSG but the club did not appreciate youth at the time. Now they have learnt from that, and although they have lost Kingsley Coman, they have fought tooth and nail to keep Adrien Rabiot at the club. They want to offer long-term contracts to youth players early and are desperate to retain Presnel Kimpembe.'

The report describes progress made at youth level with pride: 'The Paris Saint-Germain Youth Academy is committed to passing on the club's philosophy and values of possession-based football.' With their resource potential, PSG always had the capability to have the best academy in the world; QSi helped them realise that.

Step 3: Style of Play

Amid the big-name celebrity footballers signed from abroad, PSG invested in a young talent from little Pescara, in Italy's second league, and immediately looked to promote him as the poster boy of their 'style'. 'Marco Verratti, at the heart of the Parisian midfield, was once again the anchor of the team's possession-based philosophy. The young Italian emerged as one of the best midfielders in Europe, dominating national statistics with an average of 102.8 balls played per match, and 86.2 completed passes,' the report proudly declares. That 'possession-based philosophy' PSG wished to create, Cédric felt, was part of the reason Laurent Blanc was dismissed in favour of the Spaniard Unai Emery: he failed to create a style of play worthy of regard.

Success for QSi, already blessed with riches, is how they are perceived by society. They long for PSG to be a patron of the arts, worthy of Paris, which is why losing once more to Barcelona in 2017 – they being the club at football's mountaintop whom QSi also sponsor – was particularly painful. It was not the result that most displeased Parisians (a 6–1 capitulation that followed a propitious 4–0 home win), but more the shades of mediocrity that coloured the performance. Even when they won in Paris, Barça had controlled the ball in front of sponsors and VIPs, totting up 57% possession, playing how a big club should; how PSG believed they could. 'Everyone is annoyed,' said Nasser al-Khelaifi after the subsequent 6–1 loss, when Barcelona managed 71% of the ball.

Although possession football does not always necessarily deliver success, it does retain a perception of elitism. It is a proactive way of approaching games that separates big clubs from smaller ones; those who take the game to the opponent from those who react to their strengths. As Arrigo Sacchi said: 'Great teams all have the same characteristic of wanting to control the pitch and the ball.' The style PSG long to develop is one that controls the ball and therefore the outcome of the game. Because of that, former

Barcelona coach Carles Romagosa was recruited as technical director to assist in developing that way of playing.

Fundamentally, for possession football to be successful, the club decided after the Barça loss, players within the team structure needed to have better decision-making at all times. They had to know who to pass to, when, for what purpose, the weight of pass and the angle. They also had to see the bigger picture: to move the opponents in order to create space elsewhere to exploit.

Carles Romagosa, during his time at the University of Vic, worked to develop decision-making in athletes. 'With his colleagues, Carles Romagosa will implement the "Ekkono" method, a new training approach that highlights and improves the cognitive functions of the players,' wrote *Le Parisien* at the time of his hiring. The method is divided into four specific areas: the game, perception, questioning and concepts. For example, on the 'game', Romagosa explained it to be important to design exercises that follow football, so players are able to translate the content of the session into real life. In regards to questioning, the former Barça coach considers it essential to fabricate problems for players on and off the pitch, rather than providing them with solutions.

PSG's Camp des Loges academy, placed comfortably inside the national forest of Saint-Germain, next to Louis XIV's summer château, would implement a possession-based philosophy in the style of the marketable FC Barcelona. All youngsters in every age group would be trained to be confident on the ball, to play through the thirds with ease. In doing so, as Harvard's paper wrote, they would foster a more likeable image aligning with their super-club status.

Step 4: Media Control
Aldous Huxley, around the time he taught at Eton (with George Orwell one of his students), began to ponder the potential of media on civic consciousness. By the time of his passing in 1963, he'd become a great thinker on the topic. 'A society,' he wrote in *Brave New World*, 'most of whose members spend a great part of their time not on the spot, not here and now and in the calculable future, but somewhere else, in the irrelevant other worlds of sport and soap opera, of mythology and metaphysical

fantasy, will find it hard to resist the encroachments of those who would manipulate and control it.' [2]

Manipulating media to influence the decision-making and affection of sports fans, specifically football fans, that mass herd of people, would have been something of great interest to him were he alive today. By today, I mean this age of hyper-communication. Even Jean-Claude Blanc acknowledged how football is more free-flowing than ever before, with PSG able to achieve in five years what took Real Madrid 50. There is a 'sheeple' of some considerable numbers that wait quite impatiently for a team to support. Their affections are open to clubs, their location irrelevant. With the use of media, clubs are able to bypass locality and secure new fans in global horizons.

Professor Richard Giulianotti of Loughborough University is one of the leading academics specialising in the complex relationship between globalisation and football. His 2002 paper, titled 'Supporters, Followers, Fans, and Flâneurs: A Taxonomy of Spectator Identities in Football' is amongst the most insightful pieces of work written on the differences between fan types. In his paper, he introduced the well-to-do potential customers listed by elite football clubs as a campaign priority. Giulianotti broke the identity of the football 'spectator' into four different categories, describing the modes of interest each spectator type has in his or her desired club. The 'traditional' spectator has the deepest emotional investment in the football club, having a relationship resembling one that would be had with a family member. The second type of spectator is the 'follower' who is not defined by an emotional bond to a particular club but, instead, by keeping abreast of developments among clubs and football people in which he or she has a favourable interest. The third spectator type is the consumer 'fan'. Not generally localised to a football club, the 'fan' shows identification with a club and its players through the consumption of related products, authenticating his or her sense of belonging. The final form of spectator, and perhaps the most important, is the '*flâneur*'.

Described as being bourgeois and thus in pursuit of a multiplicity of football experiences, they are consumers from no set locality. Because of their resource potential, football clubs have provided them with an

---

2. Huxley, A (1946). *Brave New World*. New York: Harper & Bros.

increasingly welcoming shop window in which to gaze, thereby creating a quasi-community of cosmopolitans. 'The *flâneur* was a modern urban stroller: Male, typically in full adulthood, he would promenade through boulevards and markets. [They] adopt a detached relationship to football clubs, even favoured ones. A true football *flâneur* belongs only to a virtual community of strollers who window-shop around clubs.' [3]

Fittingly, the *flâneur* was a title given to the time-wasting window-gazers of Paris's streets in the 19th century. The inner circle of the city was a coalescence of wealthy socialites, their individuality combining to create a community of mutual self-interest. For the longest time, the *flâneurs* of Paris, whose greatest ambition was to be seen in the crowd, found football most unfashionable. Men and women of standing should go to Théâtre de la Ville or Palais Garnier Opéra, not the football game, where the hooligans from the outskirts met to fight. The Qatari takeover of PSG coincided with mass bans for known hooligans, allowing the club to transform itself to welcome both the wealthy inner community of Paris and people of financial clout globally.

'As one of the top ten clubs in world football, the Paris Saint-Germain brand enjoys global standing. This is due, first and foremost, to its extensive media coverage abroad – international broadcasting accounts for 70% of the club's overall television viewership,' so the report proclaims. Around 2.8 million people watched PSG play FC Barcelona in 2013. After the match, PSG manager Carlo Ancelotti faced questions from the press asking whether he played David Beckham (mostly unused that season) rather than the teenage Marco Verratti because of the global commercial significance attached to the fixture. He denied that Qatar had any influence on his decision-making.

The report declares: '[Our] official website (www.psg.fr) is now available in eight languages and continues to attract more and more fans. This season, it clocked up over 30 million sessions, with more than a third of them coming from abroad.' The minds of young *flâneurs* in Asia and the Americas can be subjugated by super-clubs like PSG, especially as they place such emphasis on targeting and welcoming them.

---

3. Giulianotti, R (2002). 'Supporters, Followers, Fans, and Flâneurs: A Taxonomy of Spectator Identities in Football'. *Journal of Sport and Social Issues*. 26 (1), 25–46.

Step 5: Investment in Talent

Yet even with a strong media presence, improved stadium and an excellent academy, PSG would not be a super-club. The catalyst for their modern status was an investment in high profile football names – both players and staff. At the front of their stadium, above the red carpet, mixed in with the words 'Dream Bigger', are gargantuan images of PSG's star players. They, more than anything else, define this modern giant. There is Ángel Di María, Thiago Silva and Edinson Cavani in blue and red. In the beginning, there was also David Beckham and Zlatan Ibrahimović. From May 2011 to August 2016, PSG spent £509,480,000 on players in a bid to announce themselves. Their nearest rivals Olympique Lyon in that same period of time invested only £58m on transfers (some £451m less). To emphasise PSG's excessiveness from a continental perspective, another club seeking to become 'super', Borussia Dortmund, spent £219m on transfers in that period but received £179m in sales. [4]

Cédric is a season-ticket holder – one of the lucky 'traditional' few remaining – and laments the club's gross spending as needless: 'They [the Qatari investors] were spending money as if to say "look at us, we mean business", but there were other players going for cheap, like [Philippe] Coutinho who went to England and even [Carlos] Tévez.' He is referring to two deals in particular. In the same window that Lucas Moura was signed for £30m, Philippe Coutinho joined Liverpool for £9m. Likewise, the handsome (marketable) Edinson Cavani cost PSG £48m, while Argentine international Carlos Tévez, a similar player in many respects, joined Juventus for £6.75m, twice winning Serie A player of the year. Transfers are easy to highlight in retrospect, but Cédric mostly bemoans the big-spending reputation that fans have had to shoulder since. 'We never trusted Ibrahimović, you know? We wanted to keep Kévin Gameiro instead.'

PSG and Soccernomics

So structured is football's hierarchy of wealth, even anomalous successes like Leicester City, who manage to win prestigious competitions from an inferior

---

4. All finances throughout the book taken from the reliable transfermarkt.com (unless specified otherwise).

position, struggle to retain talented players once super-clubs come calling. Simon Kuper, *Financial Times* writer and author of *Football Against the Enemy* and *Soccernomics*, predicted their struggles in February 2016, months before they had even won the Premier League. 'Their best players will be bought by the rich clubs and things will even out. They may drastically improve their future, but in terms of doing a Nottingham Forest and maintaining success?' he shrugged. 'They will fade, but perhaps not right now.' Local boy N'Golo Kanté later proved Simon right, signing for Chelsea FC.

We had met for breakfast at Café Funambules that autumn morning. Scooters zoomed past on the grey *Rue* behind as Simon stirred his coffee between questions. As a long-time Parisian resident, he agreed to discuss the evolutions in football locally since his book *Soccernomics* came out in 2009. 'You had this area of 12 million inhabitants and one bad club that never qualified for the Champions League or UEFA Cup. And if you compare that to London which has 8 million people and six quite good clubs, there was a big gap. When the Qataris came with their money they thought straight away they would get top players. The first season they only got [Javier] Pastore. Then Milan began falling apart and they signed Ibrahimović and Thiago Silva, that was when the project took off.'

Soccernomics can be used as an aid when scrutinising some of PSG's early decisions in the transfer market. In the opening few chapters of the book, Kuper and his co-author, Stefan Szynanski, identify four universal inefficiencies in the transfer market; errors that are continuously made by elite clubs. More than individual mistakes, these are 'deviations from rationality' and all relate to PSG in some form or another:

1. A new manager wastes money

'Typically, the new manager wants to put his mark on his new side. So he buys his own players. He then has to "clear out" some of his predecessor's purchases, usually at a discount.'

It was not the manager, but director of football Leonardo who QSi gave the money to at first. 'He's the one who is going to develop the club,' Nasser Al-Khelaifi told the media.[vii] Blaise Matuidi (€8m) would be a fine replacement for the 38-year-old Claude Makélélé, while winger Jérémy Ménez (€8m) looked well-suited to fill Ludovic Giuly's role. Kévin Gameiro (€11m) had scored 22 goals the previous year, but then there was Momo Sissoko (€7m), Diego Lugano (€3m), Milan Biševac (€3.2m) and Salvatore Sirigu (€3.9m) who all took a greater wage than any other player already in the squad. Javier Pastore (€42m) was the marquee signing to announce the club's arrival.

As per *Soccernomics,* findings, the transfer window would prove a failure for Leonardo and manager Antoine Kombouaré (one was sacked, the other resigned). Minnows Montpellier went on to win the league and new manager Carlo Ancelotti got rid of Biševac to Lyon (€2.7m), Sissoko on a free, Lugano to West Brom (free), Gameiro to Sevilla (€7m), and Ménez to AC Milan (free). An overall loss of over €22m.

2. Stars of recent World Cups or European Championships are overvalued

'The worst time to sign a player is in the summer when he's just done well at a big tournament. Everyone in the transfer market has seen how good he is.'

It is more symptomatic of the climate of the market in general than of PSG, that all players are generally signed after one good run of form – especially as their performances are constantly visible. In a previous age, major tournaments such as the World Cup or European Championships were the only opportunity players had to be watched. But in a globalised age, player performance is analysed all year round and has consequently led to a greater degree of athlete transferring. Rather than appearing in a quadrennial tournament, a 'purple patch' can present itself elsewhere. An estimated 300 million people watched the Euro 2016 final, whereas some 380 million people watched the 2016 Champions League final. 'Stars' therefore can emerge in annual campaigns as well as four-year international tournaments.

The transfer market now aligns, according to Rupert Fryer, with Dr Laurence J. Peter's business theory: 'The Peter Principle'. 'Everyone in an organisation keeps on getting promoted until they reach their level of incompetence. At that point they stop being promoted.' [viii] In other words, it is about a player finding his level. More than a reflection of the ambition of the athlete, it is the fault of the club that footballers are signed following a rich vein of form. In a desire to be ahead of the pack, big clubs try to sign players as soon as the purple patch begins. Rivals of the same stature compete for the player's signature and consequently overvalue him. Barcelona and Manchester United's presence drove PSG's bid for Marquinhos up to £26.69m, as did Juventus's with Marco Verratti and Arsenal's with Yohan Cabaye (the latter being a fine example of Peter Principle incompetency; signed for £21m after a good year with Newcastle but sold for £10m one season later). 'I was at a big club but just to be on the bench for me [was] frustrating,' he later told *The Telegraph*. [ix]

3. Certain nationalities are overvalued

'The most fashionable nationality of them all in the transfer market is Brazilian.'

Following the takeover, QSi appointed the Brazilian Leonardo as director of football, taking him from Inter Milan. He left in 2013, but by then the process had begun. As of 2015, PSG had spent over £137m on seven Brazilians. To create a marketable product, PSG needed exciting players, with Brazilians historically regarded as being the most flamboyant and attractive, from Pelé through to Ronaldo. As Simon wrote in *Soccernomics*, 'The nationality expresses an authority, an innate vocation for the job – whatever the natural ability.'

Thiago Silva became the most expensive defender in history at £35m when he joined PSG, then Marquinhos from AS Roma became the most expensive teenage defender at £29m. 'I am delighted to be joining Paris Saint-Germain, a club where so many Brazilians have played and helped write the history,' the 19-year-old said upon signing. But the big-haired eccentric Brazilian defender David Luiz (with 26.6 million Facebook 'likes') took Silva's title as the most expensive defender ever, costing PSG £50m in 2014. He would later be sold back to Chelsea after two seasons for £34m, perhaps proving that the nationality, while attractive, can be overvalued.

4. Gentlemen prefer blonds

'Scouts look for players who "look" the part. Perhaps in soccer, blonds are thought to look more like superstars.'

The blondest, most notorious superstar in football is David Beckham. With his celebrity wife and famous blond children, Beckham is a global icon. The London School of Marketing value him at £508m. By signing him, PSG attempted to peacock themselves to fans outside of France (the Beckham name is a byword for marketability, especially in Asia and the Americas). Despite being the oldest player in Ligue 1 upon joining, he brought intangibles central to PSG's brand promotion campaign. 'He is smart enough to know that, with his profile, it could be that he is being pressed on to a manager for reasons other than football,' Carlo Ancelotti later said.

Prior to 2011, Beckham had little interest in PSG. He was bigger than they were. But after departing LA Galaxy the family were open to a move to cosmopolitan Paris. Wife Victoria was rooted to the local fashion industry, whilst son Brooklyn was able to join the PSG academy. So apparently one-sided was the Beckham–PSG relationship, he did not accept a wage, but instead offered his £170,000 per week to local charities (his wages accounted for only five per cent of his income as the world's richest footballer). Nevertheless, it was seemingly a business (more than a football) decision to sign the blond. The day after he played against Barcelona, *L'Equipe* gave him three marks out of ten for his performance, writing how midfield partner Blaise Matuidi had to "fight for the both of them."

*

Soccernomics Changing

Soccernomics acknowledges that provincial clubs historically achieved more success than capital cities (fascist dictatorships allowed Madrid and Lisbon to be exceptions). Liverpool and Manchester United, rather than Arsenal and Spurs, dominated English football from 1960–2005. In Germany, Bayern, Hamburg, Dortmund and Schalke remain more geared for success than Hertha

Berlin. The manufacturing cities of Milan and Turin have left Rome's clubs behind. The Hague (being the political capital of the Netherlands) has ADO in the Eredivisie, but they will never challenge Rotterdam and Eindhoven. Glasgow overwhelms Edinburgh's Hearts and Hibs, while PSG are only now seeking to catch up with the title hauls of Marseille and Saint-Étienne. What propelled these provincial cities to have successful clubs was the attachment and dependency of their communities in an age of industrial escapism.

When *Soccernomics* was first published in 2009, Chelsea were yet to win the Champions League, and PSG had not yet been purchased. Because of that Simon wrote: 'Londoners do not go around singing about their city, and they don't believe that a prize for Chelsea or Arsenal would enhance London's status. Football matters even less in Paris, where it's possible to spend a lifetime without knowing football exists. Paris Saint-Germain, whose ground is not entirely within the city's Périphérique ring road, are hardly going to become the main focus of Parisian pride.'

Over time this has gradually changed. In Paris, fake PSG shirts sell alongside the traditional berets in stalls outside the Louvre. While research by Visit Britain found that two in five tourists to the UK have sport on their holiday agenda. 'It took a long time for London clubs to create a tradition and history but they are getting there now,' Simon acknowledged.

In Paris, 59.9% of tourists cite 'seeing monuments and landmarks' as their agenda for visiting. Events are cited as the reason by 9.4%, with football falling several percentages lower in that ambiguous umbrella category. Given that the overwhelming majority of tourists visiting Paris are from the United States and China (countries where football is still developing) it is fair to say that PSG will never oust the landmarks of the city. Nevertheless, the club has grown. To prove this, PSG pointed me towards their report. In it, they praise a 165% increase in ticketing revenue in the five years since QSi took over, as well as the doubling of members to 10,000 and the rise in season-ticket holders to 37,000. Even if PSG are not the focus of Parisian pride, the people are now aware that they exist.

Bourgeoisification

There has been a shift in power in football, from the traditional provincial working-class areas that dominated Europe – Rotterdam, Glasgow, Liverpool,

Nottingham, Mönchengladbach, Eindhoven, Bruges, Birmingham – success has relocated to wealthier climates like London and Paris. PSG's rise is a symbol of that. For Simon, the transfer of power is more down to a bourgeoisification of football in general than a preference for capitals. Indeed, footballers are now choosing to ply their trade in lovelier surroundings. The French game has moved away from the glory days of mining towns Saint-Étienne and Lens, and of the port city of Marseille – three working-class areas – to an age of middle-class domination by Olympique Lyon and Paris Saint-Germain. 'You have the deindustrialisation that hit them places hard,' Simon told me. 'The north is very poor now. The wealthy regions of France are the more high-tech ones with greater services, like Lyon, Paris and Toulouse, who are excellent at rugby. There are larger sponsorship bases in these areas which is significant when TV deals are lower than they are in England. There's a dependency on fans to pay good money and they can do that more in these areas. Many years ago, football was successful in working-class areas but it is now more popular everywhere, so the rich cities do well.'

Since the millennium, football has been won by clubs from wealthy climates with middle-class populaces, such as Juventus of Turin; AC and Internazionale of Milan; Ajax of Amsterdam; Bayern of Munich; Lyon and Barcelona, with Porto and Sevilla also testing the water. When Gylfi Sigurðsson and Clint Dempsey chose Tottenham over Liverpool in 2012, it illustrated a preference for the metropolis. Wealthy investors would also much prefer to take over clubs in upper-class areas, so they may enter society there. Such was the case with Roman Abramovich, who bought Chelsea FC during lunch at The Dorchester with Ken Bates, having flown over Stamford Bridge in his helicopter weeks earlier. Gone are the days of local fan owners willing to run at a loss, found at Blackburn Rovers (Jack Walker) and Wolverhampton Wanderers (Jack Hayward). Often the most bourgeois part of a country is the capital. PSG, Chelsea, Arsenal, Real Madrid and Atlético have won 68 trophies since 2000 in an era of cosmopolitan influence. (Hertha Berlin, with an average attendance of 51,000 in 2016/17, may within time prove to be another rising capital, more fanciable to German footballers than, say, factory clubs from the Rhine.) If wealthy citizens of the capital and other middle-class areas show interest in football, and investors choose to spend there, then poorer regions will struggle.

European Competition

A concluding thought would be this: throwing money at a club in order to win the European Cup, like PSG have done, is neither original nor sustainable. At one time the tournament was incalculable and there was an age when Steaua Bucharest, PSV, Red Star Belgrade, Marseille and Dortmund could overcome moneyed teams to win the competition. But massive underdogs are no longer able to sustain high performance in a 'league' structure. In that sense, PSG should have a chance.

However, there is never a guarantee of success. If we analyse winners of the tournament over a ten-year period, only twice have the pre-tournament favourites gone on to win (Liverpool and Porto were also huge underdogs when they won the Champions League in the years prior to 2006). Not only is there an unpredictability to the competition that PSG must acknowledge, the most frequent recent winners, FC Barcelona, have achieved their success through a long-term academy vision rather than exuberant spending.

Season	Favourite	Odds (source)	Winner	Odds(source)
2015/16	Barcelona	4/1 (SkyBet)	Real Madrid	11/2(SkyBet)
2014/15	Real Madrid	4/1 (ibtimes)	Barcelona	5/1(ibtimes)
2013/14	Bayern Munich	Evens (888)	Real Madrid	5/1(888)
2012/13	Barcelona	9/4 (Ladbrokes)	Bayern Munich	16/1(Ladbrokes)
2011/12	Barcelona	2/1 (Totesport)	Chelsea	12/1(Bet365)
2010/11	Barcelona	11/4 (Ladbrokes)	Barcelona	-
2009/10	Barcelona	4/1 (PaddyPower)	Internazionale	12/1(PaddyPower)
2008/09	Barcelona	5/2 (Soccerlens)	Barcelona	-
2007/08	Barcelona	7/2 (Ladbrokes)	Manchester United	5/1(Ladbrokes)
2006/07	Chelsea	3/1 (Betfair)	AC Milan	10/1(Fiso)

Usually odds are determined in favour of the reigning champions, as bookmakers set them to allow for minimal losses. Nevertheless, PSG face the same issue that Lyon had in the seven seasons prior to the Qatari takeover: competition. A team can no longer win the Champions League without playing in a competitive domestic league. Former Saint-Étienne director Damien Comolli substantiated the issue in 2011 at the time of the takeover: 'You have to ask is the French league competitive enough to give PSG a sufficient challenge, for them to compete in the Champions League?'[xi]

Sevilla came to dominate the Europa League partly due to regular competition against Real Madrid, Barcelona and Atlético, winning the competition for the third time in 2016. PSG that same season finished 31 points ahead of second-placed Lyon. It is a theory applicable to the stagnation of clubs from 'two-team leagues' such as Celtic, Basel and Ajax – the jump from competing against Ross County, Winterthur and PEC Zwolle on a Saturday to super-clubs Bayern Munich and Juventus on a Wednesday being too great both tactically and mentally for them.

Forbes described Ligue 1 as a league 'poached of broad star-talent, bereft of competition, [that] can't encourage player effort [or] promote ambition,' though one has to ponder whether QSi are concerned? Competition will arrive one day. For now, sponsors pour in, shirts sell abundantly and, most importantly for them, the image of Qatar grows in Western favour. Gab Marcotti wrote how we're in an era of dominance for the one-percenters 'and, frankly, that's not going to change, barring some kind of deep regulatory overhaul. The overwhelming power of [super-clubs] is only going to grow,' much to PSG's delight. The Harvard University paper ended on similar lines: 'One wonders if football will ever again be played on a level field?'

For the locals who read *L'Équipe* on the journey home from Opéra to Tolbiac, such sentiments don't concern them. A superiority complex has carried through this city for centuries. As Napoleon declared to his generals, 'The teeth of envy are powerless here, these achievements are granite.' Bonaparte, that corporeal symbol of French pride, would most definitely have valued PSG's cold ambition. If anywhere deserves a super-club, it is Paris.

TWO

A LEGACY FOR THE FUTURE: AULAS' LYON

The Mères Lyonnaises *(Mothers of Lyon), humble housemaids of the highest standards, drew wealthy connoisseurs from across the continent in the 1800s, eager to taste their famed cuisine. Ingredients sourced locally – olives, wines, cheeses and oils – were cooked to such a calibre that les Mères inspired the invention of Michelin guides.[5] Modest ladies of ordinary means, thriving in an age of gender oppression, les Mères epitomised the character of Lyonnaises. They believed that Lyon was home to the best ingredients in the world and were proven right. Children of future generations would be raised by their mothers to understand the requirements of excellence. Nowadays, the city retains a pride amongst its populace, a desire to be the best. It is therefore surprising that its club Olympique Lyon went so long without competing for glory. It would be a member of that future generation, Jean-Michel Aulas, born in the small village of L'Arbresle on the outskirts and raised on rich cuisine, who would transfer the messages of les Mères Lyonnaises to football, presenting Lyon with a team of champions. Housemaids would say: 'Strive to be the best; create something worth savouring; and have faith in local ingredients.' His Lyon reinforce those messages, with unwavering faith in the club's academy and coaching staff.*

---

5. Ándre and Édouard Michelin created the guides in the hope of inspiring people to drive and visit restaurants, thus wearing down their tyres.

A great plain of countryside divides Paris and Lyon. Sporadic *bourgades*, with familiar churches and small houses, offer some variation to the open green land. In these *petit* villages, life is a bubble. It is distinctively different to the concrete no man's land that divides much of Britain. The nearer one gets to Lyon, the more frequent the *bourgades* become, until eventually their marmalade-tiled roofs form a city. And a fine city it is. During the fifth century, Louis XI established Lyon as the home of silk, merchandising and then distributing the fabric overseas. The wealth associated with silk has since remained, displayed in the neoclassical and baroque architecture.

However, much like Paris, there are two Lyons. There is an affluent inner circle and a poor outskirt. The fine architecture of the old city lies between the Saône and Rhône rivers. Take a five-minute walk to the east, though, when dusk falls, and the bourgeois window-shoppers of Vieux become young gang members in hoods. In that sense, Lyon is typical of elsewhere. What is striking about the city is how the two communities (those with and those without) never cross beyond invisible thresholds; they could be of different worlds. It is this understanding of social differences that allows Lyon to be a prism through which human structures can be viewed.

The young Arab men from the poorer side of town are football-crazy. They wear Napoli, Milan, Arsenal or Real Madrid tracksuits and caps. They even wear PSG attire; anything but Olympique Lyon. Disillusionment with society is a big issue in France. Arabs see themselves as outsiders within their own cities and, in contrast to historic Lyonnais characteristics, take little pride in their locality. Simon Kuper had explained the issue from a football perspective back in Paris. 'In the 1998 era, you had rural guys who grew up in villages, like Didier Deschamps, Bixente Lizarazu, Laurent Blanc and Fabien Barthez. There is much less of that now; they are mostly non-white and from the suburbs. That is the issue with French football. These guys [Arabs] have been left out by the French nation and discriminated against, and suddenly they are wealthy professional footballers. Many French fans don't like that.' The biggest example of tensions came in 2010 when, at the South Africa World Cup, the national team went on strike. *France Football* found that only 20% of people surveyed in 2014 had a positive view of the team. The *New York Times* debated underlying racism. [xii]

Street Football

That evening as the setting sun reflected off the River Rhône, I sat on some steps at its banks. Local Arab men and boys played football together on a court underneath La Guillotière bridge. Sat with me were groups of families; the men smoked while the women chatted and watched their sons play. French rap blared out from speakers. It was a fine atmosphere for a Sunday evening and the talent on display was surprising. One boy, with his arm in a cast, breezed past the older teenagers as they fell for his drop of the shoulder time and again. He, as the person who performed the most nutmegs, was the king of the court. It is in these unstructured 'street' environments that many of the best footballers have been developed. All that is needed is a flat surface and a ball – a factor in the game's global popularity. Creativity, tenacity, bravery, flair and aggression develop on the streets, as typified by Ibrahimović and Zidane. When the boy-wonder Wayne Rooney finished training at Everton he would play on Liverpool's streets with his mates.

For the players, it is escapism; they may never find a world beyond this neighbourhood. Unlike traditional football, this game had two scoring systems: one that entailed putting the ball in the net, typically; the other rewarding a team with a goal for every nutmeg. Within this mini-court society, stardom beckons for the boy who is able to take on his opponent in the most creative fashion. Zidane's roulette was born on a dusty Marseille court. Likewise, in Rio, was Ronaldo's flip-flap. Sadly, street football in Europe is dying. Children overall come from wealthier backgrounds than before and have alternatives to outdoor participation. [6]

Economically deprived environments allow for continuous development. Youngsters in Lyon hate missing matches on the courts and long to find out the gossip of who performed the most audaciously. Because of the mismatch of ages – from 10- to 20-year-olds – younger players strive to be as good as the bigger kids, both verbally and technically. Just ten minutes spent watching the court provided an education in understanding Karim Benzema's demeanour.

In urban areas, full-sized grass pitches are difficult to come by. They are

6. Gentin, S (2011). 'Outdoor recreation and ethnicity in Europe—A review.' *Urban Forestry & Urban Greening*. 10 (3), 153–61.

not part of the landscape. Because of this, many of the rawest talents come without any understanding of the tactical side of football. They generally have poor positional sense and often look out of sorts during trials. But tactics can be taught. Natural technique, coupled with an innate desire to win, form intangibles most clubs desire. A coach with cones and a whistle cannot teach spatial awareness like street football can. Benches, swings, see-saws and moving vehicles must be manoeuvred past, whilst always being in control of the ball. The weight and angle of a pass must be so perfect that it cuts through the small space between a dustbin and a car, and on to a teammate's run. It also establishes and inspires leadership at an age when personalities are still being formed. To arrange matches requires a democracy, but is usually decided by those with the sharpest tongues. Local boys adored Zlatan when he played in Paris; a man they saw as street football personified.

Alexsandar Hemon describes the street footballer as an artist, his unpredictability an expression of his exuberant nature: 'What might be called neo-romantic football aesthetics.'[7] Hemon points out that street footballers continued their soloist unpredictability off the pitch, naming Garrincha, Stoichkov, Hagi, Gascoigne and Riquelme as examples. The apotheosis artist Diego Maradona dedicated his life towards impressing people and could not be more open in his actions, yet he still retains a mysteriousness and inspires a deep frustration that he hasn't passed on his inspirational skills. A true street footballer possesses talents that are unteachable to others; only in their natural environment can they be learnt.

Recreating street football is a challenge all Western academies now face. Young players are simply not getting enough hours of development, as per changes in society, and clubs feel it is their duty to rectify this. Feyenoord, as you will later read, open their gates an hour before training and leave 50 balls on a pitch. They tell the youngsters 'go and enjoy', offering the kind of unstructured time that is essential for social development. Sporting Lisbon, similarly, have adopted a laissez-faire approach to coaching foundation-aged children: 'We just let them play,' a coach told me.

---

7. Hemon, A (Sep 2013). *The Blizzard – The Football Quarterly*. Sunderland: Blizzard Media Ltd. 98.

By planting a scout on the Guillotière steps and telling him to sit and watch, Olympique Lyon would find many treasures on their banks. They are in a fortunate situation. Some footballers are too 'street', often struggling to adapt to an academy environment that demands rules and structure. Others, like the prodigy Karim Benzema, who was born in Lyon to Algerian parents, are willing students. Benzema was the perfect pupil – polite and courteous to staff members, but with a tough side hardened on the streets. Aged 17 at a team meeting he was told to introduce himself to the rest of the squad. Surveying the room, he saw international footballers giggling at him. 'I wouldn't laugh,' he snapped. 'I'm here to take your place!' [xiii]

'Strive to be the best; create something worth savouring; and have faith in local ingredients'

It was in 1987 that the successful IT entrepreneur, Jean-Michel Aulas, purchased Olympique Lyon. His plan, titled 'OL – Europe', was to establish Lyon, then in the second division, as a Ligue 1 force within four years. His purchase embodied a shift away from emotional chairman to thoughtful business owner. At first, Lyon were not a quest for personal glory, but a manageable company underachieving in France's second-wealthiest city. As this was the city of film, Pathé purchased a stake in the club in 1999, thus accelerating growth. Lyon's rise was not down to an owner pumping funds into new players, à la Paris Saint-Germain 2011, but more a meticulously savvy strategic plan.

Aulas bemoaned the club's lack of history and fanbase when he arrived. Lens, Nantes and Auxerre, clubs from small towns, were all more geared for success than them. Yet because of the lower expectations, he was able to invest funds patiently into emerging talents. It was a Tour de France approach: 'You can overtake the people just in front of you,' he said. Florent Malouda (bought for £3m from Guingamp; sold for £14.25m to Chelsea), Michael Essien (bought for £8.78m from Bastia; sold for £28.5m to Chelsea), Eric Abidal (bought for £6.38m from Lille; sold for £11.5m to Barcelona) and Mahamadou Diarra (bought for £2.93m from Vitesse; sold for £19.5m to Real Madrid) were considered to be sound investments, whilst Karim Benzema (from the academy; sold for £26.25m to Real Madrid) was locally produced.

Seven consecutive league titles would be won between 2002 and 2008, but it was in striving for an elusive eighth that Aulas erred. 'It was total domination,' Cédric recalled as we set off for Gare de Lyon train station. 'When they won their seventh title, we [PSG] finished three points above relegation,' 16th in fact; some 36 points away from Lyon. 'Then they spent more money – we didn't think it would ever end.' OL's downfall came in 2008 as, with ambitions to conquer Europe, they overspent on substandard players. Lisandro López, Michel Bastos, Aly Cissokho, Ederson, Jean Makoun and Kader Keïta arrived for £73m, underperformed and departed for £26m. Aulas was faced with two choices: either gamble on expenditure and hope Lyon would eventually win, or cut costs and rebuild the club organically. 'It is time for fiscal restraint and better economic management,' he decided. 'This means we will have less depreciation in the coming years.' [xiv] From 2011, Aulas sold Lyon's highest-earning players and filled the team with academy graduates.

The French press called it 'The Summer of Madness'. Lyon were mocked for offloading 19 first-team players, including the great talent of his generation, Hugo Lloris. 'The 2011/12 season wasn't a good one, and yet we'd spent nearly €135m on new players; that was far too much, considering the club's standing at the time,' Aulas explained. 'So, we decided to change our sporting policy entirely by focusing on strengthening the academy. Today, we're reaping the benefits of this investment in youth.' This Lyon, a club whose nucleus is its academy, with a first team filled with local talents, inspired by *les Mères Lyonnaises*, would be the club I visited in the spring of 2016. An old Lyon fan, who had been staring at us from across the cabin to the point of awkwardness, poetically declared as our train arrived: 'PSG have so much money they are like the dark. We resist them now, we are the light.'

Le Moderne Classique

In the old city are *traboules* – small passageways between buildings – that were used by armed locals to evade German troops during World War Two. La Résistance fighters would entice the *Sturmabteilung* into narrow streets before disappearing from sight, quite conveniently as housewives happened to drop dirty water from pails high above. It was urban guerrilla warfare. One late February afternoon we, as visiting Parisians (myself adopted), scurried through the *traboules* to avoid being recognised by any Bad Gones – Lyon's ultra group. Cédric was in town for Lyon versus PSG, a fixture of great symbolism, and was worried he'd be recognised. It was to be a battle between the old champions and the new; between a club that carefully invests and a club that spends excessively; between first and second in the league.

A metro ride, a tram and a coach was required to reach Lyon's newly built Stade des Lumières (Parc OL) arena. As darkness fell, both sets of fans grew frustrated with the length of the journey. 'They should rename themselves Olympique Decines,' one Parisian joked, in reference to the location. A stadium is part of a community, allowing match-goers to create rituals based on experiences. In academia, it is known as 'place attachment'. Scannell and Gifford created the Tripartite Model in 2010 as a conceptual framework. They defined place attachment through three Ps: Person, Process and Place. In 'Person', attachment occurs either individually or as part of a collective community based on the experiences shared. The 'Process' would occur in the dimension of attending regular fixtures, whilst 'Place' is the stadium where the community congregates. [8] More simply, Stade de Gerland, Lyon's old stadium, retained for fans a cemented love of place – known also as topophilia – that the new Parc OL was yet to have. Place attachment can take years, and is determined mostly by the success of the Person phase.

Parc OL was designed by the same architect as Arsenal's Emirates stadium. 'In many ways, several European football stadiums are the conceptual equivalents of the horseshoe parliamentary chambers favoured across the European continent that are, in theory at least, said to breed courtesy, consensus and collaboration,' came architectural correspondent Ike Ijeh's review, upon Parc OL opening. 'English stadium design on the other hand, rather like our gladiatorially confrontational House of Commons, tends to take a somewhat more aggressive approach.' English stadiums are famed across Europe for the intensity and implied oppression of their design, with steeper stands, encircling roofs and a lack of athletics tracks, said to foster a more energised connection between spectator and pitch. Parc OL, Ijeh clarified, was of British influence. Aulas, the perpetual Anglophile, looked at Arsenal throughout that period of austerity as an inspiration.

---

8. Scannell, L & Gifford, R (2010). 'Defining place attachment: A tripartite organizing framework'. *Journal of Environmental Psychology*. 30 (1), 1–10.

'It's true they went through a difficult period with a lot of sceptical people saying, "You can't develop all this infrastructure and have a strong team at the same time – the club will die," so there is definitely a parallel between the clubs.' Arsenal became both the economic and architectural inspirations for *Nouveau* Olympique Lyon. [xvii]

Mixed in with the obvious economic reasons for constructing Parc OL was a legatorial cause. Architecture is a permanent tribute to history. Stade de Gerland, Lyon's previous home, whilst decaying and in need of modernisation, was a symbol of the 60 years before Aulas. 'When we started out on this project, we told ourselves that a big club defines itself not only by its performances on the pitch, but by its performance off it, too.' Parc OL is a declaration of triumph, of wealth, power and status, but most prominently is a salute to the dreams of a man who, upon investing in Lyon, found a club with neither ambition nor fans. In February, during my visit, 56,000 people had come to watch the local kids take on the rich capital club. Good architecture radiates an absolutism; of being correct in one's approach. Parc OL for Aulas justifies his life's work: a pantheon to carry his name through generations. 'In France, there is a cultural problem,' he once said. 'Winners are not popular.'

Unusually for an owner, Aulas is adored. When he imposed austerity at Lyon the fans accepted it. If it meant a platform for the academy, then so be it. The best ingredients are local anyway. Frédéric Kanouté, Steed Malbranque and Ludovic Giuly came through in the 1990s as Lyon considered greatness. Later, graduates Sidney Govou and Hatem Ben Arfa helped secure it.

That night, Lyon defeated PSG, ending their 36-game unbeaten run, with a mostly home-grown team. Mostly; they in fact had nine academy players in the full squad. That figure would have been 12 were Clément Grenier, Nabil Fakir and the soon-to-be Barcelona-bound Samuel Umtiti available. Even their manager, Bruno Génésio, was a former Lyon player, born in the city, who was promoted from the youth academy to become manager in 2015 – harvested by Aulas to maintain his vision.

The Bad Gones *capos* waved their flags and sang throughout. Most of the chants targeted Adrien Rabiot, with him being PSG's best player on the night. Others harmonised Anthony Lopes, the goalkeeper. At a recent ultras meeting he was the only player to turn up, despite the invitation being open to all (before becoming professional he was a Bad Gones member). It is the duty of both the Nord stand in the first half and the Sud in the second to honour him vociferously. '*Pas besoin de défenseur*,' topless men roared at him, to a tune that would later be adopted for Will Griggs and familiarised here in Parc OL as Northern Ireland overcame Ukraine. Back in February, Aulas had given every fan vouchers to spend on beer at half-time. Afterwards, on the coach, tram and subsequent metro ride to the city centre, they commented that the new stadium now felt like home. Topophilia can be a capricious form of love at times.

*

Future of Football Science

Of all the species on the planet, the human is the most adaptable. In the 5 million years since early hominids emerged in East Africa's Rift Valley, man has had to adapt to climate evolution and predators. It is our survival instinct, our innate intelligence that has gotten us so far. We know how to combat threats, when to fight and when to run. Even today, the intelligent modern human must adapt to his working and social environment to survive. Some are unable to do so, finding themselves out of place everywhere, whilst others are comfortable adapting. In football – the most changeable industry in sport (English managers average 1.23 years) – the best staff adapt to survive. One man who has done so successfully is Emmanuel Orhant, Lyon's chief doctor since 2008.

'The head coach will work with a team of coaches for forwards, or for goalkeepers, and they all have their own personal way of working,' the doctor said from inside a Portakabin office at Lyon's Tola Vologe training complex. He sat comfortably, having survived four managerial tenures. 'For me, it is not possible to have the same way of working with every head coach. When the team changes its manager, the philosophy and the type of work I do changes completely.'

The city was still asleep that Saturday morning as I made my way down Rue Jean Jaurès to meet him. Lyon was yet to stir, all but for a lady stocking the window of her patisserie and an old man watering his oleanders in the coming light of day. Even Tola Vologe was at slumber as I rang its gates. After several minutes, an apologetic young man arrived and courteously introduced me to the doctor. 'You must forgive me for my lack of English,' Orhant had humbly apologised, despite producing a perfect grasp of the language.

Usually in football, staff are nomadic. If the manager departs for elsewhere he will take his backroom with him. Orhant is a constant. So talented is he, every new manager disowns his original doctor from the previous club and places total faith in him. 'For me, it is very difficult to adapt because sometimes I do not feel the same as the coach. If we think completely differently I must adapt my organisation to meet the coach's needs. I can tell him what I think in regards to how we do things, but I am a chef; if the boss wants things doing one way then I must say "okay". But that is football.' He understands that successful clubs must run coherently. Despite having beliefs to the contrary, the head coach is always right.

Outside, the injured home-grown midfielder Corentin Tolisso and a fitness coach were doing recuperation work around mannequins. They waved at us as they jogged by before stopping to check Tolisso's GPS monitor. Without prompt, Orhant explained what the pair were looking at. 'The GPS tells us if he is running at close to his full intensity. We can see if he is using one leg more than the other and if he is hiding an injury.' *Surely the use of technology in sport science has never been better?* 'No, but it still has to improve.' *How so?* 'I think football in the future will be the same as the NBA and NFL. Everything will be measured. We will know the measure of blood at every moment, or the skin, and in 20 years we may even measure psychology through technology.'

Orhant believes the doctor on the bench will be able to check his iPad and analyse whether or not the player's blood levels have reached a percentage where he is susceptible to injury, thus requiring substitution. 'We will know the top level he should be at in each moment and we can see if it is good for him to play or not.' This, he believes, works in the same way for players waiting to get substituted on – the coach can see on his iPad if his body is 'warm' enough to meet the tempo of the game. 'Science must help us to protect players. In the NFL and NBA, they have videos of each moment. The head coach has the materials and numbers of accelerations, so he knows if it is good or not good and when to make an alternation. The head coach should also have a tablet with the levels of the game, so he can see if his players are close to injury.'

Hamstring injuries cause Orhant, and indeed doctors at all clubs, the greatest difficulty. Next are ankle and knee injuries. Such strains are caused through repetitive overuse. Strength and conditioning coaches, such as Nicolai Kammann at FC Bayern (see Bavaria chapter), vary training for academy players and incorporate sessions from different sports, like judo and NFL, so key muscle groups are offered variation. At first-team level it is more difficult to implement such exercises; everything must be specific to matches. Therefore, Orhant and coaches meet to discuss strategies to minimise injury potential prior to training. 'We will talk for an hour before the session. For example, training for the PSG match was at 5:30pm, so we met at 4:30pm. We have one hour to work with each player to discuss the muscle problems with him. If there is an imbalance in the strength of the muscle, we will work on this problem for an hour.' Players at Lyon are also encouraged to take responsibility for their own physical condition. They are given cards that detail exercises to do at home to strengthen muscles. 'He knows what he should do one, two or three days before the match. We tell him to take his card and work on prevention exercises.'

The Document

It was a chilly morning despite the sun, with the doctor's office providing warm refuge. 'We have a lot of things that help us to prevent injury,' he continued, booting up his computer and settling back into his chair. 'At the beginning of the season players do physical preparation tests and we create exercises to minimise injury.' Alongside the coaches, Orhant's medical department try to discover the strength of every player's muscles and nerves, so they may match training to their physical thresholds: 'We learn about each player and how we should manoeuvre him by using balance boards and other technology.' All data is added to a Microsoft Excel spreadsheet that determines each player's athletic capabilities. Factors like dexterity, previous injuries, extendibility of muscles and biology (tooth strength and foot size), are all reviewed throughout the season. The data is there so Orhant can discover what peak condition is for each individual. Consider Alexandre

Lacazette. He had taken a knock in the previous league match versus Lille away. Orhant ran tests on the striker and compared his findings to the document. He discovered Lacazette was of sufficient athletic capability to play 80 minutes versus PSG. He did so and assisted the first goal.

'We explain to each player what he must do. And the coach and physical preparation team, they are shown the same. Over the weeks of the season, every player has this document and the coach knows how many times he sprints, the distance, energy exerted. [The document] is sectioned for attackers, midfielders, defenders and lateral defenders [wing-backs]. We know exactly what each player does and it is possible to know after training if he should play the full game or not.' GPS software (the black chest strap footballers wear in training) is used to determine whether a player is playing at his athletic potential. 'Then, during matches, when we haven't got GPS to help, we use a special camera on the pitch that shows how many kilometres every player has run and at what speed, so we can compare if he is running at maximum intensity. It is only possible to do this at home though as we do not have this technology at away games.'

Ajax believe that the best players simply do not get injured. They have found a correlation between the highest graded talents at the academy and lowest injury attainment. Simply, their best talents were found at the bottom of the chart. Therefore, they have more time to play and improve than other more injury-prone youngsters. Lyon have also found that to be true. I asked Orhant about one of sport science's most topical debates. *Are some athletes naturally injury-prone?* 'It is not because of God that they are always injured, there is a problem and we must know what this is. Psychology also plays a role. Perhaps there are things in his life that are stopping him from preventing injuries at home. We must think of everything. I have lots of conversations with my physiotherapist so we can discover everything and know where the problem lies.' Many people uphold the naïve notion of a naturally injury-prone footballer. There is, it seems, no such thing.

Age Culture

In modern football, the most important organ that coaches must consider is the brain. With advancements in the game, a greater value has been placed upon understanding footballers; their morale and aptitude. Previously, footballers were seen as commodities more than people and belonged to the club. Bill Shankly famously ignored injured players. Nowadays, coaching courses from foundation to elite level contain elements on psychology. 'I work with a clinic where the players do psychological work,' Orhant explained. 'Some players won't work with a psychologist on their sleep for example, but it is important we work with this clinic. Other players prefer this type of recovery. I want each player to find what works for him – it could even be acupuncture. I have special doctors for every field to support the players.' *So, you have some players who resist this side of the game still?* 'Yes, but my job is to propose solutions. If the player chooses not to do this, then it is up to him. The player can have a good feeling with one doctor but not another.'

Tola Vologe is a small complex with three grass outdoor pitches. It sits beneath the shadow of Stade de Gerland, quite literally over the road, and like the stadium will soon be a forgotten white elephant when Lyon move to their new complex. Doctor Orhant and I strolled back past the pitches towards reception. I had just enough time for one last question. *Why are footballers playing longer into their lives?* Forty-year-old Francesco Totti was cited as the example. 'In France, we do not have these types of players at all. After 30 years of age, they do not play as often. For me it is in the head of the player, because after 30 they don't want to work hard. It is not the same as in England or Italy. Also, the coaches do not protect these types of players; they will not tailor a training session to make it easier for them. The player must train at the same intensity as the other younger players in the team.'

With France the exception, overall footballers are extending their peaks. Yet Orhant believes it is a cultural matter. In Italy, because of the slower tempo of matches and their understanding of tactical game management, it is quite normal for players to continue until they are over 35. True greats like Paolo Maldini, Javier Zanetti and Francesco Totti will reach 40. Italian society values age more than elsewhere. Their average life expectancy is 82.94 years, higher than the UK or France, and grandparents are the epicentre of close-knit families. Culturally, out of respect, older players are allowed to train less often as the intangibles their experience brings to the team has greater value than performances. As Rudi Garcia said of Totti: 'Francesco is not only a formidable player – a '*fuoriclasse*' as you say in Italy – but also a man with great qualities off the pitch.' Marcello Lippi added: 'Totti is the monument of Italian football.'

At the 2016 European Championships, Gábor Király became the tournament's oldest ever player at 40. He shared his elixir with 38-year-olds Ricardo Carvalho and Gianluigi Buffon. Iceland's Eiður Guðjohnsen and Ukraine's captain Anatoliy Tymoshchuk played aged 37. If a footballer is disciplined, he can extend his peak for much longer. But France has socialist elements in the mentality of the populace. Not like in Italy, where older players are fashionable, everyone here must contribute equally. 'It is down to his diet, self-care and levels of intensity in training,' Orhant explained, before quickly thanking me, shaking hands and returning to work on his Excel document: Lyon's most valuable assessment tool.

THREE

BASQUE IN THEIR GLORY: ATHLETIC BILBAO AND THE POWER OF IDENTITY

Confetti fell on the smiling faces of hundreds beneath city hall. They sang songs of independence and waved flags late into the warm August night. Old-timers told stories comparing the success to a previous golden age, inspiring pride in a young generation of listeners. Not only had they won their first piece of silverware since 1984, they had done so against the great Barcelona side of Suárez, Neymar and Messi. And it was 'they' who had won it. Not a team of outsiders brought in to better the club; they were players from the community. Basque players. Men who had been raised to adore the club like fans.

For the People

The Lezama training complex is nestled inside a sun-kissed valley of Basque greenery. To train amid such a backdrop of rolling landscape must be truly satisfying, especially if you are a Basque man representing a club entwined with the history of your people. Basques are characterised as honest and hard-working. They create an atmosphere for their cities so agreeable that central France feels diffident by contrast. Red and white Athletic flags are draped from every second balcony and washing line in Bilbao; a daily display of frenzied 'cup final' fanaticism. It is as though the club overwhelms the consciousness of its citizens. On the walls of the factories on the edge of the city, graffiti writes '*3 + 4 = 1*', a sum proclaiming that the three regions in France (Lapurdi, Nafarroa Beherea and Zuberoa) and the four in Spain (Bizkaia, Gipuzkoa, Nafarroa Garaia and Araba) equal one Basque Country. Not all fans who follow the club wish to politicise it to promote independence – with many wishing to remain a part of Spain – yet the image of Athletic Bilbao as a symbol of Basque separatism remains.

That idea is reinforced by their *cantera* (quarry) ruling, stating *how all players who represent the club must have family ties to a wider Basque region.* After the First World War, during the 1920s, nationalism grew in Spain and Athletic, in an effort to embed themselves within the local community, created the Basques-only ruling. Footballers who play for the club nowadays are aware that they represent the politically attached historic identity of the region. Some argue that cantera helps foster insularity, a distrust of outside influence. However, *cantera* also protects Athletic from the emotionless face of the modern game; a merry-go-round of players and staff seeking betterment. 'Other teams all seem like photocopies,' club president Josu Urrutia told the *New York Times.*[xviii]

Ekain Rojo is a PHD researcher in social sciences at the University of the Basque Country. 'There were two major internal wars, and because of the outcome of these wars they [Baskonia] lost the right to be a country; a right that dated back to the Middle Ages,' he explained to me as we walked beside Athletic's waterside San Mamés stadium. 'It was part of a centralisation process by Spain to build up a strong state.' I asked Ekain why he felt Athletic Bilbao were sociologically cemented to their insularity, and how football promotes this mentality. He explained that the emergence of football at the start of the 20th century happened to coincide with a re-emergence of Basque nationalism. The game became a vehicle of expression for people in both Catalonia and the Basque region as Spain 'aggressively promoted' the nation state. Franco banned non-Spanish culture and changed the club's name to Atlético Bilbao in 1941 by decree. To this day, Athletic and Barcelona are united by a common enemy in Real Madrid, Franco's team (their adored president Santiago Bernabéu was a Francoist who fought against the Catalans in the Civil War). Some tension still exists today, although the threat of violence is much less prevalent than in former years.

The Last Lions

The idea that Athletic could be successful with only local players was consolidated in the 1950s when, as other Spanish clubs began to recruit foreigners, they remained competitive with locals. It is their self-imposed limitation that, by competing from an inferior position, gives them more strength. They are a David competing in a *liga* of Goliaths, 'or as the Asterix and Obelix of global football,' Hungarian anthropologist Mariann Vaczi concluded. [xix] She dedicated a year to researching the culture of football inside the region. 'Fans celebrate Athletic because it goes against the trends and laws of modern competition, and maintains continuity with the very beginnings of football.' They are the only club that could ever possibly replicate what Celtic did in 1967 with the Lisbon Lions by winning the European Cup with local players. Any European success would be hyper-significant in these times of de-localisation.

From an anthropologist's point of view, Athletic was a unique avenue to study Basque culture. 'It is quite intriguing that Athletic limits itself to a small territory in an expanding, globalising football culture that thrives on athlete migration and commerce,' she wrote.

Although using only local players can strangle potential avenues of success in Spain's competitive championship, the majority of fans back the philosophy. 'You might win games less frequently, but when you do, the joy and pride of that victory is far greater than winning with foreigners. The philosophy allows even losses to be celebrated, like the 2009 Cup defeat by Barcelona. It has redefined the meaning of winning and losing: you have to lose games in order to win tradition and identity,' Vaczi wrote. In post-modern societies, identities have been deconstructed from original nationalistic or political expressions (such as being proud to come from a certain place and appreciating the values of an area) into newer, less poignant identities; more attachments to shared experiences: festivals, social media trends, favourite TV shows and cult pop stars, for example. Football on the other hand has consistently offered itself as a firm vehicle of expression. People within a community are taken by their local sport club and see it as an extension of themselves. Athletic, unlike other clubs, reinforce that attachment. They are probably the most connected example of club and fans in the world.

The Hunger Strike

During the spring of 2016, I was invited to Lezama by Athletic. The club maintains the English spelling of its name rather than the Spanish 'Atlético' alternative in tribute to the British shipyard workers who founded it in the late 19th century. Athletic also wear the colours of Southampton FC, as it was they who provided kits for the team during their formative years. Throughout the following century Athletic forged a strong association with Britain, being coached by an Englishman 11 times. As I waited in the modern glass-walled reception that morning, I was given a magazine to read – a 20-page eulogy of Howard Kendall, their last English manager. British influence led Athletic to play a style of football that mixed local flair with John Bull grit, known locally as *la furia* or 'the rage'. It was, as one can imagine, a physical style of football with lofted passes up to a target-man striker (Urzaiz, Llorente, Aduriz). Because of the British climate here and the muddy pitches that make passing the ball on the ground difficult, players were receptive to the style of play and achieved success with it. Manager of the Spanish national team, the Basque-born former Athletic midfielder Javier Clemente, adopted the style in the 1990s and flooded the team with Basques. His physical *la furia* Spain were a direct contrast to Cruyff's passing Barcelona Dream Team of the time. 'Yin and Yang' described *El Confidencial* of the relationship between styles.

The appointment of Luis Aragonés for Spain in 2004, then later Marcelo Bielsa at Athletic in 2011, changed that. During Bielsa's stint as manager, Athletic's most successful era for many years, he changed the style of play and made it his objective to understand the names, ability and needs of every youth player aged 14 upwards, appreciating that they are the spine the club depends upon. That togetherness continues today. Walking around their huge complex, it is difficult to pinpoint where the first team ends and the academy begins, such is the club's dependence on its youth sector.

Athletic Bilbao are starved of the global ocean of talent that other clubs fish from. They instead have a shallow pool of 3 million Basques to develop (less considering that number includes women, the elderly and the infirm); a small figure compared to the other 44.1 million people in Spain and 742 million in wider Europe. It is accepted that Ajax of Amsterdam are most synonymous with youth development. They, however, are not required to produce local players. Ajax can instead drink from other wells. For example, some of their most successful 'home-grown' names have been the Belgians Toby Alderweireld and Jan Vertonghen (purchased from Germinal Beerschot as 15-year-olds) and the Danes Viktor Fischer and Christian Eriksen (likewise from Odense and Midtjylland).

Athletic's self-imposed limitations make them an interesting case in point for youth development; quite frankly it is not something they can afford to get wrong. Fail to develop talented youth players and the club is unsustainable. They do sign Basque players developed at other clubs, but according to transfermarkt.com figures, Athletic have only spent around £60m since the turn of the millennium. It is therefore quite remarkable to consider that they are the only club alongside Real Madrid and Barcelona to have never been relegated from La Liga.

Basque Independence

Spain as a nation refuses to disband. The Madrid government takes revenue from Catalonian, Galician and Basque industries (as well as every other part of the country) before redistributing it. What these autonomous states want is to be either fully independent or part of a collection of territories, depending on whom you speak with. In Galicia, where independence is less vocalised, people promote a symbolic idea of freedom. In the Basque region, they look to the UK and particularly to Scotland as inspiration. They like how Wales, Northern Ireland, England and Scotland are able to be part of a United Kingdom whilst maintaining individual identities. All home nations (bar Scotland) participated at Euro 2016 under individual guises, not as Great Britain. If the Spanish government granted such ideological independence to their territories, then they may find themselves with less forceful divisions.

The Spanish national team that won the World Cup in 2010 had a combined total of ten Catalan and Basque players in their 23-man squad. If *Euskadi* (the land of the Basques) had been able to field their own competitive team in 2010, they would have had a fine collection of players. Cesar Azpilicueta, Aymeric Laporte, Javi Martínez, Xabi Alonso, Ander Herrera, Fernando Llorente and Asier Illarramendi were all born close to or within the region with family ties but instead represented either France or Spain. Currently, the Basque Country is allowed one friendly game per year, at Christmas. The dream, as *The Telegraph* recognised in 2013, is that 'independent national elevens will one day represent autonomous regions of Spain.'

Kondaira

The head coach of the Basque national team is José María Amorrortu, a true son of the region who, in a 45-year career, has managed Real Sociedad, Athletic Bilbao and SD Eibar. There is nobody more in tune with the demands of the game in this area than him, and it shows. He is an oracle of Basque football. Alongside coaching the autonomous national squad for one game each year, he is also director of football at Athletic. At Lezama, his name reverberates off the walls, though only ever his last name, like a storied legend. 'You're here for Amorrortu?' enquired the receptionist. He arrived wearing a club tracksuit with his spectacles on a cord, much resembling Marcelo Bielsa. 'Here all of the coaches are from Bilbao,' he began as we settled in a spare glass office. 'It is not difficult for them to explain what the Athletic philosophy is and what the club means.'

Young players are educated on Basque history at school so they grow up to appreciate the significance of the Athletic shirt. 'Our model is unique in world football. Chivas have only Mexican players, but we don't have only Spanish players; we have only Basque players.' Amorrortu was a player himself for Athletic in the 1970s and a manager in the 1990s. As director of football, he has a more controlling role. 'The function of a director must be to be close to the players and the coaches. I must help, support, talk to them and understand their issues. The most important thing is that we are all moving in the same direction and that we are close.' His position differs in that Athletic's president handles finances and transfers. Amorrortu focuses purely on football development.

Basque Rivals

Over a narrow country road from Lezama is a wooden-built restaurant. Whilst it does not officially belong to the club, it is here that directors bring clients to wine and dine. The walls are lined with memorabilia relating to Athletic: pins, scarves and paintings. There are framed photos in every room celebrating the achievements of the club. One such image, from 1976, shows the captains of Athletic and Real Sociedad each carrying one corner of the *Ikurriña* (the white, green and red flag of the Basque Country), a symbol suppressed at that time due to the Franco regime. If ever proof was needed that football transcends rivalry, it is delivered in this picture; Athletic lost the game 5–0 but fans of the club revere the significance of the moment and consider it one of their most poignant images.

During the 1940s, General Franco tried to erase separatist mentalities by promoting provincialism. For a long time, the two clubs – Athletic Bilbao and Real Sociedad – competed for the honour of best representing the Basque region. Yet when Real disbanded from their localised *cantera* policy in 1989, that honour landed at the feet of Athletic. Real Sociedad fans greatly opposed the shift in philosophy (John Aldridge – their first foreign signing – in his autobiography recalls locals spitting at his feet), and as a result convinced the club to purchase European and not Spanish players throughout the 90s.

Although they dislike each other, there's an easy-going atmosphere before, during and after matches between Athletic and Real Sociedad. Both clubs belong to the same region and face the same anti-Basque prejudice from fans (despite away fan culture being mostly non-existent in Spain). Ekain explained how the feeling in derby games is similar to that of a rugby match; more a visit than an invasion. An outside perspective would conclude that, with Real Sociedad having the word 'Royal' (*Real*) in their title, in recognition of the monarchy (an obvious symbol of Spain) there would be greater tension between the two clubs. Ekain reassured me, however, that this is hardly recognised by fans in the region. Since the beginning of the 20th century the Spanish royal family have holidayed in San Sebastian, and since the time of the formation of the Copa del Rey – the Cup of the King – Sociedad have worn the Real title.

Real Sociedad de Futbol Club (the Royal Society of Football) have high standards to maintain. It would be easy for them to become a generic club that signs and sells foreign players, having departed from their *cantera* policy restrictions, but they do not. 'Basquism' matters greatly to them, with the club's president seeking to rival Athletic Club's dominance over local youth recruitment. A notable portrayal of this resistance was the signing of Rubén Pardo, one of the most courted Basque players in Spain at youth level, wanted by both Real Madrid and Athletic Club. Real Sociedad were able to sign the player and make a statement to Athletic. He was given a buy-out clause of €30m to Spanish clubs and €60m to Basque clubs. [xxi] The idea behind the contract was to show young Basque players that there is an alternative to Athletic. However, to consolidate their squad strength in recent years, Athletic Bilbao have looked to sign displaced Basque players from rival clubs. In signing Raul Garcia from Atlético and Beñat from Betis (already a product of the academy), they hoped to reinforce their identity as the true home for local players.

Educating Pride

Iñaki Azkarraga was headhunted as a teacher 20 years ago by Amorrortu. His job is to educate and instil pride in the youth players. He recognises how essential it is for Athletic Club to support not only the young players, but the families of such players, too. 'Once the decision is made [to sign for the club] we care for them as much as possible. We have two guys working on their education and one guy caring for their families. We have specialists in physiotherapy, fitness; everyone here is very friendly,' which is correct. There is a warm atmosphere at the venue. Everybody smiles and says *aupa!* (an informal greeting meaning 'go up' or 'come on') as they pass – players included. 'We usually try to tell the young guys that if they want to be a footballer professionally, this is the best place to be. The best way to reach the first division is at Athletic.' A young player can sign for the club without worrying that their route to the first team will be barred by expensive newcomers. If they apply themselves, then the opportunity will come. 'They know that we trust them and when they are young they have our faith, that if they follow the steps then they will play in the first team.' Amorrortu reaffirmed the point earlier with a spreadsheet, showing that '80% of the team here are from the academy. We offer a minimum of two league debuts per year, sometimes that is as high as five. On average our players stay for 7.2 years.'

'Why' Understood. Understanding 'How'

Walking past the freshly cut playing fields at Lezama, the gnawing question was '*how?*' How can a club with such heavy restrictions do so well? In 2016 they finished fifth in a league of giants. The Euro Club Index has them as the 18th-best club in Europe (out of 703 teams)[9], ahead of Liverpool, Porto and both Milan clubs. Tactically, they only have a limited squad of players to pick from (with an average age of 27.1 years) but are still able to outwit their opponents. Amorrortu leaned back in his chair to think about the question of 'how?' Surprisingly, he pointed towards the focus on cognitive identification at the academy, something he feels separates Athletic from other clubs. 'When identifying talent, the medical and physiological aspects can be measured but what is not clear is the mental side of the game. The tendons of the modern footballer are based on these aspects. We are convinced that our recruitment and development models at the academy must be based around identifying and improving these mental traits.' He highlights such traits on a piece of paper that he's printed for me, exclaiming the point. 'They must understand the game to make optimal decisions, not under strict instruction. The player must value what is the correct decision,' pointing to his head, 'because we are convinced that our method of improving, not so much the technical skills, but the players' sight [a reference to tactically understanding football] is the most important thing to develop. There is now a system of education for the players that is completely different to in the past. The comprehension required to make the right technical decisions is much different than before. We must keep the mind of the players clear so they are able to make the correct decisions.'

The coaches here promote a form of accountability whereby the players take responsibility for their development. It is not uncommon to see kids carrying all of the equipment – balls and cones – instead of the coaches. From this point the players are then analysed to check if they are meeting the objectives of the team. Are they performing well in school? Have they met their personal development targets? Has their physical threshold developed? 'Of course, what we want is for our players to understand the game with autonomy and take responsibility.'

The Mission
'Our mission', Amorrortu explained with a presentation on club goals, 'is the training of the players.' The complexity of training is framed in a

---

9. A website that predicts the success of a team based upon recent form and the outcome of data from recent seasons. Euroclubindex.com. Data taken November 2016.

culture based on learning, participation and critical thinking on behalf of the players; 'orientated towards improving performance with a winning attitude.' At one time, winning was seen as an opponent to development. It was seen as an opponent to development, with courses dictating that players needed to develop in an environment without competition. It was a system that allowed every kid to win, despite successful nations harnessing competitiveness. Development in actuality works alongside winning – they are part of the same family. Competition is natural, especially in an obviously competitive sport like football. It is therefore healthy for young players to taste victory, to savour and enjoy it, whilst also sampling the bitter taste of defeat. With this in mind, Athletic aim to develop a winning mentality. Amorrortu's presentation on how Athletic win was delivered in three sections:

1. Demands on the coaches
2. Demands on the players
3. Academy/Club goals.

Demands on the coaches (on this slide Amorrortu discussed seven tasks that club trainers are given):

• The first one is to be an 'expert in football'. By this he means that every coach must know all of the key factors in the game. For example, how to wedge the ball in to space, from its most basic cognitive form into a match pace demonstration. Not only that, an expert in football is able to apply that wedged touch to a tactical framework. For example, the central midfielder receives the ball under pressure and must take a touch wide into space.

• Secondly, an Athletic coach must be exemplary in his attitude, attire, language and personality. He must look and act like a professional coach.

• He should thirdly be committed to self-improvement, using spare time to educate himself on the advancements in the game.

• The fourth point Amorrortu makes is that the coach must appreciate he is working as part of a framework, it is 'we rather than I'. By this he means that the coach should not over-emphasise points or tailor sessions to place himself in the spotlight, but rather adhere to the structure already determined.

• His fifth demand is for the coach to identify himself with the *player-centred philosophy* linked to number four. The player is most important; sessions have to focus on developing a group of competitive individuals.

• The coach has a 'vocational demand' for number six, as an employee of the club.

• The seventh and final demand links the previous points together as *training of players*, analysed throughout the year as youngsters develop suitably.

Demands on the players (of which there are five):

• Educate players so they are capable of understanding the game at any level, enabling them to take 'optimum decisions consistently'. This is done through game-related sessions, providing players with real scenarios and offering them the chance to solve them. Football is chaotic and no 90 minutes of scenarios ever follow in the same way. Therefore, the job of the coach is to give players an understanding of what to do in each situation, so that they are able to make a decision in a match based on their experiences in training.

• Players must offer 'capable technical solutions to the game's demands', such as finishing in the opposite corner to the goalkeeper, or taking a perfectly weighted touch out wide to clear the ball upfield.

• Thirdly, Athletic like to emphasise that players are their own reference point for improvement – this section is simply titled *responsibility*.

• The fourth point is related to the previous in that players must learn to value their own performance and the objectives set for them. This they call *autonomy*.

• Finally, young footballers who wish to play for Athletic must have a good physical profile. They should be fast, powerful and tough, or should excel in one physical area.

Academy/Club goals

The eventual goal is for players to develop in the club framework to represent the first team. This will be staged in what the club like to call 'evolutions', something we tend to call foundation, intermediate and advanced age groups (such as U6–U10 foundation, up to U18–U21 advanced ages). The goals of these evolutions are similar to the expectations elsewhere.

Translated from Basque into English, the slide writes: 'We will establish a plan with different working sequences, oriented and executed towards the training of a holistic player, in terms of his competitiveness.' In other words, the club have three evolutions in place for the players to progress through. At the end of which the player should be 'holistically competitive', or rather he is ready to play. The first stage is a *multilateral approach to introducing basic patterns* (dribbling and passing). The second stage is *specific individuality* or position-specific play for defenders, midfielders, attackers and wide men, and the third and final stage is called *high performance* with players mastering their trade. It sounds complex but only Amorrortu must understand the entire framework; Athletic's Basque coaches only have to focus on their individual age group.

Replicating Success

Most clubs have explanatory presentations similar to that, so afterwards I asked Amorrortu outright what Athletic's secrets were. 'A lot of people come here and ask that. What is the key? For me it is difficult to explain, you must understand the character of the players here. There is a sense of importance and a pride to be a part of the project. It is a tradition from our fathers and grandfathers.' With all clubs having access to a similar degree of expertise, such as performance analysis and coaching, intrinsic motivation is of greater importance. Athletic being blessed with players who are already motivated before matches due to perceived historic political tensions, understanding that the club shirt they wear is an extension of local identity, ensures the club enter every match 1–0 up.

There are so many factors in place here that facilitate the success of *cantera* that replicating it elsewhere is nigh on impossible. A club attempting to follow the model must have a history of oppression (perceived or genuine) and a large enough pool of talent to draw from. Glasgow Celtic could attempt *cantera*, but to do so they would need to draw on archaic, unwanted sectarianism to inspire separatism. There is accepting one's difference as cultural uniqueness, and then there is the promotion of hateful intolerance. It is a fine line, but Athletic are on the right side of it. If the political economy of Italy altered we could see Napoli dominating a southern Italian state, but they lack the infrastructure found here in Bilbao (this is one of the richest cities in Spain, while Naples is one of the poorest in Italy). Palermo and Catania also come from a region where local Sicilian pride takes precedence over Italian nationalism, yet like Napoli their league is not wealthy enough for them to invest in a *cantera* youth structure. What a club needs is a strong league with regular windfalls, allowing them to reinvest in their facilities. They must be able to offer competitive wages and regular silverware to entice players to stay (Llorente left for Juventus, Martínez for Bayern and Herrera for Manchester United when the relationship between club and talent ceased to be mutual), have a strong local identity, and possess fans who support the notion. It will not happen without such factors; otherwise one would merely witness a club supported by a strong academy who produce players for sale.

Domestically speaking, perhaps in Manchester, Liverpool, Yorkshire and other parts of the North, it could be attempted due to the governmental distrust harboured by the people of such regions, stemming from economic negligence in the 1970s and 80s. Such insular parts of England have a regional rather than national mindset. However, Premier League clubs are so steeped in financial agenda that they would never allow themselves to rely on youth. Everton are quite suitable, with a similar stature to Athletic Bilbao, but their league is too competitive to try it. They would struggle to survive with a Merseyside-only team, even if the fans allowed it. Players like Wayne Rooney and Ross Barkley emerge once a decade, and whilst the club could sign players like Scott Dann and Joey Barton (like Athletic signed Ander Herrera and Javi Martínez), they're unable to break into the top four of the English game with a global pool of talent to draw from, so it's most unlikely they would be able to thrive as recluses. What Everton also lack is the politicised core that Athletic have. Players here are educated on the historic suffering of the region – and while Liverpool is insular, it is not passionately separatist. Athletic Bilbao is equipped with so many intricate factors that sustain them, they are the carbon dioxide of football.

The Secret

A grand mansion cannot be built without strong foundations. Iñaki knows this. 'I have been here for 20 years. It was Amorrortu who wanted somebody to come in and support the academy players with their studies when he was manager in 1995. We have an academy culture of people caring about their studies because it gives us a good idea about the players' levels of discipline and how willing they are to sacrifice. The Basques are different in some ways; the people are very tough, strong-minded. There's decades of history combined with us being self-sufficient that fits our identity and creates a wheel that defends our values.'

Clubs in today's game compete for marginal gains. Most are equal in terms of analysis techniques and squad depth, so must find a competitive edge in their preparation for matches. They approach each game with an intent to motivate their players, to fight for marginal gains. If a club has a squad of intrinsically motivated players, as mentioned, then they are in an advantageous position. If, like Athletic, they are in a situation whereby they can instil intrinsic motivation by educating young academy players on the historic plight of their region, reinforcing how the club they play for represents an autonomous nation of people, then they are in strong standing. 'The children are taught Basque history. With democracy, we began to discover our own values. When they learn about Basque history in school, by the time they are in the first team it means everything to represent the club.' This is the secret of Athletic Bilbao, how their weaknesses make them stronger.

Educative settings also allow the club to gauge the responsibility of each player. It is an American college approach to playing time that discounts young players who do not value their education. 'We have several players who are scoring badly in school, so we ask them to work with us in school during the week to improve, and depending on the quality of their work they may play less during matches. It is an incentive for them to do well and focus on their education.' The club has a desire to create 'first division people', not just first division players. They are amongst the most intelligent footballers around. If a player does fail to secure a professional contract then there is a contingency plan in place, allowing him to gain a college scholarship in the United States, fully paid for by the club.

Amaiera

Athletic's localised dependency remains sustainable. It is an admirable policy that projects the club against the crashing waves of money-dependent football. Their internal vision is often romanticised, yet as a club they are pioneers in youth development. On a global scale, they have gained admirers for *cantera* (somewhat ironic for a policy that stands behind a pulled drawbridge), as fans of other clubs, disillusioned with the carousel ride of comings and goings, idealise the policy. In an effort to reach out to this core of admirers, Athletic created the 'One Club Man' award, presented to players at San Mamés in front of 40,000 fans. The award is an attempt to reward loyalty in football and was won by Matt Le Tissier of Southampton in 2015 and Paolo Maldini of AC Milan in 2016.

Athletic will never forsake their traditions. Even if they were relegated they would retain San Mamés and Lezama, as well as a fantastic youth structure and a healthy organic outlook. So strong are the club's foundations that the usually omnipresent Real Madrid and Barcelona are unable to sign young Basques. This is the club of a large community, a wrap-around that Amorrortu reinforces. 'Our concern is improving our players every day,' he says. 'Every youngster from our daily work must have one aim: imagine one day you are an Athletic player! When you enter here you will find the solution from our trainers. We know from every player what the other problems in his life are; his studies, psychology, family issues, and we will support him. Our worry must be to have an interest in every aspect of a player's life, as we are going to a higher level together.'

As I walked from Lezama, the beating sun had relented, creating a calm early evening. A choir of birds harmonised my way, past the grass pitches and up the country lane. There were scatterings of white villas on different levels of hillside, their shutters either green or red – the colours of the Basque *Ikurriña* flag. Football is devoid of exceptionalism in this modern era, with a free, fluid market of players, coaches and fans moving to and fro. Through their stance, while Athletic may not always gain victory through points, they win every game. In triumph or in defeat they are football's most lovable club. Long may *cantera* remain.

FOUR

MASTERS AND APPRENTICES: OPORTO'S TACTICAL INNOVATORS

In order to appreciate the climate of modern Porto, we have to follow the paths of José Mourinho and André Villas-Boas. Theirs is a story of ambitious men who rose from obscure roles – one a translator, the other a scout – to European royalty. Neither of whom would have reached football's beau monde without managing the Dragões. It was a mutually beneficial relationship, as FC Porto continues to benefit from the legacy both men left. The story of Mourinho–Boas, from conspicuous origins to mutual acquaintances, into inseparable allies then later rivals could well be a novel theme. United by a shared vision, José and AVB had the same mentors: Bobby Robson and the tactical theorist Vitór Frade. This chapter is about a tactical methodology developed at FC Porto by both men. The club is, and has for the longest time been, a place where potential thrives.

It takes a day of travel to reach Oporto from Bilbao. The train trudges slowly through the insular regions of Vasconia and Galicia before stopping off in Vigo on the west coast of northern Spain. Outside the country, Galician independence is largely unheard of, partly due to the relative neutrality of its football teams, Deportivo La Coruña and Celta Vigo. Undeveloped tracks guide trains through the Cantabrian mountains where passengers marvel at shadows created on dark green treetops. Galicia is a fine buffer, with its language a mix of both Spanish and Portuguese. Later, on the dusty roads through national boundaries, it only becomes apparent that Spain is Portugal when orange trees are replaced by palms (and when the people in the coach begin using their phones once more). Like most of Europe, there is no security checkpoint, just invisible boundaries.

The roads cannot have changed much in the two decades since Bobby Robson's arrival in Oporto. It was 1994 and a part of him must have missed home. Sporting Lisbon had sacked the former England manager a few months earlier, despite being top of the league at the time. It was to be their loss. Oporto greeted him with open arms. As he was chauffeured into the city centre from Francisco de Sa Carneiro airport, a large statue pierced the skyline before him. It depicted a lion atop a 40-foot column, its body and front paws pinning down the helpless eagle beneath it. The lion in the statue is Britain, whose naval forces defended Portugal against the supressed eagle of Napoleon's France between 1808 and 1814. For this the people of Oporto are thankful to the British, whose intervention allowed them to call themselves *Invicta* – the invincible city. Robson was also welcomed by the climate. Seagulls squawk behind passing grey rainclouds both night and day; Oporto has the feel of a British coastal city in summertime. The sun peers out for long enough to dry the cobbles and lift the spirits, before another shower apologetically falls. Because of this, the city is crowned with an eternal rainbow.

Bobby Robson was not alone in Porto. His assistant, translator and recent friend José Mourinho had agreed to follow him north. For José, the previous ten years had been a whirlwind. He'd not stopped, progressing from a job coaching children in schools to joining the academy of his local team, Vitória de Setúbal. He'd flirted with roles as a scout and assistant manager at other smaller clubs, before applying to become Bobby Robson's translator at Sporting Lisbon. 'I owe him for so much. I was a nobody in football when he came to Portugal.' Robson taking a shine to José (they first met at the airport) would prove to be his breakthrough moment. With great enthusiasm, he followed his 'Mister' to FC Porto. There they won the league in 1994 and 1995.

Enter the Kid
According to legend, one morning a well-dressed schoolboy approached

Robson and boldly began talking to him in perfect English. He recognised the lad as one of his neighbours and gladly discussed football with him. 'Why are you not playing Domingos?' the boy asked. Robson liked him and admired his brassy introduction.

The teenage André Villas-Boas lived in a well-to-do area of Oporto with his mother and father – him a lecturer, her an entrepreneur. He spent his spare time outside of school playing Championship Manager (and would continue to do so up until his appointment as Académica de Coimbra manager in 2009)[10], so when he discovered that Robson had moved in to his apartment block, he planned to open a dialogue. The pair would continue to talk when chance allowed, with a young AVB – assured with the confidence youth brings – leaving scout reports in the Robson mailbox every Friday. Eventually he was invited to watch the team he supported train. He met the coaches, shook hands with the players and came across Robson's translator, José Mourinho. At 17, AVB was sent to gain his coaching badges at Lilleshall under Robson's blessing. He was also sent to Ipswich Town to study under their manager George Burley: 'Bobby told me the boy was going to be something special in the coaching world. He called me and André spent two weeks shadowing me. He came to all the training sessions and the meetings with the board. I thought that Bobby had found somebody special,' Burley said. [xxii]

Robson would leave Porto in 1996 to join Barcelona, taking Mourinho with him. AVB stayed behind to coach at the academy, still a teenager himself. In 1999, Robson returned to England with Newcastle; Mourinho, however, remained at Barcelona, continuing his education under Louis van Gaal. Unbeknown to outsiders, no other environment in the world was nurturing as many gifted future managers. The club was a hotbed of enlightened minds during José's time there. From 1996 to 2000, he shared ideas with players like Laurent Blanc, Luis Enrique, Frank de Boer, Phillip Cocu, Julen Lopetegui and future nemesis Josép Guardiola. Mourinho's education under Robson and van Gaal elevated him to the senior coaching staff at Benfica in 2000. He succeeded Jupp Heynckes as manager aged 37 after the German was sacked, but later departed when Benfica courted other coaches.

---

10. According to his biography by Luis Miguel Pereira and Jaime R. Pinho.

André Villas-Boas also held ambitions to work in senior football. Around the same time José took over from Heynckes, AVB applied for a role with the British Virgin Isles. He was 22 but didn't reveal his age to the association during the application process. For them it was a shock to find they had appointed somebody so young.

TP

Vitór Frade was a professor at the University of Oporto who had studied and taught physical education, medicine and philosophy. Whilst there, in the late 1980s, he combined his knowledge of cybernetics, anthropology and psychology to create a sport development programme called 'Tactical Periodisation' (TP)[11]. Mourinho had first spoken with Vitór Frade when working at Setúbal's academy. By the time he came to Porto with Robson, he reopened a dialogue and the three men became more personally acquainted; discussing, amongst other things, the lasting influence of Robson's football hero Jimmy Hagan and his legacy on tactics in Portugal (Hagan won three league championships with Benfica at the start of the 1970s). José Mourinho, decades later as FC Porto manager, would encourage his young team of coaches, analysts and scouts to study the work of Frade: namely Vitór Pereira (Rui Faria and André Villas-Boas had already done so).

In January 2001, Mourinho was able to implement Tactical Periodisation fully, having taken small club União de Leiria to third in the league. FC Porto president Jorge Nuno Pinto da Costa was building a reputation for investing in potential and brought Mourinho back to Porto in 2002, this time as manager. A small coastal city, names are remembered and discussed daily in Oporto. At Crestuma, their training base, Mourinho leant on Vitór Frade once more to discuss a methodological approach for Porto. He decided to hire the young André Villas-Boas as opposition scout, and so, in novel theme, their paths entwined once more. Without Bobby Robson as mentor, Mourinho restructured FC Porto's educative model from top to bottom, with principles of TP flowing through every age group.

---

11. It translates as 'periodisation' from Portuguese in reference to 'a period of time', specifically the time taken by coaches to integrate a game model, basing training around the technical, tactical, psychological and physical. Such time is organised in 'morphocycles' between matches.

Principles of Tactical Periodisation: Mourinho's Porto

Although TP came to be stigmatised by some in the media, partly due to its overuse as a reference, it is an approach of considerable favour amongst elite level managers. They, rather than calling it 'tactical periodisation', instead refer to it as the 'training process' and accept it as common practice, training their players as close to the game as possible and not in isolation. It is no longer a prime factor in team success (in the 2000s it was considered to be revolutionary), but is instead just how things are done – how most teams train. Mourinho popularised the approach at Porto and Chelsea, but as Timo Jankowski wrote in his book *Taktische Periodisierung im Fußball,* fellow advocates of TP have been Marcelo Bielsa, Brendan Rodgers, Jorge Jesus, Christian Gourcuff, Rudi Garcia, Mauricio Pochettino, Roberto Martínez, Jorge Sampaoli, Luis Enrique and Julen Lopetegui. [12]

TP has also been incorporated by Pep Guardiola, a man Vitór Frade greatly admires. Before Christmas 2014, Guardiola met with Eddie Jones, head coach of the Japan rugby union team at the time, and the two men shared ideas that would benefit both sports. 'The soccer approach is called tactical periodisation, in which everything is done in preparation for the game and in order, to be tactically aware,' Jones told Sky Sports. 'I watched Bayern train and had a really good meeting with [Guardiola] and I really think we can improve greatly with adjustments in the way we train.' Japan would go on to defeat South Africa at the 2015 World Cup in one of rugby union's greatest ever upsets.

TP training universalises every phase of the game, from defence to attack, and develops every moment through practice. Previously, daily football training sessions included isolated physical and tactical exercises, but as Vitór Frade explained to Martí Perarnau (author of *Pep Confidential*), 'It [TP] rejects the physical side of the game as being separate to game model training, as this leads to specificity.' Football is fluid, not specific. Quite simply, TP teaches real-life football scenarios fluidly in preference to traditional isolated training exercises, like running around fields or (Sacchi-esque) shape play without the ball. It also has the underlying philosophy of promoting team principles every day. The more realistic training is, the more able the footballer is to

---

12. Jankowski, T (2015). *Taktische Periodisierung im Fußball: Die Übungen der Spitzentrainer. Trainieren wie Guardiola und Mourinho.* Aachen: Meyer & Meyer.

transfer his knowledge into matches. *Why train for football without the ball?* In TP, no time is wasted.

José Mourinho won the Champions League with Porto in 2004 by extending the knowledge base of his squad through training. They bypassed increasingly revered paradigms of wealth structure and order – that football should be won by the richest – and triumphed with evolutionary training techniques. He explained his beliefs at the time: 'Running for the sake of it has a natural energetic wear, but is null, and as such the wear in emotional terms tends to be null also, unlike the complex situations where technical, tactical and physical requisites are demanded of the players, the complexity of [such] exercise[s] leads to higher concentration.' [13]

In Oporto, the people are open and frank; they speak their minds and swear openly, to the great annoyance of those from Lisbon. Mourinho's declarations of northern power (whilst manager of the club) stood against an internally perceived centralisation towards Lisbon, in regards to various capacities of favouritism, and were greatly in line with the civic mindset of the people. His 'us against the world' rhetoric created a darling cult around him as a leader, a man who would pull up FC Porto's drawbridge. Before fully doing so, he stocked the club with the most undervalued players in the country. Maniche arrived from Benfica for free; Derlei and Nuno Valente joined from Leiria for just under £800,000 combined; and Paulo Ferreira was signed from Setúbal for £1.5m. Nomadic loanee Ricardo Carvalho became a mainstay in defence. Mourinho's 'game model' won Porto the UEFA Cup in 2003 and the Champions League in 2004.

Underlying Knowledge

By the time he arrived at Chelsea his methods were still fresh. Didier Drogba, signed from Marseille in France, recalls in his biography his shock at arriving at training with running shoes and being told by Mourinho that they were unnecessary:

'"Where are you going with those?" the manager asked.

'"We're not going to run?" I was surprised.

'"Bring your football boots," he answered, "because you're playing

---

13. José Mourinho, as mentioned in: Tamarit, X (2015). *What is Tactical Periodization?* Oakamoor. Bennion Kearny.

football. Everything I do is adapted for the game and related to the game – and the game does not involve wearing trainers!'" [14]

Rather, Drogba was to discover 'football fitness' in place of 'physical fitness'. Outside of Portugal, TP was an unheard-of concept. It promoted, quite simply, the pedagogical principle of football being learnt in a logical structure, revolving around four moments in the game:

1. Defensive organisation.
2. Transition to attack from defence.
3. Attacking organisation.
4. Transition to defence from attack.

According to Frade, every action in football, whether it be controlling the ball or passing, requires: an understanding of the context of the game (tactical); the ability to perform the action (technical); a motor movement (physical); and concentration (mental). The very best footballers are able to select the correct action consistently within a tactical framework. For example, when and where to pass if the team is winning 1–0 with five minutes left to play. Because football requires four factors – tactical, technical, physical and mental – at any one time, Frade pondered why they were trained in isolation?

Training sessions must consider and develop all four factors in every exercise. Ruling the theme of the session is the logical structure. Meaning, if the training focus is on defensive organisation, Mourinho or AVB will work on team shape, compactness, spaces, delaying the opposition, forcing them into pressing traps, and will then add in the following transition to attack once the ball is won. All the while, the four factors are being worked upon unconsciously, such as: When to press the ball (tactical); speed of movement (physical); calmness to pass the ball (mental); and the weight of pass (technical). 'My sessions last 90 minutes perfectly calculated,' said Mourinho. 'No place for distraction; everything is under control and the player is designed to work at maximum intensity every day.'

Within TP is a universe of comprehension, but it can be broken down. Firstly, there are the four factors. Then there are the moments and transitions.

14. Drogba, D. (2015). *Commitment*. London: Hodder & Stoughton.

But ruling both like gravity is 'context'. Why work on such specific moments in the game? It is the job of the coach to determine this. He is in charge and must consider absolutely everything. Therefore, training takes much consideration and planning. But once the season begins, observations taken from matches assist him in deciding what to train.

It is the first duty of a new coach to decide upon a 'game model' – a way of playing – that he wants his team to follow. 'For me, the most important aspect in my teams is to have a game model, a set of principles that provide organisation,' Mourinho stated. 'Therefore, since the first day of training, our attention is dictated to that.' When he arrived at Porto, Mourinho's objective was to create a way of playing based upon several factors: the capabilities of the players already at the club; the desire of the board; the culture of the club; the demands of the fans; and the culture of the country and opposition teams. Once a game model is decided upon and the players are selected, the coach can then begin to tactically periodise training. As complex as TP seems, it can be broken down simply to flow in the following order:

Identify a game model > produce match-related training exercises > incorporate the transitions > consider the four factors.

The Protégé's Porto

It has been suggested that José Mourinho elevated himself from humble translator to the greatest coach in the world between 2004 and 2012 through Machiavellian means. That would detract from the years of study he acquired under Frade and Robson in Porto, and van Gaal at Barcelona. Mourinho's rise was one of pure ambition, for when a man is enveloped in that, few can deter him. In a metaphorical room filled with 100 people, one can assess their garments and exterior presentation, but cannot see what resides inside of them. Ambition is invisible. For some it fades over time, but for others like Mourinho it grows. Only he envisaged his future. Incarnating T.E. Lawrence's famous introduction, he was a dreamer of the day.[15] The translator dreamt of glory and woke one day to find it was so.

---

15. 'All men dream, but not equally. Those who dream by night in the dusty recesses of their minds, wake in the day to find that it was vanity: but the dreamers of the day are dangerous men, for they may act on their dreams with open eyes, to make them possible.' T.E. Lawrence (1922). *Seven Pillars of Wisdom: a triumph.*

Perhaps unrealised during their years together (though one would rather imagine they schemed life in the long hours between matches), Mourinho's protégé André Villas-Boas was of equal ambition; a fellow dreamer of the day. 'I was able to learn many things and working with [Mourinho] takes you to another level,' he reminisced in an interview with the *International Business Times*. 'You fall in love with him and he becomes your idol. I wanted to be like him, know everything that he knew and absorb all the information he was giving.' [xxvi]

In 2009, though, AVB chose to go it alone. The young man sat in a large auditorium re-reading the key points of his presentation, waiting for his group to enter. He knew what he was going to say – his presentation would be similar to the one he had produced for the club's president, José Eduardo Simões, several days earlier. In it, at the president's home, the unshaven Villas-Boas laid out his objectives for improving Académica, who at that point sat uncomfortably at the bottom of the Portuguese league table. What Villas-Boas delivered was one of the famous scout reports that had taken him from Porto to Chelsea and Internazionale with Mourinho. On top of identifying Académica's strengths and weaknesses, he explained for the first time in his career *how* the squad would be improved. It was a similar presentation to the one that José Mourinho delivered to Roman Abramovich back in 2004, overstepping Sven-Göran Eriksson as the Russian's man for the job. Académica, AVB explained, would be improved through a programme of tactical periodisation.

'A boat is safe in a port,' he said, stepping from Mourinho's shadow, 'but that is not why boats were made.' In his first season as manager, Académica survived relegation. By the end of his second (then with FC Porto) Villas-Boas had become Europe's hottest coaching prospect. A more recent student of Frade, AVB adapted his game model to suit a 4-1-2-3 formation (a variation of 4-3-3 with only one holding midfielder). Tactically, he turned Porto into a more dynamic squad than Mourinho's version. He placed greater emphasis on pressing quickly and generally valued speed through every transition of the game, such was his game model. Rolando and Nicolás Otamendi at centre-back played a higher line; Sapunaru and Pereira had a greater degree of freedom as wing-backs than Valente and Ferreira; Fernando, Moutinho and Belluschi were able to sustain possession for longer if required; and Hulk and Falcao shared the goalscoring responsibility left under Mourinho for Benni McCarthy. It was a style of football lauded by Vitór Frade and inspired by his football hero, Johan Cruyff.

FC Porto won the Super Cup, the Portuguese Cup, the Primeira Liga and the Europa League, remaining undefeated all season. They conceded just 13 goals, giving Oporto pride in its title of *Invicta* – the invincible city. Perfection in life is an often-unattainable aspiration. Likewise in football. Yet believing perfection can be attained often brings success. 2010/11 was a season as close to perfect as football can offer. Aged 33, Villas-Boas became the youngest manager to win a European trophy and only the 11th to win a treble. Most crucially for him, he would become the man to inspire a generation of young minds to strive for football's unattainable.

Legacy of Methodology

FC Porto have over time built up a reputation as progressives. In the 40 years after Jorge Nuno Pinto da Costa joined the club's backroom staff, Porto won 22 league titles and two European Cups. 'We have internal and external scouts, who are divided into several levels of observation, which allows a player to be viewed by several people,' explained club director Antonio Henrique. 'They work with a shadow team, which is a set of players who are identified from various leagues capable of being hired by Porto.' As well as targeting footballers with potential, Porto invest in coaches and managers and actively promote relations with the local Universidade do Porto – one of the greatest academic football environments in Atlantic Europe.

Graduates José Mourinho and André Villas-Boas carried teachings from university lecturer Vitór Frade to the club – even offering him a role developing methodology. Rui Faria was one of Frade's brightest students when he contacted Mourinho in the 1990s regarding his thesis on Barcelona. Impressed, Mourinho took him to Porto in 2002 upon returning as manager. Faria would be the man to implement periodised football fitness sessions. He became José's indispensable right-hand commander. 'The aim will always be the same,' he said of the methodology. 'To make a set of principles conscious and then subconscious in a way that we naturally display a way of playing.' [16]

---

16. Tamarit, X (2015). *What is Tactical Periodization?* Oakamoor. Bennion Kearny.

When on UEFA Pro Licence courses, coaches are tasked with creating a thesis of study. They often seek advice from Frade. He tells them simply to study what Johan Cruyff did at Barcelona as the ideal game model. 'This passion for Cruyff's game is not for nothing. We are talking about someone who [was] a milestone in the qualitative evolution of football.' [xviii] By Frade's accounts, José Mourinho was an aficionado of Cruyffian football and it was this style that he implemented at Porto in the 2000s.

Mourinho came to be seen as the antihero to Cruyffian football with his reactive style of play, but that stemmed from necessity. He understands the fragility of life as a football manager – his father was sacked one Christmas when José was a boy – and sees reactive play as a fundamental practice for survival. When he became manager of União de Leiria in 2001, Mourinho introduced the Cruyffian philosophy of resting on the ball to Portuguese football (keep possession when winning a match to exert minimal amounts of physical effort, whilst frustrating the opposition). It is mostly forgotten that in his first season at the club, Porto played an attacking 4-3-3. He and the team are remembered elsewhere for the pragmatic 4-4-2 diamond played on European nights, but domestically they were expansive. The diamond was only incorporated when, as the tempo became reduced, his players could appear between the lines of the opposition's defence with greater ease. Mourinho over time became regarded as the fallen angel of FC Barcelona, the anti-Barça opposing their relentless attacking philosophy, but when he first came into management he was of the same school of thought as de Boer, Guardiola, Cocu, Luis Enrique and the other purists.

Both José Mourinho and André Villas-Boas were involved in academy development at Porto. AVB's 'point down' midfield trio (a number 6 in a 4-3-3) is still maintained. The reason many academies develop youngsters to play in a 4-3-3, despite the first team often playing a different style, is that it allows each individual to hold a duty within the structure, whilst promoting the form of attacking instinctiveness that managers find desirable. Players are sent out on to the pitch with individual targets, as Porto academy coach Vitór Matos explained to me: 'It is always related to what we want to develop in that individual player. Imagine last week we discovered that when the ball goes to our right-winger, the opposition always tried to block it. So, in training for the next game we will try to force the game to that side and say to the winger, "You are going to be bolder, to show more initiative and win your line at least five times." It is initiatives: I say to the team that our midfielders must do ten initiatives in that game.' In a 4-3-3 formation, each player has the opportunity to meet targets. 'If they don't achieve it, we will investigate why they are not able to.'

Frade's Latest Student

Whilst in Oporto I sought out Frade's most recent protégé, Vitór Matos, to learn more about TP. At 27 he is highly regarded at the club and occupies four roles: academy opposition scout, performance analyst for the U19s, assistant manager of the U17s, and head coach of the U14s.[17] 'Such is Mourinho's influence, everyone in Portugal wants to be a coach,' Matos said. 'I chose to go to Universidade do Porto because the man who invented tactical periodisation was teaching there. In TP, everything must be connected – tactical, technical, physical and psychological – it is all attached to our game model, our style of play.'

He's a busy man. We met for cappuccino in between team meetings to discuss the finer points of the methodology. *Can a coach have his own adapted version of TP?* 'No, there are some examples of when people who do not understand TP try to add to it, but that is not necessary. It is about methodical principles. For example, we deliver exercises to encourage an aspect that we want to see happening in a game. We will want to see it happen a lot in that exercise. That is one principle. There are four principles that apply to the methodology that allows us to construct our style of play. It is very specific.' A coach can use TP and apply his own game model, but he cannot alter the approach. *Why then do people add to it?* 'On the Pro Licence [course] in Portugal there are some people who tried to discuss periodisation, but to be in a place where you can talk about it you must have spoken with Vitór Frade. It is the only way. You can understand it, but he must teach it to you.'

As previously explained, once a game model is decided upon by the coach, inspiration for training sessions is drawn from flaws in matches. Matos has a full spectrum of understanding in regards to deciding upon

17. Matos, when we last spoke, had a new role in China as the technical director for Felix Magath's Shandong Luneng.

training sessions; he is both a performance analyst and a coach. 'We call it a morphocycle week; one game Sunday and then another game the following Sunday. It is a cycle of two games. In this one week, the idea is to have a day off on Monday to recover – because in TP recovery is also emotional and psychological. You could have had a difficult game that you need time to recover from mentally. So we then have Tuesday, Wednesday, Thursday, Friday and Saturday to train, before playing a game again on Sunday.' He will devote hours towards thinking of session structures, meticulously planning and preparing the flow of every exercise, tailored towards the upcoming match.

'Imagine in the game on Sunday there were some ideas that did not work. We have to then arrange training to solve this. It becomes the focus for that week, alongside having exercises related to the game coming in the future. It is always related to the game that has gone and the game that is upcoming, in a cycle.' And so, the season carries on in cycles between matches. Matos adds that each year he will encounter 'peaks of training' and is wary not to train too vigorously too early – in comparison to a previous age when clubs overloaded the squad with fitness work before the season had even begun. 'Pre-season is the most important time in TP because from the first day you have to develop and train your way of playing.'

When scouting the opposition, the first thing Matos tries to identify is their style of play overall. He then analyses how they approach transitions. 'I look to see who the best players are. Then, I analyse where we can win the game, and where they are dangerous. The most important thing is our style of play and the individual. At U19 this starts to be something we are aware of; how can we beat the opposition using our style of play?' Like AVB did before him, Matos trains his teams to play in a model aligning with the first team.

Cruyff-like in nature, Matos' philosophy is to manipulate the ball in an attacking manner. 'I do this for three reasons: firstly, I believe that is how football must be played; secondly, I believe it is the easiest way to win; and thirdly, it is the best way to develop players. If you have the ball you have more time to make correct decisions, to dribble more and pass more times and to score more goals. If you play like this, then there will surely be more development. If you play a more negative style of football, you will not be developing the player that you want; you won't get a technical creative player.' *Why then does Mourinho often attempt to control the space instead of the ball?* 'We have to understand that each team is a separate organism. I believe all good teams have balance and fluidity and always have a good positional game. The style of play is matched to the personality of the coach. There is no right or wrong way of playing as everyone is capable of winning with their own style of play. I just believe my way of doing it is attacking and having the ball. I know that Mourinho has balance and a good positional game, and they also have danger in the side. It is just his idea, there is no better way of doing it.'

History, and José Mourinho, have proven Matos to be correct – there is no set way of approaching a match, especially not a game of great significance. According to Diego Torres' book on Mourinho, the manager believes there to be seven rules to follow in order to win big matches, rules that contrast with Matos' philosophy entirely. They are:

1. The game is won by the team that commits fewer errors.
2. Football favours whoever provokes more errors in the opposition.
3. Away from home, instead of trying to be superior to the opposition, it's better to encourage their mistakes.
4. Whoever has the ball is more likely to make a mistake.
5. Whoever renounces possession reduces the possibility of making a mistake.
6. Whoever has the ball has fear.
7. Whoever does not have it is thereby stronger. [18]

If winning is the primary focus, how then can a coach foster that mentality in his players? 'Well, football is a game so therefore it is about winning. That is basic.' At Porto, Matos has found that once players believe in the style of play and find that they win by playing it, they will invest further into it, thus feeding a winning cycle. 'Another way, in every training session, each exercise must be competitive. This will start to resonate with the players and they will know that, if they win in a five-versus-five practice, they may

---

18. Torres, D (2014). *The Special One: The Dark Side of José Mourinho*. London: HarperCollins… As cited by Wilson, J. in: 'The devil and José Mourinho', *The Guardian* (2015).

feature in the game on Sunday. It creates a culture of winning.' At Porto that culture is rich, historic, and has been developed by managers like Robson, Mourinho and Villas-Boas. Over time winning becomes part of the fabric of the club. Under Alex Ferguson, Manchester United became imbued with an infectious desire to win. Porto is the same. 'We win matches, yes, but we have to play good too. Because if you don't win and you don't play good then you have nothing to fall back on. Here that winning culture is everywhere.'

FIVE

CREATING CRISTIANO: SPORTING'S SUPERSTAR

For three hours on the late afternoon train from Oporto to Lisbon, a golden sun shone over new spring fields. Silhouettes of men could be seen from the carriage, walking amongst the crops inspecting their progress. Farmers harvest in the early morning and then later in the day when the temperature cools. The process holds historic significance as a representation of the new season. A good harvest is a matter of celebration and has been since pagan times, with festivals held in acknowledgement of the gifts of existence. Producing crops for sustainability every year can be viewed as a football analogy, especially considering youth production. It was Matt Busby who said, 'If you want football's finest fruit, you grow your own.' The job of a manager should be to blood new players into the first team every season. Few academies have placed a greater emphasis on that idea than Sporting Lisbon. They are the only club to have developed two FIFA World Player of the Year winners in Luís Figo and Cristiano Ronaldo. Because of the type of individual development players receive at Sporting, coupled with a reinforced message to be creative on the ball, they continue to produce some of the best attacking players in the game.

In addition to Figo and Ronaldo, Sporting's roll of honour includes: Paulo Futre, the 1987 Silver Ball Ballon d'Or recipient; Simão and Ricardo

Quaresma, the teenage sensations signed by Barcelona; and Nani, who had a similar whirlwind emergence in 2006 and was bought by Manchester United. All named wingers share a flamboyant style of play: two-footed, fast, direct, tricky with outrageous technique. Children naturally long to play in such a fashion but are taught to become tactically reserved as they grow older. At Sporting Lisbon, they encourage a creative freedom bordering on selfishness even into adulthood.

Despite it being mid-February, Lisbon baked in an Indian summer. I found cool solace in Ricardo Damas' blacked-out sports car that afternoon as he drove us to Alcochete, Sporting's training complex. Damas is a foundation youth coach at the club. At security and inside everybody called him 'Mister', a tradition that stems from the British missionaries who introduced football to Portugal, Spain and South America in the 19th century.

Like at most other clubs on the continent, Alcochete houses both Sporting's youth sides and first team.[19] Unlike elsewhere, the facility is not in the city. It's a 30-minute drive away in Setúbal, past dry country fields and over Europe's largest bridge: Vasco da Gama. Alcochete is not modern by any means. Its décor was inspired by the 1960s. Framed pictures of legendary players look like they were hung in the 1970s. The gymnasium appears to have been furnished in the 1980s, and the five-a-side roofed pitch outside that Cristiano Ronaldo grew up on was probably state-of-the-art in the 1990s. Parked Porsches look out of place against the plastered cream exterior. Staff concede that the complex is dated in comparison to Benfica's, but that doesn't matter. Why should it? A facility is less important than the teachings offered. Jamaica's world-famous sprinters have no hi-tech equipment and train in a gym without air conditioning. Alcochete is as humble as it is deceiving; this is one of the best talent factories in the world.

'Even at a young age our players are coached to recognise the transitions in the game. They know that as soon as we lose the ball, they have to pressurise the opponent to win it back. In the attacking phase, the guys

---

19. Many clubs in Europe house both the youth sides and senior squad together in one complex. Doing so is inclusive and makes the transition through age groups seem achievable. In Britain, the word 'academy' generalises youth football. But 'academy' has its origins in Plato's Greece and means 'a place of learning'. Europeans believe learning continues into adulthood.

know to keep passing lanes near so we can build up. At U9, they know positional sense; they know angles to create when we regain the ball so we can play out from the opponent's immediate press.' Damas explained the secrets of Sporting's generation-long success over the noise of his air-con. 'We do not let our kids kick the ball long to the front, they have to start from behind, facing their own goal, and build up by passing.' The Sporting way is a similar methodology to that of FC Porto: 'In the young teams we always look to focus on our model of playing, rather than the opposition like we do with older age groups. It's not all done in one day; we have several training sessions. Say our focus at the start of the week is passing. We begin basically, then tomorrow [Tuesday] me and my group are working on the intermediate scale and how to link between midfield and attack. On Wednesday, it will be the main scale in a seven-versus-seven practice. We have 90 minutes to coach in. I do 20-minute matches for a warm-up which will be based around our focus, then I have 21 players who I put in groups and work on the scales. We finish with a small-sided game, for example a three-versus-three, where the players score lots of goals and practice finishing.'

In Porto, Vitór Matos explained the concept of tactical periodisation. Himself a student of Frade, he commented that only those who have studied under the lecturer truly understand how to implement the methodology. Nevertheless, TP has spread across Europe and is used by most elite coaches – Damas included. 'In attack, if you have the ball you go to the goal; another player should stay behind to support and the third player has to give a different passing line to help [third man positioning]. In defence, there are the opposite principles. The nearest man goes to the ball to delay; a teammate is behind supporting, then we have balance behind. Porto, Benfica and Sporting – we all promote this within a philosophy of tactical periodisation.'

Although its implementation will be different than at Porto, the principles behind TP remain the same: 'In periodisation we have a lot of the ball – it is our model – so the main thing we work on is passing lines. For example, movement and positional play. Inside this, we work within scales of the game. There is the main scale which is the match. The intermediate scale is groups – for example, how our midfield and attack link together – then there is the microscale which we develop by playing.' Ricardo led us through to a long corridor. 'If we want a lot of passing in the microscale then we practice passing, before moving into the intermediate scale of linking midfielders to attackers. Then, finally, we move in to the main scale which is the game and having positive possession.'

A Home for the Assets

In a hidden room along the main corridor sit Sporting's national scouts. At their desks, they compile reports on the youngsters in their area, stopping only to make phone calls regarding fixture coverage and individual player progress. It is essential for all clubs across the world to build up a database of talented youngsters. Similar to in England, all of the main clubs in a catchment area happen to notice a talented boy at the same time. I found, when I worked for a domestic academy, that the very best scouts were not the ones with an eye for talent (that is the easy part), but the ones who could persuade a youngster's parents to sign. 'That is true,' Damas agreed. 'These scouts do that best in Portugal.' For decades, Benfica neglected their duty to represent Lisbon's most outstanding youngsters, so Sporting capitalised.

In a few months' time, Portugal would win the European Championships with a backbone of players scouted and developed by Sporting. There would be Rui Patricio in goal; Cedric Soares at right-back; the central defender Rui Fonte; a midfield trio of William Carvalho, Adrien Silva and João Mario; and the attacking duo of Nani and Cristiano Ronaldo (replaced early on by Ricardo Quaresma) all from Sporting's youth ranks. João Moutinho would come on as a substitute after the hour to ensure 10 out of the 14 players who featured for Portugal were developed here. No academy has ever better represented a triumphant nation.

Youngsters in England sign with a club at eight years of age and join an U9 team. In Portugal, they sign aged 14. Because of that, Benfica and Sporting have a gentlemen's agreement not to lure any players away who have verbally committed to the other club. If a player is released (as was the case with Miguel Veloso when Benfica cut ties with him due to his weight), he is free to sign for the neighbours. 'It is something that the clubs decided between them so not to create a war. FC Porto do not get involved because they have the entire north for themselves, they work alone there.'

Outside of the room, head of scouting and recruitment, Aurélio Pereira, welcomed a talented youngster and his parents into his office. Pereira is famous for being the man who signed Cristiano Ronaldo for Sporting. The national scouts will discover a player and invite him for a trial, but it is Pereira who decides whether to sign him or not. Such was the case in 1997 when Pereira bought Ronaldo from Nacional for £25,000. 'A huge price for a kid that age,' he said at a European Football Academy conference in London. 'But we saw instantly he had an amazing relationship with the ball. He had extraordinary physical and mental qualities. He came to Lisbon without any family and by his second day there he was dominating the changing room – the other players were looking at him like he was a UFO, they were in awe of him.' [xxix]

Struggling in Sunlight

In 1997, the 12-year-old boy travelled from his home island of Madeira, off the north-west coast of Africa, to mainland Portugal for a trial. Although they usually take a few weeks to conclude, he was signed within an hour of lacing his boots. At first, he was picked on by the Lisbon boys for his accent, but his dedication to the club won them over before long. Every night after practice the young Cristiano would not return to his room, but rather chose to practice tricks, turns, feints and shots until bed time. At the complex presently, young players are told stories of Ronaldo's time there. The most determined boys copy him, devoting most waking hours to the ball. In his movie (a decent measure of a person's success is if they are memorialised in film), Ronaldo spoke of his time leaving home: 'I cried every day because I missed my family. My father said: "If this is what you want then go." We suffered to achieve what I have now.' It was a dedication born from adversity that inspired him to work hard.

Back in Madeira, the council erected a statue in his honour and named the local airport after him. Staff at the academy would never openly label it as a strategy (they do not target hard-up youngsters), but Sporting have benefited greatly from impoverished boys. As journalist Tom Kundert wrote, William Carvalho was born and raised in a run-down Angolan neighbourhood where survival was his main focus. He came to Lisbon as a boy and played street football against older children. Sporting were so desperate to sign him before Benfica, they got Nani to call and convince him. Nani himself suffered from adversity. The son of Cape Verdean parents, his father left the family and his mother moved to the Netherlands when he was a boy, forcing him to find refuge with his aunt. Football became his passion, although he wasn't signed by Sporting until he was 17. By then, he was determined to succeed. [xxx]

Messages

When a young player signs for the club, he is given the best of everything. A nutritionist is assigned to him and will liaise with his family to create a dietary programme. He will also have a psychologist to talk with and a physio who offers massages before training. On top of all that, he is given supreme coaching. 'My main ideas are to have a lot of the ball, to circulate it a lot and to create chances,' Damas explained, 'because you don't pass the ball for the sake of it; only to create finishing situations. These are Sporting's main ideas, too.' I asked him about the type of flair players that are typical of the club – Ronaldo and Figo – much to his delight: 'We always play against older guys so we have to move the ball faster, as they are bigger and cover the ground quicker. We do not have the money of Benfica or Porto so we have to be different. The main idea of the club is to work on one-versus-ones. If in the game a child has the situation to perform a 1v1 then they have to dribble – it is a main rule for us.' Tactics come later (when to pass and when to dribble); at the start the youngsters are encouraged to perform skills. Sometimes they offer children 'points' for the best skill-move, other times they hold mini-competitions to see who can perform the best tricks. All of the moves are named after Portugal's best players, who fortunately came through at Sporting. It is a dream for the coaches to use the likes of Cristiano as role models. 'Can you do a Ronaldo turn?' or 'Can you do this Quaresma *rabona*?' they ask. Training isn't tailored to produce players for the modern game, but for how Sporting expect it to look in the future; with more players breaking the lines all over the pitch.

'We have two teams playing on a weekend. One who play in an upper level and one will play at a normal level.' As we step outside the sun blinds us. 'The first team will usually win by four goals and the other may win by 20 goals. We have to play in this championship as it's good locally for our Sporting name. The only game that we play that is equal is against Benfica.' National press had complained that morning that Renato Sanches was too inexperienced to play in the 'Derby de Lisboa' against Sporting. Nevertheless, growing up as a player the most important match for him, and indeed all youngsters at Benfica, was against Sporting. It was the tie that decided who won the league. Those very same newspapers the following day would praise Sanches for his role in Benfica's win – they failed to understand how well-versed in the demands of the fixture academy players are.

We paused upon reaching the training pitches. A group of youngsters were playing a three-versus-three match with two small goals. 'We do matches a lot,' explained Damas – something that flows up every age group. 'We do some one-versus-one exercises, but the main part of training is letting the kids play. Our children know that they can always dribble. In Portugal, there are many coaches who think they are developing youngsters by saying "you can do one or two touches", but this is worse for the players because they all become the same. We like to let our kids have a lot of the ball.' The proof, as they say, is in the pudding. Their list of graduate wingers is without rival. Coaches who impose limitations on their sessions often harm players. While accepting that limitations can sometimes improve the tempo of an exercise, an actual football match has no limits. With their laissez-faire approach, Sporting are showing the way forward for academies longing to create a Cristiano.

As our tour of the complex came to an inevitable conclusion, the Sporting B team were training in the sun. Scottish youngster Ryan Gauld was in the exercise, having overcome the language issues attached to his move. Portuguese teammates called his name in an Aberdonian accent, not mimicking him, but because that is how they had heard him introduce himself. The session was a directional practice with two middle men receiving a pass on the half-turn before playing it out wide. Sporting B is a ladder to the first division that links youth development to senior football. The competitiveness of the league has helped the Portuguese national team. Their U21s had not lost in three years up to that point, Ricardo said. In fact, every international major-trophy-winning nation that decade (Spain, Germany and Portugal) had domestic B teams. The Portuguese second division, interestingly, is sponsored by a Chinese lighting company called

Ledman. As part of the deal, Ledman demand that every club has Chinese players and develops Chinese coaches. Such investment and the presence of Porto B, Sporting B and Benfica B has spurred national interest in the league.

The Lyon Issue: Hours on the Street

China's money is welcome here. Portuguese society struggles to remain financially secure which, despite sounding ominous, could have its benefits from a sporting perspective. Usually there is a positive correlation between a weak economy and the amount of outdoor participation youths have. [20] Many of America's best basketball players come from the ghettos of California. Most gold-medal-winning sprinters are deprived Jamaicans, and football autobiographies usually always start with, '*We grew up poor.*' Richard Williams was conscious of the benefits economic deprivation can inspire and drew up a 75-page plan to make his daughters international tennis stars before they were born. His plan involved relocating the family from a comfortable set-up in Long Beach to deprived Compton. There, he negotiated with local gangsters to use the tennis courts for their actual use, rather than the dealing of narcotics. Serena and Venus would witness their father receiving regular physical beatings from the gang members over a two-year span, until he eventually triumphed. [xxxi] 'What led me to Compton was my belief that the greatest champions came out of the ghetto,' he said.

This may be an extreme example of a humble socioeconomic environment, but the intangibles fostered in a person's character having been raised in underprivileged surroundings are visible. Muhammad Ali, Diego Maradona and LeBron James, elite sport stars, developed resilience through hardship. Football, requiring only a ball to participate, is the sport of the economically deprived.

Portugal, however, is a contradiction to the rule. For many years, the country presented itself as a looming economic disaster, with an unstable debt-to-GDP ratio and a need for EU aid. Yet despite the poor economic backdrop, youngsters were not finding their way to the streets. In typical environments like this, children are too poor for indulgences like games

---

20. Gentin, S (2011). 'Outdoor recreation and ethnicity in Europe – A review'. *Urban Forestry & Urban Greening*. 10 (3), 153–61.

consoles and alternatively resort to outdoor imaginative entertainment. Damas debated the global street football issue. 'Culturally children are not playing any more like they used to, on the beaches and streets. Parents are working longer hours so the kids stay in school until later. When I was a kid, I could go to my beach and meet my neighbours there and play with a ball. Now there are no kids on the streets because there are too many cars and the cities are rising.' The younger generation are trapped indoors. 'I was born near a beach so in the afternoon I would ride my bike there to play and at night I would kick my ball about in the street. Now kids are not doing that. When I arrived at practice I had already played for three or four hours. Kids nowadays are getting zero hours, only here at the academy.'

Sporting Lisbon are one of many clubs trying to recreate street football. 'Our goal now is to just let them play. We believe kids learn to play by playing, so we let them have a lot of unstructured time. Cristiano and Figo grew up playing in the streets, so did Futre and Simão. Because they do not have any streets to play in, it's our job to recreate that type of football; less rules, less structure, just play. I have started to give them positional ideas but not very serious, I just want them to play.'

At the end of the season Benfica won the title and Sporting finished second. At Estádio José Alvalade (the large green Sporting stadium that sits one kilometre away from Benfica's large red Estádio da Luz), Sporting concluded by bringing several academy players on to the pitch who had achieved good grades in school. The home crowd applauded them rapturously, as though it was they who were in fact the champions. 'You would not get that at Benfica,' Damas reckons. Sporting fans know that one day such youngsters will be the crops harvested for a new season and a more prosperous era.

SIX

THE GATEWAY TO EUROPE: BENFICA'S SOARING EAGLE

Ruth Malosso, the alias he'd been given days earlier, felt like a prisoner during his two weeks of hiding in the Algarve. Benfica had stashed him there, away from the clutches of rivals Sporting, worried they'd reclaim him as their property. His real name, Eusébio da Silva Ferreira (Eusébio for short), was brought to Portugal from Mozambique by Benfica, despite the provincial club he represented, Sporting Marques, being affiliated to their Lisbon rivals. It took five months for Benfica to confirm the deal. Years later, he'd reflect a feeling of ownership over Lisbon, the home that never allowed him to leave. 'For me, Eusébio will always be the best player of all time,' Alfredo di Stéfano nostalgically remarked years later, perhaps reinforcing the influence of his era. When reading the following, it is interesting to consider how the achievements which painted Benfica red, the European Cup wins and global fame, could easily have been Sporting green. History does tend to be moulded by sensitive conditions, after all.

At one time, the ferry across the crystal blue River Tagus carried workers from Lisbon to Seixal, to pick fruit and make wine. It was here that the explorer Vasco da Gama planned his trips across the Atlantic and Indian oceans. Nowadays, the ferry to Seixal takes *Lisboetas* to Benfica's state-of-the-art training facility: Caixa. It is an architect's dream. Every tree and blade of grass is exactly where the design depicted. Six pitches grow in size for each age group and progress towards the Tagus. 'Your dream should be to get close to the water,' coaches say. The first team's pitch is on the banks of the river overlooking Lisbon. That was intentional. Architects wanted players to see the city they represent glistening in the distance.

A poet could write a volume of pieces in tribute to Seixal, laced with pathetic fallacy. The sun always shines and the people are all happy. Genuinely so. Even the security guards, often sombre elsewhere, smile and gesticulate in broken English. 'Who?' they asked. 'Sandro Carriço,' I replied. They invited me beyond the threshold and signalled for me to wait in reception. It was a large glassed room with polished marble floor and plush furniture. On one wall was a painting of an eagle coming out of flames, as if it were a phoenix. *E Pluribus Unum* ('One of Many') accompanied the eagle and referred to the Benfica members, of which there are hundreds of thousands. In 2006, they entered the *Guinness Book of Records* as the most supported team in the world, until Bayern Munich took that title from them. Benfica are by far the most popular club in Portugal (50.3% of the population support them) and in all of its previous African colonies, too: Mozambique, Cape Verde and Equatorial Guinea. During the Angolan War of Independence, bullets would cease on both sides of the battlefield when Benfica were playing, as natives and colonisers stopped fighting to listen for the score on wireless radios.

Inside

Sandro arrived smiling. He is a member of the Benfica LAB, the beating heart of the club, and has worked as a sport scientist here since 2013. He and his colleague Francisco, both in their mid-20s, would be my guides for the day. They're part of a young generation of intelligent thinkers working behind the scenes in football. Along the corridor walls are black and white images of days when Benfica dominated Europe. Eusébio, Águas and Coluna begin the montage at the foot of the corridor, while Rui Costa, Pablo Aimar and Óscar Cardozo end it in colour. 'The players who walk through here have to be inspired by our history,' Sandro said. Everything is state of the art, funded by current president Luís Filipe Vieira (in his fourth term in charge) as part of an agenda to place Benfica at the summit of world football once more. No longer will they be a buying and selling club – rather, it was in the president's mandate to reinvest into the club's foundations. The shift in club philosophy has seen Benfica retain youngsters, cease to buy as many foreigners and avoid third-party-ownership deals. So invested in their core are they, they're even building a retirement home attached to Seixal for former players to live in, offering them the freedom to explore the facilities, pass on wisdom and have a purpose in later life.

Neighbours Sporting Lisbon are worried about them. For many years, Benfica neglected their duty as representatives of the city, overlooking many talented young players. Sporting knew they were the second club of Lisbon, but were able to build a reputation as great youth developers. In truth, they had an open pool to fish in. Were Benfica interested, they would have ruled dominion. Tom Kundert of *World Soccer* explained: 'It rankled fans that Jorge Jesus [the manager who swapped Benfica for Sporting] did not trust Portuguese youth players, especially special talents like André Gomes and Bernardo Silva who went to Monaco. He always preferred older players and South Americans. The president has said that he wants to shift Benfica's emphasis to developing youth players and has taken advantage of losing Jorge Jesus. Now we have seen Renato Sanches come through.' 2015 also saw a significant citywide switch in mentality. Sporting, tired of being in the shadows, decided they wanted to win, while Benfica looked toward development.

Performance Analysis

We walked past the dressing rooms and the manager's office before arriving at a small, windowless room with a security-code entrance. 'Usually we only let the head coach and the president come in here,' Sandro said of the analysis department. It was a confined box, with little space between the four desks, where spectacled men sat watching football, their faces illuminated by screens. Five televisions along a far wall all showed different matches. Nuno Maurício rose to shake my hand. A tall, slim man, he came to Benfica as a coach in 1995 and became head of analysis. During his time at the club he has witnessed football transform dramatically. The idea of performance analysis was primitive back then, mostly limited to a notepad and self-recorded footage.

Statistics and performance analysis in football began, arguably, with Charles Reep in the 1950s. A former RAF wing commander, Reep recorded data on some 3,000 matches and found that 80% of goals came from three passes or fewer. His interpretation of the data was that clubs should, simply, get the ball forward as fast as possible – substantiating a case for coaches who sought to uphold long-ball football.

That idea rendered technique and skill futile, with tall, physical players taking precedence. One statistic Reep found that does apply to Benfica (and most other elite clubs), was that 60% of goals came from moves that began within 35 yards of the opponent's goalmouth. Many clubs contemporarily, especially in Portugal, press high up quickly having lost possession of the ball, so they may win it as close to the opponent's goal as possible in what is known as a 'counter-press'.

I had watched Paul Power, data scientist at Prozone, deliver a lecture on advancements in performance analysis several months before departing. His presentation, titled 'Quantifying Behaviour and Dynamic Relationships Between Players', offered the potential to be pioneering and displayed how far the field has advanced. Power explained that statistics can be two-dimensional with regards to appreciating on-field actions; his case in point being how the player who makes the move to create space for a goal does not receive any credit. His company had created technology that recognised the best decision a player should make at any one time. Dennis Bergkamp, throughout his career, created as many goals as he scored. He was able to ghost away from defenders into a space that caused confusion and allowed for Thierry Henry to capitalise. Yet statistically, if Patrick Vieira passed the ball, Bergkamp would not have been recognised. In his autobiography, he says, 'I thought a lot about tactics and the defenders' positioning, about finding weak spots...I really loved approaching football like that,' but his movements were unquantifiable. Prozone technology captures the expected outcomes of a situation, using stats to show a player what the best option to take is. It is this type of data that clubs now work with – a distant evolution from Reep's notepad.

Members of the Benfica LAB are young geniuses taken from various sport science courses at Lisbon's universities. The club have links with professors and the most engaged, dedicated students are chosen for placements. If they show willing, are football savvy, support Benfica and achieve good grades, they may be hired full-time. For the likes of Sandro and Francisco, it is a dream come true to work here (probably why they're always smiling). This generation of young thinkers are slowly being embraced by football, for the betterment of the sport as a whole.

The Benfica LAB is divided into four departments: Physiology, Nutrition, Observation and Performance Analysis (OPA), and Psychophysics – the fourth being a new branch of sport science that investigates the relationship of mental stimuli with physical performance. Football is yet to fully tap into the potential of science, but at least now it's trying.

The Department

The role of the OPA department is to compile reports on both the opposition and Benfica's performance. Reports are written, and in video format too. For a pre-match report, OPA will analyse between three and 12 matches of the opponent, depending on their quality and the expectations of the match, as well as accessibility. 'We played against a team from Kazakhstan and there was no footage so we had to travel there to watch them,' Nuno recalled. It is part of a process of tactical periodisation: data is gathered on the opposition over the course of a month, collated together and given to the assistant coach at the staff meeting. First-team coaches will discuss a method of training for the week with members of the OPA department. A video report is given to the assistant and he, with the head coach, will decide upon the best strategy to win. Pre-match messages are then shared; the assistant will talk about set pieces for and against, and the head coach will discuss a general theme with his squad.

After the match has ended on a Sunday evening, the OPA department re-watch the game three or four times, making notes on what went well and what did not. The video report given to the assistant manager helps to structure training, feeding a cycle based on what went before and what is to come. The analysis department produce ideas and the coaching team consider and then deliver them. 'It is our jobs to squeeze as much juice out of the orange as possible,' Nuno said, referring to match data. The men hired to work here are not qualified tacticians – analysis courses remain a chasm in football education – but are tactically aware coaches who impressed whilst on placement here and were hired off the back of their pre-existing football knowledge. Initially, a good performance analyst is somebody who is well versed in an understanding of technology: cameras, tablets, apps, coding and recording. They don't watch the movement of the ball, but instead watch the people around it; how they react and move as organisms in an environment, like a cohesive shoal. It is their job to analyse the functional movements of players in situations, scrutinising for lapses in concentration and weaknesses to exploit.

Database

At present, players are given mini-video reports to watch on their iPads in their hotel room before matches – homework of sorts. *'This is who you're coming up against, this is what he isn't good at and this is how you can defeat him.'* Nuno and his team work ten hours a day, seven days a week. He delegates duties and briefs staff on objectives. In between tasks, his team constantly update the Benfica Database. It is, as the name suggests, a systemised mass of data on players and teams worldwide. They record full matches, as well as key moments in games, showing the strengths and weaknesses of opponents. There are 2,000 players in the database, but Nuno insists it isn't a scouting tool – they have a separate department for that. Each team has around 30 to 35 slides of information collected, detailing transitions, set piece patterns, throw-in speeds and trajectories, as well as offensive and defensive structures. The database even records human traits, like the personality of the coach and his players, and their potential volatility (and subsequent likelihood to acquire yellow cards). Marginal gains win.

Benfica, like most other clubs, have WyScout – the global catalogue of matches and players – but prefer to build their own Benfica Database as a way of internalising knowledge. They take HD cameras with panoramic views to matches so they can record the entire pitch, not just the position of the ball. As Cruyff said, 'It is statistically proven that players actually have the ball three minutes on average. So, the most important thing is, what do you do during the 87 minutes when you do not have the ball?' Benfica's cameras, in contrast to WyScout footage, record what players are doing throughout every transition in the game, on and off the ball, and not just the spectacle of who possesses it.

There are two forms of data and Benfica collect both. There is video data, of strengths and weaknesses, and there is statistical data, that highlights trends. Benfica use stats and support them with videos. For example, Nuno showed a statistic on the number of successful moves into the opposition area (five). 'Now watch.' Upon clicking on the statistics, 2D dots appeared on the screen and adjoined the passing sequence, literally like dot-to-dot. If OPA want to further analyse these moves, they can watch video footage of the sequences and determine what made them successful – whether that be a cutting pass or a dribble through the lines. 'We pass this information on to the assistant manager in our report.'

The Machine

'Before you go, Daniel,' Nuno said as we stepped outside, 'we have to show you something.' He, Francisco and Sandro walked me down a gravelled path, past a collection of new cherry trees and into an opening of space. There, on its own, was a small modern building. They smiled to each other as we entered, and laughed as they saw my face drop. 'This cost us 1 million euros. No other team has one like this.' It was a 360° Football Room, walled by LED lights. A player from Benfica B was already in the middle of the room, receiving passes from a machine. He controlled the balls and passed them into the middle of a large flashing square. In the shadows beside the machine stood his coaches, recording pieces of information on clipboards like scientists. The young player was a new signing from Serbia named Luka Jović, of whom Benfica held high expectations.

When Jović and his coaches departed, Nuno flipped on the lights, illuminating every corner of the room. In the middle was a small patch of 3G grass and a white circle, enclosed by walls of thick black netting. 'Borussia Dortmund have one like this, but ours is better. Ours has over 100 different scenarios,' declared Sandro. Trenches ran around the outside of the square, positioned to mop up loose balls to refuel the machines with. There were four machines, one in each corner, that fired passes in at various speeds and trajectories. If, for example, the 'level' (or scenario) entailed volleying into the corner of the goal, the ball would be fired in at thigh height. Coaches input details like the position, height and age of every footballer and the machine compiles scenarios to help develop him. It then logs all performance information so coaches can see improvement. Once the player gets a high score, say 80%, the level grows in difficulty. It won't be long until every football-loving billionaire has a 360° Football Room in his back garden.

'Okay,' Nuno smiled, plugging in his laptop. 'Now it is your turn.' '*Me?*' I protested, pointing to my shoes and general attire. 'I'm not dressed to play football!' It was a weak rebellion, fuelled by anxiety at having to follow Jović. Yet within seconds I was in the middle of the square waiting for the lights to dim. My cold nervousness fell at the same time as the room's dark silence as I waited for the ball to arrive. The first level required me to listen for a whistle from one of the machines, signalling where it was coming from. I was then to control the ball and pass it into the body of a moving LED teammate.

First of all, to show me the machine's full capacity, Nuno commanded it to fire a pass in to me at around 60 miles per hour. It bounced sadly off my foot and into a trench. 'That's more for shooting first time,' he apologised, smiling knowingly. He then loaded another level up in which ten balls were passed in to me from the left and right. I was to control the pass, look up and shoot into one of two squares in the corner of the red illuminated goal. As I stood waiting, the sound of a crowd began belting out around me. 'We want to make it as realistic as possible for our players,' said Nuno afterwards. Every time I scored the machine crowd cheered, thus making me feel more confident, but booed when I missed, making me tense. '*This is how Ali Dia must have felt,*' I muttered to myself beneath the haze of noise.

'The young guys who live here can come in any time they want,' Sandro boasted as we stepped out into the Lisbon sun. It seems pioneering, a clear glimpse into the future, which is, after all, what this Benfica is all about. The staff are young geniuses, the facilities are extraordinary and the elderly have a home here. The sun-kissed trees that glisten beside the River Tagus are a symbol. They are there to represent elitism, an image of Benfica as the best team in Portugal and beyond. One feels, having visited, that if football's financial hierarchy allowed, Benfica could be the best club in the world.

SEVEN

LIGHT IN THE SHADOW OF A GIANT: PACO, RAYO AND A PHILOSOPHY OF RESISTANCE

Nicholas of Morimondo: 'We no longer have the learning of the ancients; the age of giants is past!'

William of Baskerville: 'We are dwarfs, but dwarfs who stand on the shoulders of those giants, and small though we are, we sometimes manage to see farther on the horizon than they.'

The Name of the Rose, Umberto Eco. [21]

Paco Jémez is a special manager who, at the time of my visit to Rayo Vallecano, was in charge of a special club. The atmosphere at Vallecas was positive. Yes, Rayo were in a relegation battle, but they were used to that. Everybody believed they would stay up. On the final day of the season, however, results elsewhere relegated them. Paco stood and cried. He knew he would be leaving after four demanding years. Every season, Rayo were one of the poorest teams in La Liga, with an annual budget of around £5.5m. Advisors for betting companies always tipped them for relegation. But in tribute to their fans who resist gross capitalism in football, they defied the odds. Finishing 8th, 12th and 11th, they

21. Eco, U (1980). *Il nome della rosa*. Italy: Harvest.

even qualified for Europe in Paco's first season, but were too poor to enter. Rayo's time in the sun, though short-lived overall, was exhilarating for two reasons: the fans and the manager. It was a rare and perfect coming together of two unique bodies that perennially displayed the middle finger to sceptics.

As a boy, Paco Jémez would watch his father dance on stage to the sound of castanets, clapping and soft guitar, illuminated by the amber lights of night-time villas on Las Palmas' hillside. He would marvel at the reaction of the audience towards his Flamenco-dancing father and promised himself that he too would perform when he was old enough. Paco just wanted to make beauty. Life had other plans.

He grew to be a talented footballer and was taken from Gran Canaria to Andalusia, the mainland, in his teens by Córdoba CF. His playing career was successful – he represented Spain 21 times and won the Copa del Rey three times; once with Deportivo and twice with Zaragoza (he watched from the stands in Barcelona's Olímpic Stadium in 2004 as a young David Villa destroyed the Real Madrid of Figo and Zidane). Jémez came to be regarded as a tough, no-nonsense defender; typical of his era. It was not until after his retirement that Lionel Messi made his Barcelona debut and Andrés Iniesta was allowed to become a cog in 'tiki-taka' – seen by many as the beginnings of Spain's technically brilliant age.[22] Back in Paco's day, Spanish football was robust. But even as a player he wanted to make beauty. At La Coruña in the 1990s, he was instructed by his manager John Toshack to keep things simple – rarely play out from the back, put the ball into touch. One day in training Jémez approached the Welshman with an injury: 'Mister,' he said, 'it hurts when I touch the ball.' Toshack looked him up and down. 'Paco,' he replied, 'it hurts us all when you touch the ball.' [xxxii]

Never fazed, Jémez continued to play passes into midfield and attack, to Fran and Bebeto in 1996 and then a young Rivaldo signed from Palmeiras in 1997. 'At Zaragoza, I would give the ball to Kily González and watch him do magic,' he told me from the press office at Rayo Vallecano's training complex. At the time of my visit he worked there as head coach. I'd been

22. For many, 'tiki-taka' was not the philosophy of play it was misconstrued to be. It was, rather, the visual form of 'positional play'.

drawn to Rayo because of the style of football he'd developed at the club. In September 2013, he became the first manager to have more possession than Barcelona in 316 matches (five years – 51% to 49%), having done so with a bits-and-pieces squad made up of free transfers, loans and old heads. His style, known as *Juego de Posición*, resembles Barça's developed under Pep Guardiola, and drew attention from tactics enthusiasts worldwide to one of La Liga's poorest club.

'Possession is based on two things,' he explained, when asked how it was done. 'Firstly, how long can you keep the ball? And secondly, how long do you allow the opposition to have the ball? Most people think possession is only having the ball, but it's also the speed at which you can win back the ball. So, what we did very well against Barça was that not only were we able to have possession of the ball for a long time, but we also won it back quickly. We forced them to play into areas where defensively we were stronger.' Paco beat Barcelona at their own style of play. Though possession football does not always equate to success, and can at times be frustrating, having taken Barça's greatest weapon from them – control – Paco forced them into an unfamiliar context. Despite losing the match, he won. Afterwards, as fans walked home, they talked about him as a potential suitor for the job, rather than the Argentine, Gerardo Martino.

The Visit

Vallecas, the Madrid neighbourhood that Rayo call home, is the most left-leaning area in the city. It feels like Brooklyn in the 1970s, with vast open spaces freshly made by demolished apartment blocks. The whistling dust attacks your eyes and mouth as mini-sandstorms come and go. Local children play on the debris while stray dogs sit and stare. Ciudad Deportiva, the Rayo training ground, is a modern complex slap bang in the middle of this setting. Of all the clubs I visited, no facilities were as paradoxical. The gates to the complex are always unguarded and open to the local community.

First team training was due to begin as Bebé pulled up in his red Ferrari. Vallecan children, playing football inside the car park, obliviously ignored the former Manchester United man as he walked towards the entrance. Seconds later, a stray pass sent their ball under the back of his expensive red sports car and, instead of all running away in fright (as expected), the children sent the smallest boy to scoop it out from underneath using his legs. Many can relate to having done this, but never to a Ferrari.

All age groups begin training at the same time, from U9 to the first team. Parents stand and watch from a long runway above the pitches, which grow in size from left to right in a symbolic ladder towards professional football. Sadly for Rayo, by the time the young players reach 18, the very best talents have already been pinched by Real Madrid and Atlético. In a gesture of goodwill, both clubs then loan back the 18-year-olds to Rayo to provide them with first-team experience. Because of the tactical education given to them by Paco Jémez, the standard of loans has improved over the years (Atléti mutually negotiated Saúl Ñíguez's loan to Rayo in 2014 as part of his line of progression). Halfway along the runway is a cafeteria overlooking the first-team training pitch. It was here that I met my translator, Neil Moran. Bebé was there, with another former Manchester United player, Manucho. They took selfies with the families of young players willingly, understanding that Rayo depend upon that friendly atmosphere to survive. When both men trained at the hidden village base of Carrington behind acres of trees, they were untouchable. Here, they belong to the people.

What Makes Paco

As the footballers relaxed in the café above him, Paco set up his training session. He had a full-sized pitch to work with and, despite having a team of coaches waiting to help, insisted upon setting everything up by himself. In his head, he was thinking about the transition between exercises, the space between cones and the outcome that would be produced. Jémez is a perfectionist. Every elite manager has first team coaches who deliver sessions for them. 'Hands-on' means doing sporadic training sessions each week and offering pointers to players. In a few weeks' time, I would watch Jémez's fellow countryman and philosophical kindred spirit, Pep Guardiola (considered to be the archetype example of a 'modern coach', rather than a traditional manager), work in Munich, but even then, Pep let his right-hand man Lorenzo Bonaventura set up and deliver his practice.

Jémez anomalously refuses to concede any control over training. His approach is beyond rare; it is abnormal. Neil and I spent ten minutes watching him reposition mannequins and cones. He carried heavy metal goals on his shoulders and placed them, before squatting, circling them and scrutinising their position as if they were pieces of contemporary art. Young coaches note the dedication he has towards his craft. As the session began, many of the families on the runway turned away from their children and fixed their gaze upon him.

His practice evolved from a warm-up into two 'rondos' (opposed exercises that have players inside a small area trying to keep possession of the ball). The rondos mirrored each other, with three groups of four players. A four-versus-four took place inside one rectangle, with four other players waiting on the outside to be passed to (making it an eight-versus-four for the team in possession). Paco stood facing one rondo, but was intently listening to the one behind him. After several minutes he turned and whistled – so loud that even the children on the far end of the complex stopped playing. He was furious with the sound of the exercise behind him and couldn't hear the noise of the ball circulating fast enough – the *tap-tap-tap* of passes too infrequent for his liking. All of the professional footballers stood with their heads down like naughty schoolboys as he shouted. Having intervened, the tempo of Paco's session improved instantly. Standards can always be taken from 95 to 100%, as Rinus Michels famously said.

The session moved on to an opposed (all in) 11-versus-11 match. Jémez's topic was based around improving offensive play, creating options for the man on the ball. From above it looked like chess. Every player was a pawn to be manoeuvred and gambled with. By this point, the U8s had finished training and were stood along the edge of the pitch watching – mini Rayo fans in the making. The opposition were playing a back four, so Paco positioned three attackers to stand inside the channels between the four. This pinned the full-backs back, preventing them from pressing the ball (they knew to defend both in front and behind them). Paco's team played out from the goalkeeper. His centre-backs were so deep they stood on the touchline alongside the keeper. The three of them played more passes than anybody else, waiting for an opportunity to progress forward. The deeper the possession phase begins, the more space is in the middle of the half for midfielders to exploit. Yet, as would be expected, play was congested.

As a solution, Paco shouted a number as a pass travelled back to the goalkeeper. In an example of Americanisation, the shout triggered a sequence. The deep-lying midfielder pulled away from the centre-backs and moved higher into the centre circle, taking his marker with him. The central midfielder, instead of dropping deep to receive from the goalkeeper, as a 'double-pivot' usually would, pulled out to the left wing and created an overload out there. As the goalkeeper stepped back, looking to play the ball into the overloaded space, Bebé, the left-winger whose space was full, ran to the edge of the box to receive the ball from the goalkeeper. His marker, the right-back, conscious to defend the space behind him, was cautious of moving into foreign attacking territory so chose to let Bebé go. The Portuguese man was then free to receive, turn and carry the ball forward. This triangular rotation had fooled everybody. If it was confusing to read, it was even more so to defend.

His Philosophy

Afterwards, Neil, a gentleman steeped in football, was excitable. He had moved to Madrid years earlier to discover how football was developed in Spain. He quickly became familiar with Paco's aura; the man is as well known as Cristiano in this city. Yet despite being a football man, or probably because he was one (Neil was scouting Madrid for Karanka's Middlesbrough), he was anxious to meet a pioneer like Jémez. 'You must send Aitor my greetings,' Paco said during our introductions: he knows Karanka well. Football circles are small. We met inside the press room where Paco intimidates journalists. A stocky man, bald, with a firm gaze, they call him the 'Pitbull'. He spoke no English, but Neil and I had discussed the theme of the interview prior to our meeting: to discover the cogs of his coaching philosophy.

A philosophy is defined by the *Oxford Dictionary* as 'a theory or attitude that acts as a guiding principle for behaviour'. The term was popularised in football by the great thinkers Johan Cruyff and Louis van Gaal in the 1990s. For them, their philosophies were as much a way of separating themselves as they were an approach that defined their beliefs. In a way of crediting success to the third person, they would not receive acclaim personally, but would instead praise the philosophy. It became a buzzword in the modern game made less credible by its overuse.

Every manager has a philosophy of how football should be played. It applies also to communication with the squad; use of youth players, tactical methods, media handling and an overall vision for the future of the club. A manager will deliver his philosophy during the interview process, usually by a PowerPoint presentation, and if the board of directors feel that his philosophy aligns with theirs, they will offer him the job. Nowadays, fans are able to recognise the differences in managerial philosophies, from José's to Jürgen's.

First of all, Paco says his philosophy is to dominate the ball. But he does not want possession for possession's sake – that would be futile – rather he uses possession to manipulate and control the opposition. His teams play a complex style of football called *Juego de Posición,* or 'Positional Play' in English. In *Pep Confidential,* written by Martí Perarnau, Guardiola explains to the author that only Barcelona, Bayern Munich and Paco Jémez's Rayo are brave enough to adopt Positional Play. [23]

It is difficult to pinpoint JdP's beginnings. Passing the ball to teammates was invented in Scotland in the 19th century as an alternative to kicking it long, while Rinus Michels recognised space and how to create it in the 1960s. Various aspects of the style have been seen in many teams throughout history, since its Queen's Park Glasgow beginnings. Each of these teams (Huddersfield, Honvéd, Ajax, Barcelona and so on) added ingredients to JdP, gradually evolving the style. Such teams and coaches aspired to achieve the same outcome – quantitative superiority between the lines (having two or more players behind the lines to combine and sustain possession) – but did so differently. [24]

Aspects of the modern version of *Juego de Posición* were first installed at Barcelona in the 1990s by Johan Cruyff and were built upon by Louis van Gaal, though both versions differed. Louis van Gaal said of his: 'Each player needs to know where he has to be, and that is why there needs to be mutual understanding because you need absolute discipline. This is a sport played by 22 men, and there are 11 opponents out there playing as a team. Each individual needs to know who he has to beat and be there to support his teammates.' [xxxiii]

Pep Guardiola was a prominent player in both the Barcelona sides of 1992 under Cruyff and 1997 under van Gaal. A studious man, Guardiola

23. Perarnau, M (2014). *Pep Confidential.* 2nd ed. Edinburgh: Arena Sport.
24. Research from Gareth Flitcroft.

seemingly treated his playing career as an apprenticeship of sorts. Yet it was not until 2005, when he moved to Mexico to end his career with Dorados de Sinaloa, that JdP was contemporised. There, Guardiola worked with theorist Juan Manuel Lillo – a fellow Spaniard – and the pair spoke for hours after training on the importance of retaining possession and how it could be done. 'Pep and I are intent on the same thing – gaining superiority from position. What use is good play between the lines if it does not take out opponents?' Lillo said. [xxxiv]

Historically, most evolutions in football tactics have involved formation changes, such as the shift from Herbert Chapman's 3-2-2-3 of the 1920s to Márton Bukovi's 2-3-2-3 of the 1950s. *Juego de Posición* is different. In it, the formation is irrelevant, disregarded as nothing but a telephone number by Pep Guardiola. Rather, in JdP the position of the ball determines where players move, contrary to the ball being moved by players within their shape. If the ball is on the edge of the box, for example, players position themselves in set zones. If it moves to the right wing, they move into new predetermined positions.

Its most modern adaptation gained notoriety in the 2009/10 season as Sergio Busquets became a central player in Pep Guardiola's Barcelona side, constantly positioning himself behind where the ball was expected to arrive, thus sustaining the possession phase. Busquets, despite his youth, was of the same school of thought as Brazil's Sócrates, believing clever players needn't sprint – they should already be positioned correctly. In the following years, aspects of *Juego de Posición* were adopted by Thomas Tuchel at Dortmund and Jorge Sampaoli at Sevilla, as well as Guardiola, Lillo and Paco Jémez. 'Positional Play is a musical score played by each team who practise it at their own pace, but it is essential to generate superiorities behind each line of the opponent's pressure,' Martí Perarnau told Adin Osmanbasic.

In JdP, the pitch is divided into zones. Players have responsibilities to perform whilst in these zones and know where the next pass should go when they receive the ball. Earlier that year I gained an insight into JdP from Scottish coach Kieran Smith at an 'Inspire' event in London. Smith had lived in Madrid for several years coaching local club Alcorcón. He also studied Simeone's Atlético and watched Paco's Rayo.

He reinforced to the audience that in Positional Play, it is the location of the ball that controls the team. He apologised to us for not having long enough to fully explain the philosophy: 'It would take days to explain and months to implement.' Which is part of the reason as to why Paco Jémez's teams start slowly in the league: every year at Rayo he was given a new squad of players to coach as they scrimped for loans and free transfers.

According to Smith's presentation, there are seven pillars of wisdom to understand about JdP. They are:

1. *To create superiority behind the opposition line of pressure.* 'Can we provoke the press so spaces appear and we can play out?' Smith showed a clip of Xabi Alonso facing his own goal – an obvious pressing trigger – before playing a pass back to Jérôme Boateng. The centre-back was then pressed by the runner, so Alonso peeled to the right and received a diagonal ball in metres of space, able to play forward.

2. *To play out from the back and create superiority in the initial phase.* Through circulation (passing the ball), the team travels up the field together. This allows for teams to counter-press more effectively when space is condensed during the build-up phase. 'If the pass is only ten yards away, it is easy to press only ten yards.'

3. *Use possession to unbalance the opponent.* As Pep and Paco reinforce, the intention is not to move the ball but to move the opponent. Every pass should have a thought behind it.

4. *Create width and depth so channels emerge to play in.* In the 1980s, Johan Cruyff tasked Gary Lineker with creating width. Thierry Henry, David Villa, then Neymar years later positioned themselves out on the far touchline to spread the opponent's backline. 'That is a principle of JdP.'

5. *Position players at different 'heights' on the pitch.* If one thinks of the pitch in a vertical sense, the striker would be the highest player most of the time. Having players on different diagonal receiving lines at various heights provides more options, but also confuses the opposition as to who should press the ball. Staggering lines creates 'triangulation', allowing the team in possession to circulate better.

6. *Dribbling runs.* 'This is not just a passing mentality.' Many of Messi's dribbles are horizontal across the opposition backline, enticing and pulling

opponents out of shape. Again, in the 1980s Cruyff instilled the idea of inverted wingers, with Gheorghe Hagi and Robert Prosinečki dribbling infield with their stronger foot to cause confusion.

7. *The third man and his movement.* The third man is often the free player in space. Finding him provides the team with time to make correct decisions.

Jémez

'I've been coaching now, including this season, I think for nine years, and since the beginning I've had this idea [to play positional football],' Paco explained in a fast-paced accent. 'It's true that over time you change things, you modify things, you see that there are some things that you can do better, things you can take out or put in, because it's a constant evolution. But it's true that since I started to coach at Alcalá [a Madrid team in Tercera Division – Spain's fourth tier] I had the idea that I wanted my team to play football in a certain way.'

Whereas Guardiola credits Cruyff as the inspiration for his style of play, Jémez feels he developed his alone. 'I think it's the experience of a lot of years as a player, seeing things, seeing ways of playing football, seeing another style, and in the end when you become a coach, you have to choose the road you want to go down. I chose this one because it was the one that I could identify with the most. It was the one with which I felt most comfortable.' One of Paco's most famous quotes, when explaining why his Rayo team continued to play so openly against bigger teams despite losing comprehensively (a few months before my visit they had lost 10–2 to Real Madrid) is: 'They're going to kill us anyway, so why forsake our principles in the face of death?'

'It's a way of playing in which you probably need more time. It's true that when playing out from the back you undertake more risk, but I think it's a very nice way to play. It's something all of the players are involved in, and they enjoy that way of playing. We understand that possession itself isn't really important, a lot of people only look at possession. If there's no progression toward the other half of the pitch, then possession is a problem in the end. Having the ball for a long time in your own half means you have more chance of losing it, so the idea is to have possession but always looking to progress, to get in to the opposition half, to be able to attack the opposition goal, and this is something that we make really clear to the players.'

Speakers at the 'Inspire' event, all working at academies, bemoaned how British players lack confidence needed to sustain possession for a decent period of time. 'Technically they're competent, but tactically unaware' became the theme. 'We work [with our players] a lot,' said Paco on the matter. 'They know that having possession is good, but possession on its own is not going to win you a game. What's going to help you win a game is getting the ball in situations where you can generate play, close to the area to score a goal. As much as there are other ways of playing, you'll see in our training sessions that we try to work every day on what we are going to need later in the competition and one of those things is of course possession.'

Circulation

There are a lot of passing moves in Paco's *modelo de juego* that appear to be fluid, but when asked if he works on combinations in the final third, he says that such phases are unstructured. That they come from the instincts of his attackers. 'We are a very natural team. It's true we need to be organised, but we're capable of losing that organisation very quickly and then reorganising ourselves. In that respect, I think we're a very fresh team, very natural. Lots of the situations that come about are down to the talent of the players. I've always said that the job of a coach is more important above all when the team doesn't have the ball. When you've got the ball you're more dependent on the players' talent.'

Most important for him is the message he gives his players. In training, they work on playing through the thirds, with different rotations to get the ball further forward, but in the final third he allows for freedom and imagination. Good players make good decisions, he feels. 'It's true that you can train different things but above all what you should train are habits. If something comes off or not depends on the imagination and talent of the players themselves. However, on the defensive side, you need to do a more thorough job. Everybody needs to know where they have to press, everybody needs to know when they have to defend. Everyone needs to know when they have to drop back in, and that's where I think you have to work most. Afterwards, for our way of playing, it's important to circulate the ball, to play the ball out from the back. From an attacking point of view, I think that especially with teams like us who are cool, more natural, we just give guidelines to the players for where they have to move, to be able to be in situations where we can do damage.' In other words, to be in the correct position.

Much of Jémez's training is Sacchi-esque in the sense that his players are walked through rotations of what happens from one pass to the next, as if Jémez has the gift of precognition. Unlike Sacchi, he does so using the ball in live contexts. Once more, this is a principle within TP – to train as closely to the game as possible, ensuring situations are ingrained in muscle memory. It is vital for Jémez to do this as his players arrive at different times in the season and have varying levels of understanding. For him, it can be like Groundhog Day. 'It's true, we're a team that changes too many players each season. Every year around 18 players will change. It's a difficult job for us because on top of that the players come in at different times; three players one day, another the next, so that's a problem because we don't have much time. I'd prefer to keep most of the group together and add only four new players but we start from scratch every year.'

Rayo players train for longer than any other Spanish team. Across the city, a reason Carlo Ancelotti lost his job was because Real president Florentino Pérez felt they trained too little. Here, Rayo work in the morning, spend time in the video room in the afternoon and do a public training session several evenings a week. Because time is so valuable, retaining players who are already embedded in the system is of maximum importance. Central to the education process are Raúl Baena and his fellow midfielder, the captain Roberto Trashorras. In 2015, Trashorras played more accurate passes than any other midfielder in Spain – 2,338 out of 2,699 (86.7%), ahead of Toni Kroos and Sergio Busquets. 'They speed the process up. They're an extension of the coach out on the field. They tell new players lots of things – where they need to position themselves – because they already know how things work so they save us a lot of time.'

In the rondo session, Trashorras hardly moved but played more successful passes than anybody else. When Jémez was silently watching, it was the captain who talked the most. As a naval country with an ancient structure of delegated roles and titles, the position of captain has added importance in Britain. He should be the embodiment of club values, with passion and drive. In Spain, however, they democratically select the captain, with the team placing secret votes. At Rayo, because of his devotion to the club, the captain is an obvious choice.

Arithmetic

Neil and Kieran Smith are friends. They were fellow coaching expats seeking a more intense education in Madrid and would often come to watch Rayo train, dissecting the finer points of *Juego de Posición*. Given the opportunity to do so in person, Neil asks Jémez about the first pillar of his philosophy: the formation. Paco, like his ally Guardiola, dismisses the notion as arithmetic. 'They are a way of putting the players out on the field. For me it's not the most important thing. The important thing is how the team moves on the field, how they attack, how they defend, how they press, how capable they are to disorganise and then reorganise themselves again quickly, so that the opponent can't do any damage.'

More important is the message given to players within the system. 'In the end, a team is something that is alive, isn't it? So you can't categorise it in one system or formation and say that it always has to be this way. Teams become disorganised when they play and a lot of the time it's important to be unorganised in order to then disorganise the opposition. Formations are a starting position, but the teams never end up playing how they started. We are able to change the formation many times, you know? It's got importance, but for me it's not the most important thing. What's important for me is how this formation modifies itself; transforms itself in relation to what is needed in the match.'

*

The European Capital of Football

At one time, there was only one giant in the Spanish capital, with the smaller Vicente Calderón romanticised as the beacon of light that pierced the shadows of the despotic Bernabéu. Under Diego Simeone from 2011, that light grew sharper until, in their own right, Atlético became a giant too. As if to demonstrate their rise, club shareholders voted to purchase 34% of RC

Lens in July 2016, establishing a monopolistic process of internationalisation (they also franchised a club in the Indian Premier League, Atlético de Kolkata). Forgotten beneath the giants of Madrid, though, are 25 local clubs living off unwanted players. Most recognisable are Getafe, Alcorcón, Leganés and Rayo. When José Mourinho became Manchester United manager in May 2016, rivalling his nemesis Pep Guardiola at Manchester City, Patrick Vieira declared Manchester to be the 'Football Capital of the World'. His opinion was upheld by many in the British media, though in actuality the title most befitted Madrid. The Euro Club Index, a system ranking clubs on their domestic and continental performances over three seasons, had Real (4,413 points) in first and Atlético (3,967) in fourth at the time of Mourinho's appointment. City (3,522) were seventh with United (3,106) twentieth. [25] As a result of Diego Simeone's inspirational leadership, Atlético and Real played each other in two Champions League finals in three seasons (2014 and 2016). Never before had two clubs from the same city even contested a European final. This Madrid domination was the backdrop in which Jémez had to operate.

The city is the highest capital in Europe, surrounded by mountain ranges. It is the political beating heart of a fractious country. Surprisingly for a capital, there is strong left-wing presence. The hip socialist *Podemos* party, with their young ponytailed leader Pablo Iglesias, gain an abundance of support from the wider Madrid region. Vallecas is the neighbourhood in Madrid that best represents a devotion to leftism – 250,000 working-class people live here, all with a strong sense of community. They use Rayo as a vehicle of political expression. Sociologists would discover a lot by walking around the Campo de Vallecas stadium. There is anti-racism graffiti on the walls – '*ama al rayo dia de el racismo*' – and anti-capitalist graffiti on betting shops – '*Madrid es castilla pese al capitalismo.*'

During the week, the stadium is open to the community and is a hive of activity. Inside is a boxing gym, a billiards room and a function suite, hired out mostly by older-aged badminton fanatics. St Pauli stickers have faded

---

25. Methodology: 'The Euro Club Index (ECI) is a ranking of the football teams in the highest division of all European countries, that shows their relative playing strengths at a given point in time, and the development of playing strengths in time. The ECI makes it possible to calculate the probabilities of different match results (win, draw, loss) for football matches in the near future,' euroclubindex.com.

on the rustic red metal sheets that hold the stadium together. 'Homeless people take shelter underneath one of the stands and on matchdays are given food,' Rubén, a man who claimed to be the only Real Madrid fan in Vallecas, told me as I wandered around the stadium. 'When new players sign for the club they are taken on a tour of the community by the *Bukaneros* ultras.' Rayo know that they can't compete with rich clubs, so have to do things differently. Entrenching themselves with the community offers sustainability.

Paco Jémez and his players would cook for the homeless at a local community centre several times a month. One day when shopping, Trashorras was approached by a fan and told about the plight of an elderly lady named Carmen. The 85-year-old was due to be evicted by the police because her son couldn't pay the rent, so Trashorras gathered the squad together after training and convinced them to make donations. Eventually, the club raised enough money to financially support the elderly woman for life.

In the same month that Carmen was rescued, as Rayo moved closer towards their local support, Real Madrid moved away from theirs by removing the crucifix from their badge to welcome Middle-Eastern consumers. 'We should do more for our communities like they do,' Rubén the Real fan said. Los Blancos have an estimated annual budget of £469m while Rayo average around £5.5m. 'If we cared as much as they do, then the city would be better.'

*

'*Cinco minutos más*,' Fernando, Rayo's burly press officer interjected. Jémez had other arrangements, and it was getting late. He'd been here since 9am, having arrived some 11 hours earlier. Neil looked at me. 'What shall we ask?' We negotiated with Fernando to ask just two more questions. He checked his watch dubiously, but Paco showed willing. 'Go ahead,' he said. *What characteristics are needed to play in* Juego de Posición, *and are academy players identified based on these characteristics?* 'Yes, yes, but not at the start. In the first few years, what we try to do is help them improve technically, because they're really young and we don't know what their potential could be. But it's true, when they advance and are in the *juveniles* (U17–U19), they start to be incorporated in the B team and that's when we begin to look at what players are going to fit. And you ask what is required to play the system? Mental and physical fitness; decision-making; technique to pass the ball first time; and tactical understanding. We ask our players: "Where is the next pass? Who is the free man?" For our way of playing, above all we need brave players who are happy to take risks. And we truly need people with a good technical level because our main virtue is having possession of the ball for a long time.' They also need to be able to win it back quickly, so need players who will sacrifice themselves. 'People who understand that when we don't have the ball, nobody can rest. Everybody has to press to win it back so they can have the ball again. In every situation, in each position, it's obvious that we need players with particular qualities, but this is the same in all teams. I think it would be a serious mistake to try to bring players who are not right for that way of playing. For us with our modest budget, we try to bring in players that we think will fit in in each position.'

Neil and I looked over our notes. There were seven questions left to ask – it is advisable to over-prepare – but only one slot remaining. 'Ask him about his transitions,' I requested. 'Well, we try to achieve it so that transitions don't exist,' Paco answered. Neil smiled; I remained oblivious to the conversation. 'That's to say when we lose the ball we press instantaneously, because the long and fast transitions are when you end up tiring, because you have to cover a lot of distance. There are times when you can't avoid it; times when the opponents play on the counter-attack with very fast players who, when they win the ball back, play in behind quickly, and we have to send the whole group back again. What we try with these runs is to prevent them as much as possible, because they're very long runs and we're a team that play really close together. What we try to do above all is press in the zone where we lose the ball. There, the runs are much shorter in distance trying to force the opposition to lose the ball, so they kick it out or they play back to their keeper which gives us time to push out into the opposition half. We try to make it so those really long runs, when you play against teams who like to play on the counter, like Real Madrid with Gareth Bale and Cristiano Ronaldo, don't happen. They've got really fast players. If we have to be running 50 metres during the whole game, when we get to the

70th minute our players are exhausted; they're dead. So, the shorter, more intense runs are a lot more effective.' His message is run together, run less.

The night Rayo had more possession than Barça, they worked hard to win the ball back in transition. Their possession stats reflected the amount of times they successfully pressed Barça more than the minutes they retained the ball for. Upon winning the ball back, Paco had variety in the transition to attack. Some coaches, like Claudio Ranieri when he was at Leicester, base their system around counter-attacking instantly. Others, like Louis van Gaal used to, often slow the transition down and look for numerical superiority. Paco prefers for his players to have game-sense, so they can identify what the correct decision is: 'It depends where we win it back a lot of the time. When we win it back in our half, first of all we need to have some possession of the ball (circulation) to allow us to take up good positions. It also depends on our players, but normally if we win it back in the opposition half the idea is to always try to commit to an attack to cause danger. But mostly it depends on the players who you've got on the field. There are times when you've got more direct or faster players on the field, so you try to make the most of this speed. And there are other times when you've got players who like to link up and combine more, players who'll come inside, so when you win it back you need to have a bit of possession to be able to attack.' This is part of match preparation. Managers will look at the strengths and weaknesses of the opposition and will discuss with their coaches what the best form of strategy will be, in regards to winning the transitions. They then train this throughout the week.

Tunnel Light

As our interview concluded we managed to squeeze in one more question and asked Paco about the pressures of his job. 'I say it to all the people who come here, because lots of coaches come and study us, if they want to work at an elite level they should have a good think about it. It is a profession that has bad moments, because the manager has to take on almost all the responsibility of what has happened. There are a lot of situations where you find yourself alone. But it also gives you a lot of satisfaction. If anyone is able to arrive at the moment that we're in now, to be able to play amongst the best teams in the world, I think it's a moment to enjoy.'

In a few months' time, fans would wait outside Rayo's stadium for over an hour at the end of the season, chanting for Paco to stay. Perhaps Rayo should have played a more reactive style of football. Through pragmatism they could have prolonged survival, like that effective Stoke City beast did for so long before reinventing themselves. In every match, Rayo were vulnerable. Their squad constantly reloaded with new players adapting to their system. It became tiresome for the coach. An unsustainable policy. But without the beautiful ideas of Paco Jémez and men like him, constantly told they're mad, that it can't be done – that pragmatism is a greater approach – then football would be less. It is through visionaries that society evolves. Michels was a madman, as too was Sacchi. When history is recalled, it is rarely the names of pragmatists that are mentioned. Perhaps it's best it ended this way. Had Rayo survived, they would have been forced to become more commercialised to gain profit. It is the St Pauli dilemma: win and lose identity, or lose and retain it? For Rayo, winning is too obvious an outcome, too predictable. It is instead more poetic to sustain, to remain, to be unchanged in the face of giants. Theirs is a light that will never go out.

EIGHT

BARÇA:
AN EMPIRE'S PALETTE

'We crossed spacious streets, with buildings resembling palaces. In La Rambla promenade, the shops were well illuminated and there was movement and life... I did not decide to go to sleep, even though I wished to, so I could rise early and contemplate, in daylight, this city unknown to me: Barcelona, capital of Catalonia.'

Hans Christian Andersen, 1862.

Arguments for Art

Antoni Gaudí, the Catalan-born artist whose work continues to draw tourists to Barcelona, believed the city was so receptive to art and architecture, both grandiose and simple, because of its fortunate location. 'The inhabitants of places bathed by the Mediterranean feel beauty with more intensity,' he wrote at the turn of the century. It is, as Andersen found, a city most alive. Its football team, FC Barcelona, has, at least since the days of Johan Cruyff, sought to please locals with artistic displays of attacking brilliance in line with the vibrancy of the city.

On 22 August 1973, at 11am, KLM flight number 254 from Amsterdam to Barcelona landed carrying Cruyff. At the time fans were worried. Here was this skinny guy who smoked like a chimney and had cost six million

Dutch guilders – a world record – supposedly to stock Barça's dusty trophy cabinet. They hadn't won the league since 1959 and the region was still mourning the loss of Pablo Picasso, who had passed away four months earlier, in a period between artists known as *el vacío*. What could Cruyff do? Barcelona were fated to underwhelm as long as Franco ruled. But the Dutchman had a Provo spirit and believed the world around him could be changed. 'I was here under the Franco dictatorship: I understand how Catalan people think,' he later declared. Through his performances, attitude and his significant personal-life decisions (like giving his son a Catalan name), Cruyff revolutionised football in the same way Picasso had art. [26]

Both men lived with a shared creativity. Barcelona won the league in Cruyff's first season as he showed fans 'four-footedness', unseen before, using the inside and outside of both his left and right foot to pass and shoot. In a match against Atlético Madrid the December following his arrival, he scored *el fantasma gol* (the phantom goal), contouring his body to score with his right heel whilst levitating two metres in the air. Fans on the Mediterranean (Gaudí's receptors of beauty) would study the goal for years to come, treating Cruyff like an unknown sculpture.

His artistic way of playing football carried through into his management career. Returning in 1988 to create the 'Dream Team', Cruyff won Barcelona's first European Cup. Giorgio Vasari wrote the below in 1568 of the scientist, artist, inventor and architect Leonardo da Vinci, but his words apply in a football capacity to Johan Cruyff:

> The heavens often rain down the richest gifts on human beings, naturally, but sometimes with lavish abundance bestow upon a single individual beauty, grace and ability, so that, whatever he does, every action is so divine that he distances all other men, and clearly displays how his genius is the gift of God and not an acquirement of human art.

---

26. It is important to understand that before Cruyff managed them, Barcelona were a deeply underwhelming, underachieving club with no fluid style of play or understanding of the commercial face of the game. In fact, when the attacking midfielder José Mari Bakero passed the ball backwards or wide in the late 80s and early 90s, instead of turning and shooting, fans in the stadium whistled him. It was only when trophies followed as a consequence of their style of play post-millennium that fans came to appreciate it, and the modern elegant Barcelona regarded contemporarily as a benchmark of visual, sporting and commercial success came to be.

Whereas da Vinci chose Florence, Cruyff selected Barcelona and its mountainous backdrop as the canvas on which he would work. 'He got a blackboard and drew three defenders, four midfielders, two out-and-out wingers and a centre-forward,' recalled midfielder Eusébio. 'We looked at each other and said, "What the hell is this?" This was the era of 4-4-2 or 3-5-2. We couldn't believe how many attackers were in the team.' It was daring and revolutionary, and would prove to be lasting.

Fountains

When Albert Capellas was a junior coach, he spent his time watching Cruyff's team train rather than attending university lectures. 'I was a dreamer,' he confessed to me when we met. Capellas would later become youth co-ordinator of La Masia, the academy farm home next to Camp Nou, tasked with carrying through Barcelona's attacking style implemented by Laureano Ruiz and cultivated by Johan Cruyff.[27] [xxxvi] Capellas oversaw a period of blinding success for La Masia. In the 2009 Champions League final, Barça won it with seven home-grown players in their starting XI. Capellas and his colleagues' work was further recognised in 2010 when the three Ballon d'Or nominees, Lionel Messi, Xavi and Iniesta, were all La Masia produced.

'Barça wants 50% of its team to come from the academy; this is because they know the culture of the club and they come with *time* already invested in them,' he explained. One thing a manager can never possess is time. He works daily to justify his position – creating a club philosophy is not always feasible, therefore *time* must come from below. 'And 15% of players must be top internationals, like Michael Laudrup, Hristo Stoichkov, Ronald Koeman, and the Brazilians: Romário, Ronaldo, Rivaldo and Ronaldinho. Then the remaining 35% are signed from the nation to fill the gaps we cannot produce.'

Capellas was smiling. 'Our message we said was: "If we run together, then we run less."' It referred to pressing the ball immediately after losing

---

27. Laureano Ruiz was named La Masia co-ordinator in 1974. It was he who aligned the playing style of the academy for every age group and began the succession plan of recruiting technically gifted players – even if they were small – rather than physically outstanding boys, as had been the case previously. He credits himself with introducing 'rondos' to the club, saying he invented them in 1957. According to the late Tito Vilanova, Barça had throughout the 1970s and 1980s continuously developed technical youngsters but the style of the first teams differed. It was only when Johan Cruyff replaced Terry Venables that the pathway opened. In other words, Ruiz planted the Barça style, Cruyff nurtured it, and Guardiola reaped its rewards.

it to avoid sprinting back into their own half, like Paco explained at Rayo. La Masia's *el Joc de Posició* methodology was based around what Capellas describes as 'the three Ps': Position, Possession and Pressure. Position on the field, possession of the ball and pressure (on both the man on the ball and the space around him) to win the ball back as quickly as possible.

He looks like a politician, or a businessman, or a lawyer perhaps, but a man of stature for definite. 'In July 2007, when I first met Pep Guardiola before he started coaching with Barcelona B, I asked him how he would like his team to play. He told me, "I only know two things: that every player in my team will run, and we will try to move the ball faster than the opponent." It is obvious that Pep knows much more than just these two things, but it is our jobs to make complex football simple.' Capellas' role was to make the difficult understandable for children at La Masia. 'You must have tears in your eyes when you talk about football, it is organic, no two situations are the same.' Therefore, the job of coaches at the academy was to familiarise players with situations to help them make correct decisions often; like Andrés Iniesta, who Capellas coached. 'He is always thinking what is the best for the team, but never what is best for himself. His technical and tactical skills are outstanding. We were so lucky that we were in the right place that we could spot him. You only get a player like him every 40 years.'

Arguments for Science

Good art inspires wonder. The components that come together to create a masterpiece, whether they be palette shades or the use of light and shadow, require a process of creation – a science. Picasso was a receptor of the environment around him. Living in Barcelona, he acquainted himself with anarchists and radicals and as a consequence began to move away from classical techniques to form his Cubist style. He would work from 2pm to 11pm without eating and drew from memory, before stopping, staring at his work for an hour or so, and going again. That was his process: the science behind the art. A similar approach applies to all pieces of great art. Be it Vermeer or Matisse, they all had a way of working, a science, that goes undetected beneath the canvas.

Pep Guardiola said of Johan Cruyff: 'He painted the chapel, and Barcelona coaches since merely restore or improve it.' [xxxvii] To discover that science, the Barcelona science – patterns and movement, angles and distances – that created a chapel of art adored by fans worldwide, I met with Albert Rudé.

I'd first encountered Albert in 2012. My university class had travelled over to Barcelona to discover the culture of both the city and its club during a study visit. Albert was one of the speakers, well versed in the methods of La Masia, and opened our minds to the tactical inner workings of Barça. We had, naively, watched the spectacle of play and admired the ability of the players; but Albert dissected every move and showed us, in a morning presentation that ran into the afternoon, how and why every player moved as individuals within the collective. We were awestruck. That was at the University of Vic-Universitat Central de Catalunya where he was a lecturer. At the time of my return, he was assistant coach at Mexican side Pachuca working alongside the Uruguayan, Diego Alonso. In 2016 they won the league *Clausura* championship, finishing ahead of Monterrey.

But in March he was back in Barcelona visiting family and agreed to meet to dissect the club once more. Beneath the shadow of the stadium, he explained the science. According to him, no matter who the manager is – whether that be Frank Rijkaard or Luis Enrique – the team is a self-organised system. 'Barça have a holistic perspective and each component [each position in the team structure] has to contribute. The coaches are just able to guide the learning of their players and manage the emergence of the team. Therefore, it will be the environment and the team itself which will teach the players.' By this he means that each player in the team must base his decision-making on the football environment happening around him – the positioning of his teammates in relation to the zones on the pitch. 'It is negentropy, you know? The degree of order in a system.'

It could be argued that if a club's style is dependent upon the players more than any individual coach, it could potentially wane as they age and inevitably retire. Albert believes, though, that many of the core aspects of their play will remain – either through new talents emerging from La Masia or through their style becoming embedded as tradition.

More than technical brilliance, there is mathematics that has carried through Barcelona's teams – from the first Rijkaard-built squad of Deco, Ronaldinho and Giuly; the Guardiola team of Henry, Eto'o and Messi and most recent one of Suárez, Neymar and Messi – which will continue to be visible in future years. It involves angles, distances, measurements, weight and timing of movements. 'The main difference which marks Barcelona out from other teams is that they understand that, while the system is being adapted to the environment, the environment is also adapting to the system,' Albert said. Tactically, they consider the shape of the opposition, spaces, the position of the ball (*Juego de Posición*), and the time of the match for tempo.

'When in control of the ball, Barça's shape is 1-(goalkeeper)-2-3-2-3 with as many lines as possible. The man in possession of the ball, whether he is the lateral defender or the *delantero* [striker], always has 100% of play possibilities,' or rather he has three options to pass to. Backwards to the goalkeeper (or generally to the next line behind), inside to a midfielder, or forwards to an *extremo* (wide forward, like David Villa or Neymar). It is about creating numerical superiority around the ball to support the man with it. Barcelona overwhelm the pitch both horizontally and vertically, ensuring there are players positioned within each line. Tiki-taka, as it came to be known (a word Capellas tells me is frowned upon at La Masia), was not an exercise in totalling up how many passes Xavi and Puyol could get, as it was often interpreted, but was part of a process of enticing the opposition towards the ball so spaces emerged elsewhere to exploit.

'There are four phases to Barcelona when they are in the offensive tactic,' Albert said, consulting a page of documents. 'Phase one is the position of the teammate to maintain possession. Two is moving (having considered space within the environment) to support possession. Phase three is creating overwhelmed zones near the ball so the man in possession is able to switch it into space; and four is having offensive cover for the next transition so players are in high density zones to press.' In March when we met, Barça's Positional Play was unique to them. It had been fostered at the academy and developed years earlier by Pep Guardiola as manager.

However, new imports raised elsewhere in different styles of play gradually diluted its effectiveness. For all his talent, fans said Ivan Rakitić could never be as influential as Xavi in Barça's *modelo de juego*. [28] 'Obviously, we're adopting a different sporting model with transfers given

---

28. Eventually, Barça will move away from their unique way of playing and come to rely on individual brilliance when teams learn how to defeat them (and when influential players who have pillared the style for many years retire). They'll sign outstanding talents as they did before, and will certainly continue to win, but they will do so differently.

more importance than the youth system. Is the playing style at risk? Is it sustainable?' presidential candidate Victor Font pondered. The number of La Masia graduates in the first team at the time of his campaign was Barça's lowest total for many years (eight players). Fellow candidate Toni Freixa similarly complained about self-gratifying transfers: 'This is an inexorable trend that makes the club just like any other.' The press came to reference an old Spanish saying, '*pan para hoy, hambre para mañana*', meaning 'bread for today, hunger for tomorrow'. In other words, by overlooking La Masia as the club's prime focus, Barça could starve in the long term. [xxxviii]

That afternoon, a Barcelona side trapped between ages picked Getafe apart. To give 100% of passing options for Iniesta, if he received a pass in a central position, most players made a move of sorts: Piqué dropped deeper to give him a safe outlet; Alba moved higher up and began to make a run, confident in Iniesta's ability to keep possession; Turan stepped forward into the next line; Neymar moved wider and Messi dropped in to face him. Through their positioning, they maintained possession. Other players would remain static within a zone, knowing that the ball would eventually find them in the next phase. Sergi Roberto and Munir were staggered on different lines on the left channel, with Neymar just ahead of them, waiting for the switch of play to come. 'Their body position and the way they are facing is a form of unspoken motor communication,' Albert pointed out. When the ball got passed wide right to Messi, Neymar stayed on the left touchline. Only when Messi began to dribble the ball infield did Neymar begin to move, making a blind-side run behind the defenders towards goal, just like Thierry Henry and David Villa did so successfully in the years before him.

Modern Empire

Eighty thousand members of the public would gather in the Colosseum, that giant oval amphitheatre, to watch gladiators destroy their sacrificial opponents. It was built to project the power and wealth of Rome and was used by emperors to keep the mob satisfied through entertainment. Its shows – reconstructions of famous battles, or the introducing of exotic animals taken from across the empire – were used to inspire patriotism. Gladiatorial schools were traditionally built next to the Colosseum for future generations of Roman legends to emerge (much like La Masia). 'Never, in its bloodiest prime, can the sight of the gigantic Colosseum, full and running over with the lustiest life, have moved one heart, as it must move all who look upon it now, a ruin,' wrote Charles Dickens upon visiting. Perhaps 1,000 years from this age, given its resemblance, cultural similarity and lusty life, writers will stand outside Camp Nou and be moved by stories of Cruyff, Maradona, Rivaldo and Ronaldinho.

Like the Colosseum, Camp Nou is a den of political expression. Outside of it, Catalan flags hang on the balconies of apartments – a response to a perceived invasion – with almost all of them featuring the blue or red triangle of independence: the *Estelada*. On 17 minutes and 14 seconds, fans sing about Catalan freedom (*independència!*), in reference to 1714, the year they lost the war of succession. Newspapers used to fearmonger people that if Catalonia became independent again, FC Barcelona would not be able to play in La Liga. Many believed them, so an agreement was had between club and country to keep FCB in Spain before any future referendum.

Although they would say otherwise, FC Barcelona need their rivals Real Madrid – that great symbol of Spain – to prosper, and likewise. It is syntax and semantic identity: you are what you are not. FCB and RMCF uphold the rivalry for both marketable and competitive prosperity. Yin needs yang. Spain is peculiar in that fans have a main team who they support, be it Zaragoza or Betis, but everybody picks either Real or Barça as their second team. They're institutions of huge cultural significance.

'Real Madrid are the second-most supported team in Catalonia, ahead of Espanyol,' Albert Juncà, PdD of UVic-UCC, told me. 'A lot of Spaniards who supported Real came here from the south because it was a good economy.' I had also met Juncà in 2012 and did so again at the Getafe match. Inside the stadium, players' faces appeared on a big screen as the team was announced; not their actual faces, but those from the video game *FIFA*. The atmosphere was theatrical, accommodating the often tabooed 'Mexican Wave' when Barcelona scored. The Scandinavians and Americans sat around us took great delight in it all. Qatar Airways sponsor a shirt that for over 100 years refused to yield to commercialisation. Because of the presence of all factors, I asked Juncà whether FC Barcelona could still justifiably brand themselves as '*Més que un club*': more than a club? 'My brother is a member, so are some of my friends. They are definitely concerned with these issues. But we also want a budget to sign great players. In some games, when Barça are expected to win 10–0, the *socios* [members] may not be there. But in the big games they are. There is a ten- to twelve-year waiting list for season tickets and the stadium capacity is being expanded to 105,000. We had elections and some candidates proposed to remove the sponsorship, they asked all of the *socios* who said Qatar were okay – not to worry. They're aware that they need them to have Neymar or Suárez.'

Messi is the modern gladiator. Getafe on that day were his sacrificial victims. He scored one, provided three and missed a penalty kick to send Barça 11 points clear at the top – a position they would remain in all season. Simon Kuper described him as a *pibe*: 'A figure Argentine football fans have had in their heads since the 1920s.' [30] *Pibe*s are small and creative with dirty faces and can dribble past an entire team. They belong to the people. My Catalan friends told me of a similar boy who they imagined, of a *nen prodigi*, who, instead of being a dribbler like the Argentinian *pibe*, was, amongst other things, a gifted passer of the ball, able to make fools of Franco's Real Madrid. Such legends become flesh maybe once in a lifetime, if the people are lucky. Barcelona are beyond that. They had a *pibe*, Messi, and a *nen prodigi*, Iniesta, in the same squad for over a decade. Thirty trophies were won in that time: four Champions Leagues and eight La Ligas.

'Artists do not need monuments erected for them because their works are their monuments,' Antoni Gaudí wrote, perhaps expecting Messi and Iniesta. Whether it is science or art, there are no fresh superlatives left to be written about FC Barcelona and the aesthetics of their play. They're majestic; poetic motion. The dictionary defines art as 'the expression of human creative skill, appreciated for beauty or emotional power'. It also applies, conceptually, to Barça. For how long that will remain though is yet to be seen. In time, they will move away from the *Juego de Posición* style that made them unique, as teams discover a way to counter it. Such evolutions are natural in football; from the end of Pelé's Santos to the conclusion of Sacchi's Milan. Coaches will leave and players will age. Only when analysing how long success was sustained for can greatness be measured and compared. The end of Barça's

29. Kuper, S (2011). *The Football Men: Up Close with the Giants of the Modern Game*. Great Britain: Simon & Schuster.

reign will be a celebration, inspired not by disdain but by appreciation. They prolonged triumph for longer than any other team in modern history. If Barça were to remain at the mountaintop there would be a complacency of affections – a process of getting used to and eventually tiring of them. Because Rome fell, history appreciated its influence. When Barça falls, fans will be able to look back at them as football's greatest ever team. As football made art.

NINE

HAGGLERS, MERCHANTS AND MEDITERRANEAN DREAMS: THE AGENT OF MARSEILLE

'A lo loco se vive mejor! A lo loco se vive mejor!' reverberated around the stadium. 'You live better being crazy' was the chant. It was a tribute to Marcelo Bielsa, the former Athletic Bilbao and Marseille manager, sung in unison by Basques and Marseillais when they played each other in February 2016. Adored in both cities, Bielsa became a symbol of rebelliousness. In Stade Velodrome, his face was painted on banners in the style of his fellow Argentine, Che Guevara. The fusion of cultures within Marseille has offered a platform for leftism to thrive. That standing was cemented by the racist responses from elsewhere. Clubs like Lille, Nantes and Strasbourg would chant xenophobic bile at Olympique Marseille when they visited in the 1990s. When anti-Semitic attacks broke out in France, Marseille ultras began wearing kippahs to matches in support. Upon arriving in the city contemporarily, the train doors slowly open and people pour out into what can only be described as a chaotic hotbed of passionate life. Somehow, in this disorderly environment, a football club survives.

A map would suggest it to be a simple journey from Spain to France. It is not. It is a complex trip from the unrecognised state of Catalonia to the consciously separatist city of Marseille. Alexandre Dumas described the Catalans as settled seabirds with their own tongue who arrived in Marseille centuries ago. The fort walls of the city remain open to Catalans today, and to Italians, and North Africans; after all, Marseille is a melting pot of everywhere else. One local with a Catalan family, the mysterious Eric Cantona, is the city personified. His defiant nature, passion, aggression, artistry and philosophic detail is deep-rooted in the character of the people. He could be from nowhere else. 'Sometimes you get submerged by emotion. I think it's very important to express it,' he once said when describing his playing style. 'My ancestors were fighters, something I have inherited.' [xxxix]

Industrial port cities and towns in Europe often hold cultural or political tensions with their nation: Barcelona, Marseille, Bastia, Palermo, Bilbao, Naples, Rotterdam, Hamburg and (half of) Glasgow mostly prioritise civic pride over national duty. A self-reliance stemming from maritime exploits – of commerce and trade – ensures many major port areas regard themselves as the exploited. Rich cultures historically emerged from tales and insights born afar, fostering a strong individual sense of purpose. Here, the French do not fully embrace the city of Marseille and the people see themselves as outsiders. The great irony is, whenever 'La Marseillaise' (the national anthem named after the people of Marseille who marched on Paris, spurred by patriotism to fight in the French Revolution) is played in public, locals jeer it. Marseillais are a proud people. Being referred to as 'Africa', a dig at the number of Tunisians, Algerians and Moroccans living in the city, as well as being regarded as criminals by the rest of France, with the media reinforcing negatives, has seen a process of drawbridge-lifting.

In psychogeography, academics study the relationship between place and people, notably how a place can influence the mentality of a group and vice versa. [30] For this topic, Marseille offers itself as an excellent case in point. Its citizens are shaped by the insularity of its geography: a cul-de-sac town facing southern Europe and North Africa with a fear of being stabbed in the back.

What's more, the French do not believe Marseille. An 18th-century legend satirises how the people here told outsiders that a sardine had blocked the port entrance. They were ridiculed and called liars – *how can a sardine block the port?* In actuality, *Sartine* was one of Louis XVI's frigates sunk by the

---

30. Erdi-Lelandais, G (2014). *Understanding the City: Henri Lefebvre and Urban Studies.* Cambridge: Cambridge Scholars Publishing. 228–9.

British at the gates of the port, preventing traffic from coming and going. That paranoia within the city became infectious. Napoleon built a palace here on the highest point to scout for enemies on the horizon of the Med.

Protected by two forts, a distrust of outsiders has plagued the community, even those who work at the local football club: Olympique de Marseille. A mutual connection had arranged for me and the then president Vincent Labrune to meet during my visit. OM were cautious to begin with, then performances declined further and our meeting was called off. That's football, unfortunately. If it were a fluid game we wouldn't be as infatuated with it as we are. Because it is flawed, with winners and losers, it excites us eternally.

Before Qatari money arrived, Olympique Marseille were the greatest club in France. The raucous dedication of their fans and the beauty of the Côte d'Azur enticed the very best footballers in France. In 1993 they won the European Cup, defeating Milan, with Didier Deschamps, Marcel Desailly and Fabien Barthez in the side – future cogs in upcoming French triumphs. Since the 2000s however, OM have been in a state of perpetual decline having won only a single Ligue 1 title since their European triumph.

Money moved away from the south of France and Olympique Marseille got left behind. Yet throughout the barren years, the club and city remained staunchly proud. With good reason. Marseille is a wonderful place. Like New York and Rio, its stories, climate, location and people make visitors feel as though they're in a city of substance. I stayed in Vieux-Port (the Old Port). In the coming months, it would be the scene of hooliganism, but during my visit it was a location that stimulated writing. Tourists stood day and night gazing out beyond the forts and port, daydreaming. Indeed, it would have been extraordinary to have at one time witnessed tall ships coming and going; their magnificent sails carrying Mediterranean enterprise. Back then there was a romantic idea belonging to the sea. The unknown world was made thrilling by tales from afar. Nowadays, Vieux-Port accommodates white yachts on glistening water that journey wealthy gentlemen to Monte Carlo and back in a day.

While the buildings around the port have changed, the sea air remains. It carries the smell of prosperity. The sound of haggling merchants with their thick accents has been a staple of the city for centuries. Generations of Marseille seamen long since forgotten instilled a treasure-hunting nature into their children. The people now quite naturally long for prosperity. The great decision of a young man's life is whether he will pursue a criminal or legitimate form of career. The local hero Yazid, known elsewhere as Zinedine Zidane, is a source of pride for both his financial and footballing success. [31] *The French Connection* was born here, but not all criminals are from here. Most Marseillais are honest, straight-living people – the rougher the setting, the warmer the folk. In the dusty Castellane projects where Zidane was raised, there were more good kids playing football than there were playing with guns.

One such honest person I met was an agent called Mehdi Joumaili. Surprisingly, given the overwhelming presence of football on the people of Marseille, coupled with their desire to escape financial hardship, the area has few football agents. Mehdi does well in the city because he is from here. He understands what it is like to be a Marseillais: 'We are Marseille before we are French. Marseille first. Basically, Marseille was historically the naughty one. Louis XIII – I think it was him – turned the cannons at Fort St Jean on us during his reign and not out to sea! We are not like the rest of France, that is why we are so paranoid.'

He embraces that paranoia. Football is an often mistrusting industry, especially in this part of the world. He was a footballer in his youth – playing alongside Samir Nasri for a while – but studied marketing when it became obvious he wouldn't make the grade. During high school, Mehdi would sneak off to Stade Velodrome to lay out *tifos* with the South Winners 84 Ultras. Because of his background, the usually sceptical Olympique Marseille trust him. He represents players from OM, South America and the rest of Europe, and offers them psychology and nutrition coaches. These are modern times and he's riding a wave of change in football. 'You have to watch your players on Snapchat, Instagram, Facebook and Twitter. My marketing experience helped me to connect with my players on these platforms, to understand them. You have to be kind to your players and defend their interests.'

Because of the overwhelming nature of the sport now, footballers need assistance. The demands placed upon them by interior and exterior forces make them vulnerable. Most agents enjoy cordial relationships with

---

31. Zidane is also loved because he remains a Marseille fan (he named his son Enzo after the Uruguayan Francescoli), and all of his achievements, according to locals, are a toast to the city's greatness.

clubs, but that isn't newsworthy, so fans only hear stories of greed and gluttony. Mehdi is trying to improve that image: 'You have to be good with your players and constantly think about their interests. I talk to my players once a week, even if it is by text saying, "Have a good game and give your guts." Then I look at their performance afterwards. I have a guy playing with the first team and the U19s, so he is playing a lot. I found out he scored and they won 6–0, so I contacted him immediately to say well done.' In 1967 the Beatles had a song that opened with 'La Marseillaise', which Mehdi cites as a guide in his methods: young footballers – all they need is love.

But there is more to being an agent than regular contact and support. It often goes unnoticed how important females are in a footballer's life. In the beginning, one head of recruitment told me, it is the mother (more than the father) who decides what academy a youngster joins. He's later encouraged to marry young by his club, eager to keep him focused on his career. Later, his wife will have a major input in where he plays. Mehdi knows this. 'You don't want to come between the player and his woman, so you have to work with her to know what she is thinking. With one player in Marseille I spoke with his girlfriend and asked her if he was going abroad. I asked is that okay with her? She said yes, it is fine. "So tomorrow if I have a contract in Germany are you okay?" You need two yeses, the player and the partner.' He laughed and gave me a look that implied we were members of a secret society of males. 'It has always been hard to manage a woman, right?!'

Perhaps women are more *difficile* in Marseille. People here are a little crazy from baking under the Mediterranean sun. As we ourselves cooked beneath it, our conversation led to one of OM's heroes, the *loco* ex-manager Marcelo Bielsa. 'He had hot blood like us and stood up for himself and that is part of our identity; an eye for an eye. He managed to score goals, which is what the fans wanted. We did not win any trophies, but the atmosphere was better.' Bielsa, believed to be the perfect Marseille fit, capable of both the romantic and the erratic, would sustain that belief by quitting his next job as Lazio manager after just two days.

I met Mehdi at the chic Dallayou restaurant for coffee. Outside on the boardwalk, comfortable families came and went. A man stood leaning on the rails facing out to sea; his back both literally and figuratively turned on the land behind him. Mehdi, in a shirt and sunglasses, projected success. 'There are two ways that agents make money. You have a representation contract with a player where you negotiate bonuses and salaries and external contracts with him, like a car and sponsorship where you take a percentage. And secondly, a club will give you a mandate to sell a player and you can take between 6% and 10%.'

When a player is transfer-listed it's up to the agent to find him a new club. 'If a scout has seen my player then he will send an offer to the club. The club will then tell the player, who will inform his agent. It trickles down. If club "A" want to buy a player from club "B", then club "A" will contact club "B" and ask if he is for sale. "Yes, okay we will sell for £15m," "Oh, we only see him as being worth £8m." Then they will agree. They will contact my player, who tells me. I will then speak with club "A" regarding his salary, image rights and accommodation.' With third parties like Doyen Sports a transfer becomes more complicated. They own a percentage of the player, so a club cannot sell him unless Doyen agree.

Mehdi has also, rarely, experienced the club contacting him directly. 'They say "we don't want your player here next season", so if the agent has been contacted by other clubs then they are free to negotiate. It's a lot easier for clubs to see who the agent of every player is now thanks to transfermarkt.com[32] – they can find out what a player is valued at.'

I ask him how transfers come to happen. Later, in Turin, Juventus explain how the scouting process works. Here, Mehdi describes the agent's involvement. 'There are three different ways. Firstly, a club can give you a mandate. Secondly, they may contact you if they want to sign your player. And thirdly, the two clubs contact each other and you step in to negotiate a salary and image rights.' Signing a player is a complex piece of business. Not only do the two clubs have to agree on a fee, say £10m, there is also a levy that is paid to the league (around 4% usually, so £400,000 in this case) and solidarity payments as well. An agent will then come in to negotiate the player's basic wage, his signing-on bonus, as well as performance-related bonuses. For example, a goal bonus of £10,000 or a clean sheet bonus of £5,000 – it depends on the position. Players also have targets to meet within a team that can produce bonus payments, such as top-four qualification or

---

32. Football finance website. Used throughout this book for transfer fee data.

cup wins. A growing trend in football is for clubs to offer a lesser basic wage with plenty of bonuses as incentives.

Companies working alongside both clubs will take a fee, as too will the agents involved in the deal. Increasingly significant is the image rights of a player. As 'thesetpieces.com' explained, a club will combine all fees involved in a transfer (transfer fee, agent costs, image rights and other payments) and divide them over the length of the contract. For example, a player who cost £40m on a four-year deal will cost the club £10m per year. That is how a club looks at it. On top of his fee will be his wage and image rights. Say they add up to £50,000 per week. Multiply that by 52 weeks in a year and an additional £2,600,000 will be placed on the club's budget. In total a player who costs £40m is viewed by clubs as £12.6m per year – not £40m up front.

Often, the selling club is happy for money to be paid over in such a format as it offers them a steady flow of income. It took just shy of a decade for Everton to receive the full amount of Wayne Rooney's Manchester United transfer fee. Former Real Madrid president Ramón Calderón on the other hand spoke of his bemusement when selling Robinho to the newly wealthy Manchester City. He told them the fee he wanted and they agreed straight away, paying all money up front in one lump sum. Naïve practice on their behalf, Calderón felt. [33]

'A lot of things are moving in the background. Especially here in Marseille, there are a lot of people around who take percentages,' Mehdi said. Transfers at an elite level have moved on from the traditional fax system used for decades. Previously, clubs would fax each other and wait for confirmation. They would then send a fax to FIFA, who would issue a certificate to each of the two clubs' leagues. After that, the leagues would offer out new registration papers. It was laborious, arduous, time-consuming, and could take days for a transfer to happen. Since 2010, however, clubs agree a deal and both type the same passcode into FIFA's TMS database. Instead of a transfer taking days, it now takes minutes. As a regrettable consequence of TMS's efficiency, the commercial 'transfer deadline day' spectacle that fans presently endure was born. The bad reputation agents have is a side effect

---

33. The Big Interview with Graham Hunter, available on soundcloud.com/thebiginterview. See *Ramon Calderon: Making the Deal* (Part Two).

of TMS. Because transfers are so easy to do, selling clubs hold off until the very last moment. The buying club has already been assured by the agent that his client is willing to sign and, in the closing stages of the window, panic ensues, driving up the fee paid to all parties. Gary Neville several years before his Valencia job tweeted that transfer deadline day is a good indicator of poorly run clubs. For agents, it is Christmas in August. [34]

Growing a Name

Mehdi has free rein over the southern coast of France. He will attend matches at Olympique Marseille, AS Monaco and Nice, as well as at smaller clubs like Cannes and Nimes. The idea is to identify and approach the best young talents while they are available. 'It is easy to manage a Ligue 1 player; sponsors are coming, clubs are coming. It is more difficult to take an U17 player and help him become a man with responsibilities. You always have to defend young players. I speak with his parents over coffee and ask them, "What do you want for your son?" It is good to have a plan. I talked with a young player who said to me "I want to go to England." I told him he needed to learn his strong basics in France first. "I won't put your career and my reputation in balance. Stay close to your family and let's see how you are from that point."' Monopolising youth talent is normal in continental football. In Britain, players do not get an agent until they are nearing professional ages. Here, it is common practice for agents to try and tie down the best young talents as early as possible.

In Portugal, as I discovered, super-rich agents have 'spies' watching academy players as young as 12. Mehdi has a good relationship with the coaches at Olympique Marseille, ensuring he does not step on any toes. 'I have friends [coaching at OM] who I played with. They know I am not a snake and that I have a good reputation. When I say I will do something, then I will do it; if I cannot do it then I will not say I can. You have to do your best to prove your word. If you do not know about me then ask around and you will see, I have a good name.' Having a good name is more important in a city where everybody knows everybody. 'We call it a village. I am only one person away from Zidane if I want to speak with him.'

---

34. Tweet: 'What the transfer deadline gives you is a clear indication of which are the badly run football clubs.' 31/08/2012.

Having a good reputation has also allowed for growth. Not only does he drive across *le Midi* attending matches, shaking hands and signing players, Mehdi also manages footballers in Brazil and Britain. Globalisation has allowed for instant communication. His pool of talent has grown thanks to social media apps in a global age: 'Players contact me on my Instagram and send direct messages. A young player from AC Milan contacted me two weeks ago to find him a new club because he was having financial issues there. AC tried to sell him to Ukraine but he did not want to go. They [other players] may have an agent already but are not happy. They also speak to me on Twitter. Players are talking a lot between themselves and will mention my name.' Clubs also contact him. In Europe, he talks with some clubs who want him to sell on players they own, while in South America the clubs ask him if he has any.

We settled the bill and stepped out on to the bustling streets of the city. Mopeds beeped at traffic lights, a white canopied market spread on to the road, and women in shawls stood talking as their children ran amok. Whatever misconceptions people have of Marseille, there are few cities in Europe as alive. Whatever misconceptions they have of agents, their presence is more than essential.

TEN

THE SECRETS OF SCOUTING: HOW JUVENTUS DOMINATE ITALY

'Juventus are like a desert flower. They may seem dead, but all they need is a drop of water to burst back into colourful life.'

Fabio Capello.

'They are like a dragon with seven heads. You cut one off but another one sprouts up in its place. They never give up and their recovery is beautiful.'

Giovanni Trapattoni.

The *Bianconeri* are eternal. I had spoken with my friend Luca Hodges-Ramon, an editor for *The Gentleman Ultra*, about this modern super-club Juventus prior to visiting Turin. It is now largely forgotten, but the *Calciopoli* scandal that saw Juventus relegated was just ten years earlier in 2006. They lost Fabio Capello as manager, as well as stars Fabio Cannavaro, Lilian Thuram, Gianluca Zambrotta, Patrick Vieira and Zlatan Ibrahimović. The only first team players of substance to remain were Alex Del Piero, David Trezeguet, Pavel Nedvěd and Gigi Buffon. Since then, Juventus invested smartly in the right players and coaches, without ever spending beyond their means.

'Quite clearly, they have built a reputation for securing players with high potential for modest fees and then cashing in later down the line,'

Luca said. 'This is a refreshing philosophy in this modern age of footballing mercantilism and outlandish transfer fees. What it ultimately boils down to is the club's hierarchy and prudent business model. Run by the Agnelli family since 1923, Juve is very much a family business.' One cannot, for example, envision a situation in which they would overspend funds that they do not have in the short-sighted pursuit of glory.

'Their patient recovery following *Calciopoli* is an example par excellence. Many Italian clubs have fallen foul to short-termism and extravagant spending, which has ultimately cost them – Parma under Calisto Tanzi's *Parmalat* empire, Lazio under Sergio Cragnotti's food conglomerate *Cirio*, and Torino under Gian Mauro Borsano in the early 1990s. The list goes on – and look how it ended for each club. Parma in financial ruin, Torino relegated to Serie B and Lazio on the brink. This would simply not be allowed to happen at Juve.' There is a sophistication associated with the Agnelli family's long-term outlook.

Our car travelled past the Agnelli-owned FIAT factory on Corsa Giovanni Agnelli toward Juventus' training complex. FIAT's presence in Italian society, most specifically within Turin, cannot be understated. They own Chrysler and Jeep and thus dominate the Italian car market. Historically, with factory workers being paid a wage by FIAT, they loyally chose to support Juventus (second fiddle to Torino throughout the 1940s) in a reinvestment of love. The Agnelli family would later make up one third of *tre grandi*, the big three families that controlled Italian football in the 1980s and 90s, alongside Berlusconi (AC Milan) and Moratti (Internazionale).

Such is the passion for football in Italy, families of wealth and power chose to purchase the teams they supported. Roma, Lazio, Sampdoria, Palermo, Genoa, Udinese and Napoli all had familial ownership since the 1990s. Such models began to dissolve around 2010, though. Previously, great importance was placed on a familial corporate structure. Nowadays, only the Agnelli family remain as owners of repute. Their model is encapsulated on their website in a statement: 'Juventus strives to maintain stable relationships with its shareholders by creating profits through the development of the Juventus brand and enhancement of sporting organisation.' [xli] This cool, business-savvy approach is what separates the Agnelli family from the hot-headed Mediterranean owners of elsewhere, and is most of the reason why the club is eternal.

*

How to Sign

He stands holding his new shirt up to the flashing bulbs, smiling numbly for the tenth time that day. A thousand deafening 'tweets' carry his image worldwide. Fans react in shades of adulation and deploration, without fully understanding the context of why he arrived. For most, the process of a player joining a club is blanketed in mystery. It is long, complicated and considers factors such as age, value, contract, image rights, game-model culture, agent relations and rival offers, determining whether or not a club will bid for a player. Or at least it should consider such factors.

Good clubs, like FC Porto and Sevilla, analyse potential signings for a long period of time and have backup contingencies for other players, should negotiations go beyond their predetermined threshold. 'Every month we produce an ideal XI for each league. Then in December we start watching players who appeared regularly in different contexts – home, away, international – to build the broadest possible profile,' Sevilla director Monchi explained. Likewise, Porto have over 300 scouts worldwide working at various hierarchical levels, who help to compile a 'shadow team' of players ready to be signed once a current first team starter is sold. [xlii]

Yet Sevilla and Porto are able to be more adventurous in their purchases. They can afford for certain signings not to adapt as their revenue is not sustained by silverware. Juventus, a club that constantly recruits perfect-fit players, has less room to get expensive purchases wrong, as their current position as a super-club is only upheld by the quality of their rota. In 2014, Juve were firmly the best team in Italy and finished 17 points ahead of Roma. The following year they again finished 17 points ahead of Roma, but in 2016 Napoli threatened them and finished just nine points behind. So, quite astutely, to strengthen themselves and weaken their rivals, Juventus signed the best players from both clubs; Higuaín from Napoli and Pjanić from Roma. 'A significant statement in taking assets from their only legitimate threats' wrote the *International Business*

Times of the deals. Both purchases were covered by the sale of Paul Pogba, a Frenchman who had been cheaply recruited from Manchester United's reserve team years earlier.

Responsibility for Juventus' purchases belongs with Fabio Paratici, the sporting director. It is Paratici who talks with Andrea Agnelli about transfers, and who arguably is the man most responsible for recreating this efficient modern Juventus machine. He arrived in 2010 from Sampdoria tasked with freshening up a stale squad that harboured Momo Sissoko, Miloš Krasić, Vincenzo Iaquinta and Amauri. Working alongside Andrea Agnelli, Paratici identified what players were retainable. The club was looking to redefine itself as a European force once more following the *Calciopoli* affair and decided that Gigi Buffon, Gio Chiellini and Claudio Marchisio should be retained. Everybody else was disposable. 'I treat Juventus' money as if it were mine,' Paratici said. 'It's part of my personal and professional ethic.' [xliii]

Major catalysts in Juventus' resurgence, having finished seventh in 2010, were the cheap signings of Arturo Vidal and Andrea Pirlo. Vidal, bored of living in industrial Leverkusen, ran his contract down under the advice of his then coach Jupp Heynckes, who planned to take the Chilean with him to Bayern Munich the following season. 'We came along and Italy became his preferred spot. His agent was very intelligent to understand the situation,' Paratici said. Andrea Pirlo, aged 31, they knew of. Vidal took analytic scouting. Stats showed he covered more ground than any player in Europe's top five leagues. 'Any man who can train for hours on the pitch and then go home to ride horses to release excess energy is made for this Juventus. We need his energy, his inspiring stamina. Perfect for [the] hard-working club [we're] trying to build,' Paratici told ESPN. Leverkusen would not sell Vidal to Bayern so he landed in Turin. From seventh the season before (and with Antonio Conte now coaching them), Juventus won the league.

Fine Wines
Pirlo was 31 but still young in an Italian context. Unlike in France where, as Dr Orhant explained, every player must pull his own weight and contribute regardless of his age, Italian clubs see older players as a luxury to be savoured. Their experience is viewed as an intangible, essential for team-building.

Juventus would end the 2016/17 season with Gianluigi Buffon aged 39, Andrea Barzagli 36 and Dani Alves 35, mixed in with the 22-year-old pup Paulo Dybala. Luca Hodges-Ramon had explained this age favouritism to be both a cultural and tactical phenomenon.

'Firstly, I think it is important to point out the general relationship between Italy and age. By that I mean culturally, Italians lead a healthy lifestyle and have a very good diet. Italy ranks in the world's top ten in terms of average life expectancy [82.94 years]. From personal experience, I can remember my *nonni* [grandparents] being extremely active despite their age. My *nonno* Bruno, for example, continued to work at the Poli Grappa Distillery in Schiavon well into his 70s, perhaps even 80s. There's a small village called Acciaroli in the south-west of Italy where one in ten residents live beyond 100 years due to their healthy diet, consisting of plenty of rosemary and an active lifestyle.' Studies found over 300 of the 2,000 residents of Acciaroli reached 100 years old, with 20% of that number reaching 110. Good wine, small duties and little stress, as well as family support, were found to prolong life expectancy. 'I think this cultural tradition has to be factored in. Indeed, it has a direct correlation with the nation's athletes because they are obviously socialised and fostered within this culture. I am sure Italian players tend to eat more healthily than the average British player, for example.'

Furthermore, Luca acknowledges Italy's tactical lineage which allowed for Francesco Totti, Paolo Maldini, Luca Toni and Roberto Baggio to hit 40. 'I'll use the example of Andrea Pirlo and the *regista* position. The first signs of a player with *regista*-like responsibilities originated from Vittorio Pozzo's *metodo* system in the early 20th century. Having spent time in England, Pozzo grew to admire the way Manchester United centre-half Charlie Roberts played. Roberts was capable of starting attacks, which was something Pozzo wanted from a centre-half by the time he was in management. At this point, centre-halves were only just being accommodated as part of a three-man defensive line, having initially been seen as the centre of a three-man midfield in a 2-3-5 formation. Pozzo adapted the 2-3-5 in his own way, refusing to incorporate a third back. Instead, he wanted his centre-half to be able to distribute the ball; he wanted a conductor, or in Italian, a *regista*.'

Luis Monti became Pozzo's *regista*, despite having played for Argentina in the 1930 World Cup. By 1931 he was living in Italy, having joined Juventus from San Lorenzo. 'With Italian heritage,' Luca explained between sips of water, 'Monti was called up by Pozzo to be his *regista*, his centre-half, in the 2-3-2-3 *metodo* system. He was in his 30s, overweight, and lacked agility and dynamism. But he was just what Pozzo wanted. He dropped deep when Italy did not have possession and then would embrace the role of creator when they had the ball.'

Pozzo would go on to win the 1934 World Cup. 'This creation of a specialised position in which an older, less mobile player could thrive was the precursor for Pirlo and his appropriation of this role. He is a player who has combatted age masterfully of course, using his intelligent positional sense and nonchalant style to preserve his years.' Juventus were able to sustain Pirlo's career as a *regista* as the cultural environment of Serie A, with its slower pace and tactical emphasis, allowed for it to happen. Nor did Pirlo need to run – he had Vidal to do that for him.

Passione e la Velocità

'The hard-working club' would come to dominate Italian football. Vidal became a template for every purchase to follow as the scouting department rethought its approach to recruitment. That began with Roberto Brovarone, scouting officer at the club since 2004. I met with him at Juventus' Vinovo facilities in March 2016 during a period when his department were narrowing down on potential targets for the summer; Dani Alves' name sat atop most report sheets. Vinovo, the small town where Juventus train, follows one straight road from Turin centre that begins as *Corsa Abruzzi*, becomes *Corsa Giovanni Agnelli* (home of the FIAT factory) and ends as *Viale Torino*. As I travelled south towards Palazzina di Stupinigi, the 18th-century UNESCO protected hunting lodge six miles outside of Turin, the white-topped Graie Alps came and went, flashing between apartments and wide open streets on my right-hand side. It's easy to see why Vidal chose to swap Leverkusen's factory fumes for Turin's clean air.

Roberto witnessed the *Bianconeri* emerge from the ashes to become a super-club. His work behind the scenes identifying both youth and senior players has been, alongside Antonio Conte's tactics and Fabio Paratici's recruitments, a factor in Juve's rebirth. Every scout at Juventus has to compile reports on players to add into their *Vecchia Signora* database. There are few players in the world they are unaware of, especially U20s. A Juve scout report is split into physical, technical and tactical profiles, with a final conclusion: 'For us we like to give our scouts some liberty when they do those reports,' Roberto said when asked about the areas he covers. 'Normally there is not a "Juventus" profile of players. The scout is able to make his own graphic of players to give us an image. We have scouts who are skilled as analysts, and we have other sensible scouts who have a good sensation [gut feel] of a player. It is important to have a mix between the both.'

His phone lit up as we talked. So polite is Roberto that, instead of answering what was most likely an important call, he placed his phone face down on the desk. Regaining his train of thought, he explained Juve's recruitment approach, from local kids up to international superstars. 'We have three departments. The first is the international first team scouting department. The second is the international and national youth department, and the third is the regional Piedmont scouting department. Up until 14, we can only sign players from Piedmont. In this local department, we have nine younger age scouts. They are like the chiefs of the region, and they have 38 volunteers working below them who attend matches in Piedmont. We are the strongest club here [out of Torino, Novara and Pro Vercelli] so we have to do better than our rivals to make sure we have the best players in the region.'

His phone rang again, carrying a greater degree of importance. Roberto watched it vibrate, picked it up, declined the call, and put it in his desk drawer on silent. Classy. 'The second department is the national department,' he continued. 'They are composed by one chief: Claudio Sclosa [a teammate of Paul Gascoigne at Lazio]. He has worked with us for four years. We have 17 scouts who work in each region to pursue the best players aged 15 up to 19. We also watch around 80 matches each week and focus on our targets. From an academy point of view, we know what the needs are for each team. For example, if a central defender is needed for the 1999 team we focus on the best central defenders in Italy. We can also sign players outside of Italy [provided they are part of the European Union] when they are 16 years of age.'

There are two areas for international scouting: first team scouts (of which they have three), and international U20 scouts (of which they have four). South American players can only be signed once they have turned 18, and Juventus are limited by legislation stating that Italian clubs may only sign one non-European each season.* Whether he be Dybala, the Argentine, or Alex Sandro, the Brazilian, he must be one of the best players in the world. 'These four U20 scouts follow the most prestigious competitions in Europe, the UEFA development tournaments and European Championships, and they also attend the best international friendlies. We follow U18 leagues in Switzerland, France, Germany, Spain, everywhere,' explained Roberto. 'We are looking for the best players in these categories. We have to increase the technical level of all of our teams. Different work is done for the first team because the three first team scouts go to the best five leagues in Europe and South America in order to focus on who are the best players to suit our first team. Here in Europe, each week we will go to three or four matches in either England, Germany, France, Spain, etc., and once in a month one of our scouts will go to South America. Our chief scout is Javier Ribalta. He is a young Spanish scout who has been here since 2012. He is working in South America a lot now. We mark players for the next window, this is our organisation.'

The Spaniard

'Speaking of which,' Roberto stood to face the door. Pablo Longoria entered right on cue, having arrived from the airport. He had been in Argentina observing a player and would spend the rest of the evening updating Juventus' database. Pablo is something of a prodigy in football. By the time he was 21 he was Newcastle's European scout, having performed well in similar roles at Recreativo de Huelva and Racing Santander. From Newcastle, Longoria worked for Atalanta (Juve's main rivals at youth level) and Sassuolo, where he identified players for the club's ambitious and wealthy owner, Giorgio Squinzi. Still in his 20s, Pablo manages scouts across Europe for Juventus.

Once introduced, he explained the use of technology in contemporary scouting: 'It is a pyramid process. At the bottom, you have the videos and you watch the player. If we are going to go to Romania, then we watch a

---

* Legislation in Italy regarding the number of non-EU players a club can sign is complex and varies.

game on WyScout first. After that we will make a walking video of the player over two or three games, then we will go to Romania to make the sensations [gut feeling] and two or three scouts will go to see if they have the same sensations.'

Traditionalists will be reassured to find that clubs still scout players in the flesh. Factors such as work rate, determination and selflessness are more visible live than they are on screen. 'Then we will talk with the chief scout and we propose this player to the sports director at the top of the pyramid. It also goes down in another way. If the SD likes a player, he will tell us and we will follow the procedure for that player. In the minor championships our system is to start watching the players when they are 15 to 16 years old when they play for Romania, for example. It is a risk to spend money to go and observe a game before having seen the player several times.'

In the six years following Fabio Paratici's hiring Juventus won five league titles, two Copa Italias and reached a Champions League final. Compared to the years before him, they twice consecutively finished seventh. Agnelli could only look on as both Milan clubs reigned supreme. Since then, they have risen to fifth in UEFA's coefficients for the 2016 season, having been 43rd (below København and above Espanyol) the year he arrived. Nine of the starting XI (Buffon and Marchisio aside) to have played in Berlin in the 2015 Champions League final were signed by Paratici, costing:

Name	From	Season	Cost
Andrea Barzagli	Wolfsburg	2010/11	£255,000
Leonardo Bonucci	Bari	2010/11	£13,180,000
Stephan Lichtsteiner	Lazio	2011/12	£8,500,000
Andrea Pirlo	Milan	2011/12	£0
Arturo Vidal	Leverkusen	2011/12	£10,630,000
Paul Pogba	Manchester United	2012/13	£800,000
Carlos Tévez	Manchester City	2013/14	£7,600,000
Patrice Evra	Manchester United	2014/15	£1,620,000
Álvaro Morata	Real Madrid	2014/15	£17,000,000

Of Carlos Tévez, unwanted in Manchester, Paratici told the press: 'Believe me, somewhere inside that man is a need to prove his doubters wrong. He needs to be remembered in a better way and there is still so much ambition left in him, he just needs a team and a coach who believe in him. He is really a star, a spectacular player.' Juventus' scouts had 'sensations' about Tévez, Pirlo and Evra and consulted those working around the players to discover if they had the desire to be a part of the new Juventus machine.

It is a 'people-centred' scouting approach that has long been associated with the club. 'Think of Gigi Buffon, a stalwart and club legend who has made his £32m price tag look like a bargain,' Luca had said. 'Pavel Nedvěd is another man who springs to mind. They paid Lazio £35m for him, but he is another who has become a club legend and is now vice-president at Juve. This reinforces the idea that Juve aren't just buying players who they think can bring them success on the field, they are buying players either with a view to future profitability or sustainability. Players who fit the Juve mould and buy into the club's family ethos.'

Advancement

By way of contrast, in *The Secret Diary of a Liverpool Scout* – one of few books written on traditional scouting – the author Simon Hughes described the process undertaken by chief scout Geoff Twentyman of recommending a player in the 1960s, 70s and 80s. His method was uncomplicated: 'If I see the slightest hint of ability I will compile a report on a player. Go back to check him out again. Make sure he doesn't slip through the net.' Liverpool signed players from the north of Britain throughout their most successful era, with Twentyman tasked with driving for hours on end to watch matches (lower league, reserve, Sunday league) several times a week. He kept a notebook full of names of players and the dates he watched them play, with some comments on the player for later reference. Of Phil Neal, whom he watched four times, he commented 'done well, good prospect'. Neal was 23 and played for Third Division Northampton Town, but Twentyman was impressed with his two-footedness, plus the fans spoke well of his personality. In October 1974, Twentyman told Bob Paisley he was going to see Neal again. Paisley trusted Twentyman's word that the player was good, just like Shankly had before him, and arranged for chairman Peter Robinson to contact Northampton Town. Their secretary drove Neal to Melwood and the deal was done for £66,000. Four European Cup wins and eight league championships later, Twentyman had scouted a gem. [35]

---

35. Hughes, S (2011). *The Secret Diary of a Liverpool Scout*. London: Trinity Mirror Sport Media.

Nowadays, the process of scouting a player is much different, but the rationale for doing so remains the same. It is to gain an advantage over the enemy. Historically, the idea originated in militia with the use of reconnaissance, whereby generals sent cavalrymen to scout the terrain of the enemy, gathering information on their strengths and weaknesses. In football, scouts working for rival clubs are all aware of each other and are still in a war of sorts. Scouts work to find the best young talent before rivals, meaning the player can be signed for less money. Three things that have not changed between Twentyman's approach and Juventus' contemporary one are: it still involves constant communication (Twentyman posted letters then whereas scouts have mobile phones now); it requires a trust in contacts (many people want to force an agenda), and; it involves heavy year-long travel. The difference nowadays however is that Juventus and other top clubs pay software developers (such as WyScout and Scout7) to compile footage of players worldwide. Meaning before they fly, they watch a footballer on-screen first. Twentyman, when driving up and down the M6 on winter mornings, had no idea who or what he'd find.

'Mr Paratici will talk with the scouts and the coaches to analyse what players they should follow and whether we can go and watch them more with other scouts,' Roberto told me. 'Once a month we will do a little report in which we write what players should be focused on during that month and we will analyse the best games to watch them in. It is a simple organisation. At the start of the season we also work with videos because before we travel to watch a player, we watch them play on WyScout. Each scout will watch a lot of matches from all leagues – Hungary, Greece, Belgium – because we have to see interesting young players before our rivals do. In England, particularly, they will bring players in very quickly and very young.' Juventus have to move quickly in South America to find out what players there have Italian family heritage. If an Argentine has an Italian grandfather, for example, Juventus can sign him.

Pablo Longoria opened his laptop. A typical report compiles the technical, tactical and physical profile of a player, as well as comments from other scouts who have watched him. Yet despite Juventus having a specific game model and tactical make-up, they do not look only to players who suit that model (3-2-3-2), but rather scout every talent, wingers included. 'Normally we speak to them [the scouts] about different skills to analyse. For example, for us to profile a top right-back, they have to be maybe a right-winger beforehand and have adapted to play further back, so they have attacking qualities. All those players who were wingers in the past have a particular skill-set that our scouts should analyse. So, we say if they are looking at a winger, does he have the quality to play as a wing-back?' Dani Alves at Bahia and Patrice Evra at OGC Nice both began their careers as wingers. The department look to see if a player is adaptable in another position before signing him. They were well aware Leonardo Bonucci grew up playing as a midfielder in Inter Milan's youth teams and later benefited from his passing ability.

If he were interested in a player, Geoff Twentyman would watch him play away from home to see how he coped with pressure. It was a small tactic that helped combat one of the only risks in scouting. One can assess a player's technique, physicality and tactical positioning, but cannot scout his mental attributes. Pablo, whilst accepting that it is indeed difficult to understand a player's mental fortitude, explains that, at Juventus, they try to scout a player in various situations, like Twentyman did, assessing how he performs outside of his comfort zone. Juve will also ask if it is possible to watch the player in training to see how he works day to day. Twentyman did not have such access, so he would speak with fans in the crowd to see what they knew of a player.

When courting Carlos Tévez, Juventus had heard that he was a difficult personality (a factor contributing to his valuation). They carefully investigated and found he was a footballer with incredible determination and desire. He sustained the *Bianconeri*'s success, helping them win two more Serie A titles in 2014 and 2015 and was named as the Serie A player of the year for 2015.

The Ambition of Coaches

The following day I headed back to Vinovo to meet representatives of the academy. Along *Corsa IV Novembre*, Juventus fans had gathered in their hundreds outside Torino's newly built Olympic Stadium in anticipation of that afternoon's derby, chanting and lighting pyrotechnics, creating a quite ebullient atmosphere. It was 10am. Kick-off would not be until 3pm.

Ultras in Italy were protesting en masse to create a united body of resistance against earlier kick-off times (for Asian viewers). This by Juventus' ultras was a portrayal of fanaticism during Catholic Mass hours to prove to the league their derby rituals would not be diluted.

In Britain, working in youth football is often seen as a rite of passage before management – Brendan Rodgers at Chelsea, Mark Warburton and Sean Dyche at Watford, Eddie Howe at Bournemouth – Italian culture, however, dictates that young coaches and retired players should bypass academy coaching to focus on senior management. To do this, they start at a lower level. Marcello Lippi led Pontedera, Siena, Pistoiese and Carrarese in the amateur divisions of Italian football before coaching Cesena, Lucchese and Atalanta in the bottom half of Serie A. He would go on to win the World Cup. Antonio Conte managed Arezzo and Bari before Juventus. The shoe salesman Arrigo Sacchi managed Rimini and Parma before Milan. Never a player, Alberto Zaccheroni managed Cesenatico, Riccione and Boca Pietri in the eighth division of Italian football before eventually rising to AC and Inter. World Cup winner Enzo Bearzot began with Serie C side Prato, and the father of Milan, Cesare Maldini, managed Foggia and Ternana before Parma.

Juventus' head coach Massimo Allegri worked at SPAL, Grosseto and Sassuolo, and would tell *The Independent*: 'That time in the provinces is invaluable. It gives you the fundamental experience needed to be a successful coach, because while everyone dreams of a big club, you first need to learn how to do the job.' [xliv] Carlo Ancelotti began at Reggina and spoke of his first leadership role as a time of uncertainty in his autobiography: 'For a good part of the first season at Reggina I didn't have a coaching licence. Understanding and accepting that I was the boss was very difficult for me. I knew my own inadequacies, my own vulnerabilities, and I could not believe others could not see that.' [36]

Such emotions are natural for any person starting out in a new job. The above Italian managers were wise to work on their shortcomings away from the judgemental spotlight. Instead of accepting a managerial job at an already

---

36. Ancelotti, C; Brady, C; Forde, M (2016). *Quiet Leadership: Winning Hearts, Minds and Matches*. Great Britain: Portfolio Penguin.

successful club, beginning at the bottom is by way of contrast an opportunity to focus on one's weaker points.

Sir Alex Ferguson, a man revered by Italians, made similar remarks in his autobiography (the first one) about his initial venture into management with East Stirlingshire in 1974, back when he was still known as Alec: 'I was learning something new about management every day and, although I was making mistakes, I was not repeating them.' [37] The journey to the corridors of history has to begin somewhere. In Britain, it begins in academy football, but in Italy it begins in lower-league management.

Yet while Italian managers following such a path allows for them to master their trade, knowledge becomes top-heavy and, as a result, diminishes the quality of the youth sector. At Vinovo I discussed the issue with technical director of Juve's academy, Stefano Baldini. 'It is a question of mentality. In my opinion the best coaches in the world are Italian, yes, but only for men's football. I'm not sure we produce the best coaches in the world at youth level. They are two different games. I agree that Italian coaches are the best, but I know in other cultures like in Holland and Portugal they work better with their youth players. In Europe, there is another feeling or attitude towards youth football. That is just my opinion.' The knowledge acquired at Coverciano, Italy's Oxbridge headquarters in the Florentine countryside where would-be coaches philosophise on tactical matters, does not influence youth football as much as it could. For Baldini, a lack of focus on youth development is curbing Italy's potential.

Technique or Tactics?

The Juventus Centre is another facility that houses both the first team and the academy. Baldini was a silhouette stood in front of a dominating window, watching the Juventus versus Milan U11 match below. Juventus compete with Atalanta for the title of 'Italy's best academy', but they strive for more. It is Baldini's job to help Juventus become Europe's best, not just Italy's. After all, the word '*Juventus*' derives from Latin for 'youth'. 'One of the problems we have is that in Piedmont we don't have a lot of competition. We play Torino and Novara, but we must organise tournaments around Italy and

---

37. Ferguson, A (1999). *Managing My Life*. London: Hodder Paperbacks.

around Europe so we have real competitors. This is something we are trying to change. Two or three years ago we began to travel around the world. At this moment, our 2004 first group are in Brazil, the 2004 second group are in Portugal. The 2005 group are in Switzerland.' In smaller nations, competition is not an issue. The catchment area in London houses famed academies like Chelsea, Arsenal, Tottenham, Crystal Palace, Charlton, QPR, Fulham and West Ham. They play regular fixtures against each other, allowing for a greater quality of co-operation and development. Larger nations, like Italy, where clubs are more dispersed, face difficulty in arranging competition. One factor in Holland's rich history of youth development is the concise arrangement of its clubs.

Nowadays, Italy still produce tactically intelligent players, but football has evolved. Speaking about the culture of developing tacticians and the dilemma Italy now face, Baldini said: 'I think it is a question of the methodology. We speak a lot about choice with the children. We speak a lot about thinking and being tactical. In the Italian mentality, we think first about developing tactics and later about developing technique. That was historically the main thing for us. Now we want to change a little because we want to improve the technical part of our players, as well as their tactical understanding. In the last ten years, our football has grown quicker as a game. We have a little problem in Italy because we think a lot, but if we play slow then we have a problem. In the future, we have to find a balance to work on both.'

Germany develop players who are gifted both on and off the ball, embodied by Müller and Götze. 'In German academies, there is a big emphasis on being tactically and technically knowledgeable,' Bayern coach Nico Kammann would later state in Munich. For Italy, a balance must be struck; the danger for them is if they go too far towards focusing on technique and neglect their tactical heritage they could become Brazil, a team of technicians without discipline (who were beaten 7–1 in the 2014 World Cup by Germany in what was, for viewers, the 'Red Wedding' of football). Baldini believes Italian academies must continue to coach tactics, but also find a way of developing technique, too. He explained how this will be done in technical practices by the coach: 'It is more about asking the players, "Why did you come here?", "Why did you pass back?", "Why have you run forward?" We ask them to think, think, think. You can start this when the guys are six years old –

why not? They are little, not stupid.' Isaac Newton's third law determined that every action has a reaction. At Juventus, they coach their youngsters to understand this from an early age; their hope being they grow to appreciate the actions needed to be champions.

ELEVEN

STYLE, HISTORY, PRESTIGE, MILAN

It takes all but one hour to reach Milan from Turin, via the home of Italian football's early champions, Pro Vercelli. The first impression of Milan is grandiose; Centrale Station was designed to represent the power of Mussolini's fascism in the late 1920s. Centrale could be a palace, with its marble domes and statues atop podiums. Except at the back, where the thrones should sit, high-speed trains come and go. As one exits the main station a huge screen stands facing, advertising Dolce and Gabbana. Boutique shops of black exterior sell Calvin Klein and Versace. Booming catwalk music accompanies passengers down escalators. Nobody rushes, everybody is cool. It is as though Milan has an image of herself to present. The stylish self-confidence of the city is infectious; a man of no real pretence might take up smoking for the visual effect of it. At tables outside a bistro, groomed couples drink wine; the men in shirts and the ladies in jumpers, everybody in oval sunglasses. Paparazzi whizz by on mopeds to snap a seemingly famous lady, yet the couples hardly break conversation. Sophistication is a state of mind. Only football, more than fashion or food, has the power to stir the senses of the Milanese.

Throughout the 1980s and 1990s, AC Milan grew in notoriety as the club who best balanced global superstars with academy graduates. The club's top three record appearance holders all progressed through Primavera (Milan's youth team): Paolo Maldini (647), Franco Baresi (531) and Billy Costacurta (458). Over the years, Milan, as if to strengthen their relationship with those professionals, whilst maintaining an image of grandeur, invested in an elixir of sorts. In 2002 they funded the 'Milan Lab' following the disintegration of gifted midfielder Fernando Redondo's career due to injuries. Jean-Pierre Meersseman, a Belgian chiropractor, was hired and installed a fresh perspective: 'Age doesn't exist. What counts is that you are physically and psychologically ready to play,' he declared.

In 2007, with a starting line-up averaging 31.3 years old, Milan, thanks to Meersseman's Lab, avenged Liverpool in the Champions League final. [38] For the best part of a decade their players were viewed as demigods, capable of performing well beyond what many would consider 'peak'.

However, the very same approach that brought success would eventually become their downfall – Icarus in flight. Such an over-reliance on aged players blinded Milan and they lost focus on youth development. Sir Alex Ferguson told the Harvard Business School, 'The idea is that the younger players are developing and meeting the standards that the older ones have set before.' Milan, instead of fuelling the cycle, created a glass ceiling. Their decline from 2010 to 2016 was reflected in their neglecting of Primavera. In 2011, they had the oldest squad in Serie A with van Bommel, Inzaghi, Seedorf, Nesta, Ambrosini, Abbiati and Zambrotta; the average age was 31.2 years. Five years later, in 2016, Silvio Berlusconi told his new head coach Vincenzo Montella his final dream for Milan over dinner. 'I want a young squad, mostly Italian who came from our academy.' [xlv]

Montella's Milan became the third youngest in Serie A: 24.4 years. Former player Filippo Galli, head of Vismara (the academy complex on the outskirts of the city) was the man at the forefront of Milan's youth resurgence. Vismara once again became central to Milan's model of development, with Gianluigi Donnarumma and Manuel Locatelli impacting a first team dangerously close to breaking the glass. At the entrance of the complex stands a silhouetted image of a footballer, his body made up of Milan

---

38. Their starting XI consisted of: Dida (32), Oddo (30), Nesta (31), Maldini (38), Jankulovski (29), Gattuso (29), Pirlo (27), Ambrosini (29), Seedorf (31), Kaká (25) and Inzaghi (33). They still had Cafu (36) and Costacurta (40) in their team that year. Maldini would retire aged 40, Inzaghi 38, Nesta departed aged 36, Seedorf likewise and Gattuso moved to Sion aged 35.

academy graduate names: Aubameyang, Coco, Abate, De Sciglio, Cristante, Maldini, Albertini, Borriello, Casiraghi, Antonelli, Cudicini, Baresi, Galli, Donadel, Donnarumma, Matri, Costacurta, Paloschi, Darmian. They placed the silhouetted man thoughtfully at the entrance so young players arriving for training would be inspired to add their name to the image.

The Resurgence

After several calls back and forth, Galli and I settled on a time to meet. A mild Italian sun began to sink that late afternoon. There was no security and the doors to the main building were open to passers-by. Coaches, analysts, physios and a degree of other busy staff members smiled as they went about their business, all clad in the famous red and black uniform of Milan. Vismara is a friendly, relaxed, but determined environment. Filippo Galli looked up over the top of his glasses to the knock at his door. 'Daniel?' he smiled, inviting me to come and sit. Before we began discussing Milan's youth resurgence, he told me how big a fan he was of English football: 'Watford is in my veins, even though I have supported Milan since I was five; and I have loved Liverpool since 1984 when they played Roma here.' He then proceeded to name the entire LFC starting XI from that evening in under ten seconds. The spectacled head of academy was almost 40 when he played for Watford under Gianluca Vialli, in an era of English football's first sampling of European influences. 'What was great for me was the atmosphere in the stadium. I am sure that if I go back to Vicarage Road I will cry.'

Galli won three European Cups as part of football's greatest ever backline. He is royalty in the game. At Milan in the 1980s, his teammates were Baresi and Maldini; Gullit, Rijkaard and van Basten. As a player, he learnt from Arrigo Sacchi and Fabio Capello and now continues their teachings with Milan's youth. It is important at this club to preserve heritage. Galli is a link between contemporary Milan and the glory days of old.

'Of course, these two coaches [Sacchi and Capello] are part of our history, and we always need to keep what they taught us in our minds, but I think it is not enough [to look at the past]. What Sacchi gave us was new at that time in Italian culture, then Capello built on that.' But now Milan must win playing what Galli describes as the 'philosophy of Berlusconi': 'To win displaying effective and entertaining football.' They promote Sacchi's hard running off the ball in between transitions, to step up high and press from the front, as well as Capello's impeccable standards. According to Gabriele Marcotti's biography of Capello, *Portrait of a Winner,* the differences between Capello and Sacchi are of personality. Capello, who was trained to work in business by Berlusconi, had a white-collar understanding of professionalism. Sacchi was a revolutionary tactician. 'Defensively, it was all about pressing, the flat back four and the offside trap. But in the final third players had more opportunity to express themselves,' with greater freedom given under Capello than Sacchi.[39]

Galli played under both men. He was a pawn in Sacchi's without-the-ball training exercises and also received many of Capello's long, wise talks. Most of all, during his playing days, Galli was a listener and a student of football. He is steeped in Milan's values as an institution and, having been part of the club's glory years, is valuable to their resurgence. 'Here we work day after day, keeping in mind the macro-principles of the game,' he said, listing the simple key points taught to youngsters at the academy from a young age. They are:

- To recognise the spaces
- To occupy them in a rational way
- To recognise the numerical condition of the game (overloads or underloads)
- Timing of each decision.

Sacchi had taught Galli, Maldini, Baresi, Tassotti and indeed all members of Milan's great squad to recognise and exploit space. His high compact play was pioneering for the time: 'If your team moved as one, each player continuously adjusting to what was happening, it would almost be like playing with 13 or 14 players,' he had told Marcotti. When coaches studied Sacchi and Capello's Milan and, in many ways, copied their methods (Rafa Benitez is an unashamed disciple), the game caught up with and eventually overtook them. Galli however remained studious. At senior level, he later worked under Leonardo and Carlo Ancelotti, particularly observing

---

39. Marcotti, G (2008). *Capello: Portrait of a Winner.* London: Bantam Press.

how they communicated with a new generation of footballers. 'There are principles to train. The tools we have are the part of the game or the moments of the match that we must translate in the training session, such as build-up, possession and finalization. Then, there are the drills that are split throughout the weekly training schedule.' Milan's youth sides have a tactically periodised programme of development, not too dissimilar to that discussed in Porto.

Being a former player here, Galli believes that if a retired footballer is also a good teacher, he can transfer to youngsters what it means to play for the club. 'It is important for us, [especially] once the ex-player realises that it is also about the future of the club and not just what they have done in the past. Then, when they put their experience at the service of the young players, we benefit.' Berlusconi longs to preserve the link to Milan's glorious era, believing that former players understand the values of the club more than outsiders. Since the millennium, Milan have been led by retired former players: Cesare Maldini, Mauro Tassotti, Carlo Ancelotti, Leonardo, Clarence Seedorf, Filippo Inzaghi and Cristian Brocchi.

While acknowledging that it is a benefit for coaches to have been steeped in the culture of Milan, Galli feels they must provide new ideas, too. 'They have to start from zero. It is good to have been a good player, but you need to be a good teacher. There is a difference when it comes to teaching football. The relationship between coaches and players is very important in the learning process. Players of the academy can also read about our history on the internet and, in general, through the media. In these ways, the young players realise that they are training for a very important club and are wearing a glorious shirt.' Seventeen-year-old Donnarumma had posters of Abbiati (his teammate and the man he displaced as number 1) on his wall, while the 18-year-old Locatelli is spoken of as a future captain in waiting (an honour more significant here than at most other clubs given the immortalised legacies of Maldini and Baresi).

Most of the former players mentioned had long and glorious careers at Milan. Seedorf retired aged 37, as did Nesta. Inzaghi was 38, Paolo Maldini was 40 and Alessandro Costacurta was 41. A number of factors contribute to the extension of careers, as Luca had mentioned when speaking about Pirlo: Italians culturally hold a great appreciation for age, the tempo of Serie

A is slower, and managers tactically seek to accommodate the intangibles older players bring.

Galli, who himself played until the age of 40, feels that the most important factor in sustaining a career is mental. 'We had an organisation and the opportunity to recruit the world's best players, but the secret was to have big men, not only big players. Big Italian men, like Maldini, Baresi, Tassotti and Donadoni. They were big human beings with a desire to improve. So of course, you have to be talented to reach this level, but to stay there you need to have values and determination.' Fitness helped, but a positive mentality was most important.

It aligns with Carol Dweck's *Mindset* research and the differences between having a 'fixed' or 'growth' mindset. In short, she believes some people are fixed in their outlook and view effort as futile. Others, however, have a growth mindset and seek to overcome predetermined views of what is achievable. [40] 'In a growth mindset students understand that their talents and abilities can be developed through effort, good teaching and persistence,' she explained. Her theory applies to sport and ties in with Galli's comments on longevity. His teammates had long, successful careers because of their desire to not only sustain themselves, but to improve.

Moving Forward

Filippo Galli takes off his glasses and asks about English football. He'd love to see Anfield, he says, and declares his admiration for fans in England. Outside, green leaves on mostly bare trees threaten to replace winter with spring, offering optimism for the future. As our interview becomes conversational, I become a humble fan. *Has the art of defending died?* No, he replies, but it is different. 'At the academy we are trying to change the perspective. We want to build up from the back, which is weird for Italian football, but we want to do this because it's the club's philosophy; when you have the ball, you can master the game.' *Then what makes a good defender?* 'He needs to have personality, to be brave to also ask for the ball from the goalkeeper and to start the build-up play. He has to be very good at concentrating, to be aware of the situation around him and he has to roll up his sleeves and work hard. At AC Milan, we need a defender who is very

40. Dweck, C (2012). *Mindset: How you can fulfil your potential.* Hachette UK.

good at defending one-versus-one with space behind him. He must be able to keep possession in short spaces.'

A degree of ambiguity is attached to the word 'brave' when discussing defenders in the modern game. They must be brave in two ways: to put their bodies into dangerous situations where they might get hurt, traditionally, but they must also be brave to receive the ball and play forward. John Stones, as the chastised forerunner of the modern role, who continually holds faith in his abilities despite fan disapproval, is braver than most. *So, for him to be good at defending with space behind him, he needs a sweeper-keeper, because for Sacchi all positions are linked?* Galli smiles. He knows I am talking about Donnarumma. The whole world is talking about Donnarumma. 'He started here when he was 14 and has worked a lot on building up from the back. He is more than a goalkeeper because we trained him to use his feet a lot.'

At 16, Donnarumma became the poster boy of Milan. His face adorned scarves outside the San Siro on the night of the Lazio match (when I visited) and the ultras sang his name. Typically, a goalkeeper is trusted to break into the first team between the ages of 21 and 25. There are exceptions, of course; Casillas was 18 when he first started for Real Madrid and Buffon was 17 when he made his Parma debut, but very rarely are goalkeepers 16 – especially at a club of Milan's stature. 'Everyone was looking at him, every club, but we had the advantage because his brother was already playing here. Then, the club was smart to reach an agreement with his parents.' Because of Donnarumma's size (he is 6ft 5in tall), he always played several years above his age group. When he was nine he played U13; aged 14 he represented the U18s; aged 16 (at my time of visiting) he was in the first team. Considering his rival for the goalkeeper position, Christian Abbiati, was 38 (at the time) Donnarumma was competing against somebody over 20 years up. Yet his emergence was not unexpected. He'd cost the club €250,000. According to *La Gazzetta* his brother Antonio, nine years his senior and a goalkeeper at Genoa, would coach his young sibling in the back garden and inspired him by showing him YouTube videos of Buffon and Casillas. [xlvi]

In Rotterdam, Feyenoord's head of academy would explain that a youth player cannot be rushed into the senior squad too early as his development could stop. *How did you know he was ready?* I ask Galli. *How do you know young players are ready in general?* 'His attitude was fantastic to play in such a big stadium. Mihajlović (the head coach) and the first team goalkeeper coach realised he was ready, so the manager played him.' He pauses. 'We knew here he would be ready; he had played underage in our youth teams and never played with his same age group. He always played with older kids. He is a natural talent and we helped him to show his talent here.' Donnarumma bypassed consensual logic that young players need gradual exposure to first team football. 'We took out his talent. Education in Latin is '*educe*', which means to take out, to pull out the talent. So, of course he had this talent, but his coaches gave him opportunities to show this.'

*

Chronicle of a Game

On the night of my arrival, Milan were playing SS Lazio. San Siro was still home, despite the club not owning the stadium. They and Internazionale instead pay rent each season to the local council for the privilege of playing there (€4.1m). This became a factor in the club's stagnation: Juventus own their ground (on land they were given for free) and receive income, while Milan have expenditure.

The atmosphere inside the San Siro felt more genuine in the absence of a man on a microphone, in contrast to what had been found elsewhere in Europe. *Capo* ultras at every football club position themselves to face the crowd with their backs turned on the spectacle behind them, beginning chants from a mic. They generate an atmosphere by dictating what songs should be sung. In Britain, songs are a dedication to moments in the game – a corner or a shot on goal – sung with spontaneous desire. Here, the fans buy tickets and are led into chants by ultras. But it works. In Britain, there are long silent moments between occurrences, while on the continent ultras fill the silence throughout.

Luca Hodges-Ramon, as an Anglo-Italian, is best positioned to comment on the parallels and differences between English and Italian spectatorship, having spent a long time sitting amongst ultras at Siena in the Curva Robur, studying their culture. 'When Siena conceded, some fans would naturally get disheartened and go quiet. This is when the *capo* ultras (positioned directly behind the goal, often propped up on the barriers or fences) would come into their own, screaming about not giving a shit about the result, and that the team needs the Curva's support.' Luca points to the dedication of the *capos*, acknowledging that they are irregularly loyal to their club with a duty of support – in comparison to many consumer fans in Britain who pay money and expect to be entertained (see the Giulianotti references in Chapter 1). 'In Britain, the preoccupation of most fans – even those who produce the atmosphere with chanting – is often the final result of their team. Having interviewed a number of Italian ultras groups, their outlook is slightly different. You will often hear them talk about the *mentalitá* ultras [who] ensure that the Curva is a constant cauldron of noise and support for the team. *Capos* lead the chants with microphones and barely watch the game. Others are tasked with waving enormous flags for 90 minutes. Let me assure you, this takes some commitment.'

The demographic in attendance that night in Milan contributed largely to the volume created; they were male, aged between 16 and 30 and disenfranchised. It is this demographic that is largely priced out of regular football consumption in Britain. A parallel between Britain and Italy is the increased demand for safe-standing areas in stadiums as an alternative to sitting. At the San Siro in the Curva Sud, seats are a dangerous inconvenience. They are only there to be stood on, and if one wishes to sit down, then a copy of *La Gazzetta* must be placed on the dirty plastic seat. The danger arises when Milan score and the fans surge forward. At best, they hurt their shins, at worst they fall over the rows.

Upon ascending the spiralled stairs, my eyes were treated to the view of one of football's greatest cathedrals. The two side stands were mostly bare, but in the Sud stand 100 flags waved majestically as pyro smoke filled the air. A flare is a symbol of resistance, a harmless anti-authority spectacle-creator used by the disengaged. The smell of marijuana lingered and no stewards could be seen. Despite that, the atmosphere was superb; raucous with an anti-establishment edge – a continued ritual for traditional supporters. The largest banner read 'Baresi 6' and soared high above a sea of red and black. Franco Baresi is AC Milan more than any other player. He was there in Serie B and was there in '88. The concept of ultras is as much a declaration of self-worth as it is a response to invasion. Italian football is highly politicised and Milan must demonstrate their strength to the Lazio ultras in attendance. It is regionalism shown through fandom.

Milan continue to receive high levels of sponsorship, with Audi, Nivea, Emirates, Dolce and Gabbana and Adidas advertising along the pitch side. They earned that season around €102.1m in commercial revenue according to Deloitte, which is considerably more than the €85m Juventus earnt. The Japanese midfielder Keisuke Honda was their most technical player that night. As well as offering talent, he brought a weight of support to the stadium. Japanese fans clapped out of tune at the back of the Sud stand, comically receiving constant tellings-off from ultras for taking photographs of the flags. 'NO FOTO' asserted one banner. In the second half, the Nice-bound maverick Mario Balotelli returned from injury and immediately looked to be the best player on the pitch (alongside Lazio's Brazilian Filipe Anderson), which in itself was the most telling illustration of the game. It ended 1–1. The 33,000 in attendance left abruptly to make the already bare stadium seem a lot barer. Within minutes, the San Siro became a hollow shell of blue seats. They would finish seventh a few months later. Siniša Mihajlović would be sacked and replaced by Vincenzo Montella, refreshing a stale club with Manuel Locatelli, Suso and M'Baye Niang.

*

The Transfer Man
He stands holding his new shirt up to the flashing bulbs, smiling numbly for the tenth time that day. A thousand deafening 'tweets' carry his image worldwide.

Yet the first tweet, the one that began the carnival, was pushed into the phone of Gianluca Di Marzio. It is he, son of former Napoli coach Gianni Di Marzio, who knows when a transfer happens first. Just shy of a million Twitter followers await his confirmation.

The following bright Milanese morning after AC's draw with Lazio, my translator (*La Gazzetta dello Sport* writer Dario Vismara) and I arrived at the Sky Italia studios in the city centre – a mammoth complex with security to rival Geneva's UN headquarters – and waited in the lobby. 'Have you heard the news?' Dario suddenly asked, looking down at his phone. 'Cruyff has died.' Within seconds the complex came alive as groups of workers frantically began producing a montage of the great man.

Di Marzio arrived wearing jeans and a hoodie and shook our hands. 'It is terrible,' he said of Cruyff's passing – we all thought the Dutchman was recovering well. Di Marzio's English was mostly perfect, yet Dario proved to be a welcome addition. The transfer man took us both on a behind-the-scenes tour of Sky Sports News before our talk. There, we silently watched from behind a teleprompter as presenters discussed Cruyff's passing. Sadness overtook us as his montage was played. In Italy, he is remembered as the embodiment of *Totaalvoetbal* (Total Football), the tactical system that ended Italy's dominant *Catenaccio* age.

Di Marzio is an adjective for reliability with an international reputation, known for releasing the details of a transfer before any other media outlet – usually beating a club's official website. The fascinating question is how he manages to gain information from clubs? *Do they contact you with stories for their agenda?* 'Sometimes. We collaborate. The most important thing in the relationship with my source is to gain credit for the news, and for them to know they can trust me, and that I can trust them too. For example, last year when [Roberto] Mancini became the new Internazionale manager, I had the news before everybody else. It was a Thursday night and I had two options: I could have gone public live on television with it, but Internazionale trust me, so I spoke with the club and they told me not to say anything because [Walter] Mazzarri [the manager] did not know. So, for me it was a risk because another journalist could have run with the story. Nevertheless, Inter told me that once Mazzarri found out, I would be the second person, so they told me out of respect for contacting them. If I went public first it could have built a lot of problems, so I like to have this relationship with my sources.'

It is a conflict of interests for you… 'It has happened, when I was really sure of my news but I was not 100%, that I had to verify with the club. Sometimes I am really sure and I have news from the agent and the player, so sometimes I do not need to verify with the club, I can go live even though it can cause problems. This happened last year with [Juan] Iturbe, when Genoa were sure they would sign him from AS Roma. I went on TV with it and all of the Roma fans went crazy because they didn't want to lose the player, so then the deal was cancelled! The president of Genoa rang me and said "Gianluca, this was all your fault!" But for me I had to go live.' Iturbe ended up going on loan to Bournemouth, where he played just two league games. *Do agents ever get in touch and say that their player wants to leave a club?* 'Sure.' *Then what do you do if you have a relationship with the club?* 'Look, it's not a problem for me, it is a problem for the club. I will break the news and say that the player wants to leave, that he is in a difficult moment and will consider other offers, but I try to say it in a balanced way so I confirm nothing. It is my strength; I am balanced and I'm not aggressive with the news. It's very difficult. I always do things the right way. I do not want to create problems for anybody.' Sometimes that isn't always possible for him, though.

Di Marzio tells me that in the modern game clubs look to manipulate the media for their own agenda. *So theoretically, would a club contact you if they wanted to sign a player, to create a rumour and turn his head?* 'Si, it happens, but not frequently because clubs prefer to do their business without any public attention. They tell me usually not to say anything, but the first thing I say to a general manager is, "You can never tell me something is a lie if I know it is the truth myself. If I arrive at a name, it is not your problem, I just want you to know that I know." Then the contact can say to me: "Okay, it is a difficult time, keep it under wraps for now so we can do the deal," instead of them saying "No, it is not true," and then it becomes official. Sometimes clubs tell me not to say anything, and then when it is the right moment they will call me first and I will announce the news. I want to arrive first at a story ahead of *Gazzetta dello Sport* for example.' Di Marzio's reputation is built on the quality of information he gains. Having a father as a manager got him so far, but to progress to the level he has done took *ambizione*.

What happens then if a source is lying to you? 'It happens. Sometimes an agent will want to break the news that his player is scouted by Real Madrid so he can, for example, get a move to Juventus. He will tell me because he has an agenda, so I try to discover if it is true or not. After 12 years, I know who is telling me the truth or who is lying for their purpose. If they tell me they need my help, then I can do favours. I can say that their player is scouted by Real Madrid, then I will go live with it so in return they will tell me first when he signs for Juventus. If a club are dragging their feet then I will break the news as a favour, so the club will follow through. Then I am the first to announce when he signs for his new club one or two hours before it becomes official. When it is official, it is not news.' *Then what do we believe?*

American actor Denzel Washington best summed up the motives of the modern liberal media, of which Di Marzio is a member. 'If you don't read the news you're uninformed. If you do read it then you're misinformed,' he told a red-carpet reporter. *What do you do?* She asked. 'Well,' he began, 'what is the long-term effect of too much information? One of the effects is the need to be first – not even to be true. We live in a society now where people just want to be first; we don't care who it hurts, we don't care who we destroy, we don't care if it's true. Let's just say it, sell it.' Di Marzio confirmed for us that agents sometimes promote false rumours to push a deal through, and that he will run with it in order to be in their favour. Apparently, it is a legitimate negotiation strategy. That's not Di Marzio's fault, such is the influence of the circus. Society, as receivers of mass media, have a duty to challenge news providers on the sincerity of their claims; to be more thoughtful as consumers. An unquenchable hunger for news from a trough – true or false – perpetuates a dangerous cycle that transcends football. A lot can be learnt from the Milanese. For them, sophistication is a state of mind. As too is its relative perceptiveness.

TWELVE

CASTLES, KINGS AND FABLES: BAYERN OF BAVARIA

At a narrow road with no cars to be seen on either side, a crowd of people gathered waiting for the signal to cross. For minutes they stood, staring unblinkingly, urging red to become green, all the while suppressing a deep urge to step on to the road. As more people congregated the frustration grew, yet nobody satisfied their impulse. Jaywalking is illegal. There are rules to be obeyed, a structure to adhere to, that makes German society so effective. Green will flash eventually. The country's politics and football are so lacking in controversy – in contrast to the fickleness of modern Britain – they make boring seem like a breath of fresh air. Bavaria has one of the largest economies in Europe, with only 4.1% unemployment, and constantly sits near the top of quality of life polls. Locals talk about being independent but never mean it seriously. This is a region of fables and folk tales, designed to offer moral direction. Britain has legends, Bavaria has lessons. Perhaps, given that Britain now quite likes Germany (post-war tensions are dissolving on the continent on the whole), they might choose to learn from them.

To discover how Bayern and Germany win I travelled to Säbener Straße to meet Nico Kammann, a strength and conditioning coach at the academy. For all of England's ineptitudes, we decided that one of the key differences between players from both nations is game management. When the Germans embarrassed Brazil 7–1 at the World Cup, they did so against players whose technique was as good if not better. To borrow a quote from elsewhere: Oscar had Ferrari feet, but Müller had a Rolls-Royce brain. Germany produce footballers who understand the game at every moment. They are tacticians on the pitch; academies here have perfectly blended the balance between coaching tactics and technique to young players, something that Italian clubs are working to do.

'In German academies, there is a big emphasis on being tactically and technically knowledgeable,' Nico said. 'Americans are good tactically with a tremendous work ethic but they can't pass a ball – to exaggerate a bit. Brazilians are amazing technically but sometimes lack elite tactics or strength. If you see it as a triangle of athleticism, sport-specific skills and tactics, I think in Germany we are good at all three corners of the development model.'

Nico believes that German youngsters are also taught to cope with mistakes better. On courses in Britain the coach must identify and 'coach' a mistake as soon as he sees it. Here, they understand that mistakes occur, and should be allowed to happen as part of the learning process. Only when errors are repeated several times should they be considered a flaw worth coaching: 'So it contributes to Germany being the best, and I think our players learnt to make mistakes and not to worry about them. We try to create an atmosphere where players are allowed to make mistakes once or twice.' Even at senior level, Mats Hummels and Jérôme Boateng are allowed to give the ball away now and then.

Self-critique was identified as something all German academies should encourage in their players by staff at Hennes Weisweiler Akademie in Köln, the epicentre of coach education. It resulted in Bayern creating Thomas Müller, one of the most intelligent footballers on the planet. With his black boots, low socks and industrious work rate, Müller is a throwback to a humbler generation. 'His football IQ is up here,' Nico stretches his arms high above his head. 'When we played Barcelona he basically did a basketball move by blocking a player. I know that he was helped by being produced in an environment where it was important to win. We teach work ethic a lot. You have to teach children that losing is important and a part of the game. But you should never lose because of laziness. If you're lazy, then there are 1,000 children who would crawl here on their knees to play for Bayern, so you have to work hard.'

The Spectacle

Säbener Straße (Sabener Street) is a quiet part of suburbia. Numbers 94 and 96 are large, Swedish-themed detached homes, built on a long road with high trees and gentle birdsong. Over the road, at number 55, is a complex of modern buildings most resembling a sore thumb. They belong to one of the world's most renowned sporting names, FC Bayern.

Residents are seemingly unware of the famed athletes who train halfway up their street; one woman was tending to her daffodils as sports cars breezed past. Families walking their dogs cut through the arrangement of buildings, past the training pitches, and on to the woodland behind. The openness of training for public viewing is so shocking, so forward thinking, that it could only be a liberally German concept. Conservative British clubs would never dream of allowing fans to watch a training session. Many supporters of Premier League clubs do not even know where their team facilities are. FC Bayern on the other hand put step-by-step maps of directions to Säbener Straße on their website along with weekly training schedules.

The complex is worth showing off, housing six outdoor pitches, a restaurant, a shop-come-Audi dealership, several large roman-numbered Hublot clocks and a beach volleyball court for Douglas Costa and Thiago to play on. There is a dreamy atmosphere here that managers grow to love. Nico and I met outside the *biergarten* beside the main training pitch. Fans sipped lager as part of the experience, watching as first team coach Lorenzo Bonaventura set up his session (Guardiola was still in charge at the time). Not only could fans watch their beloved players for free, they could drink beer at the same time. The same thing was possible at Rayo too, of course, but Rayo do not contest European Cup finals. To be a Bayern fan is a blessed thing. Tickets are cheap, they're active in the community and they always win. 'We do not think the fans are like cows to be milked,' president Uli Hoeneß told the BBC. [xlvii]

When the players came out to warm up, the hundred or so people in attendance applauded favourably for several seconds, then fell silent. There was no hysteria, no chanting, no longing for celebrity attention.

There were hardly even any photographs taken. Pep Guardiola had by this point informed the club of his intention to leave at the end of the season (becoming only the fourth manager in 45 years not to be sacked). He was yet to announce his decision to join Manchester City. Initially fans were offended – 'we have given him everything' – but on this day they had forgiven him and politely clapped his entrance on to the pitch. Time had healed the wounds. He was wearing a red gilet, hands in his pockets, more relaxed than before. By this point of his tenure Pep was confident that he had passed on his philosophy to the players. There was no need to scream and gesticulate like he had at the start.

As the technical practice began, Pep stalked around the outside of the session, scrutinising every pass. At one point, he stopped it – the players fixed their gaze upon him. Javi Martínez was coming off the mannequin to receive the ball too early. 'It is not real!' Pep shouted before demonstrating perfect form. He whistled and play resumed with greater effort. The supporters on the rails began watching him more intently. Forgetting Lahm, Ribéry and company, it was he they had come to see. Pep grew into himself, praising his squad. Xabi Alonso and Javi Martínez responded, the three of them talking the most in Spanish-German. After several minutes Pep whistled, signalling for his players to walk over to the next practice. It was a possession exercise with four versus four, and four more on the outside of the square, similar to the one Paco Jémez had eavesdropped upon. The team who lost the ball swapped with those on the outside, signalling the transition from attack to defence and vice versa. It had to be Pep to feed the ball into the session. He commanded the tempo: a leader at work.

In a city that has welcomed Mozart, Wagner, Strauss and Orff, Guardiola was the most exciting composer in Munich. He had injected a fascination into public training sessions unseen before. His style of football is classical music in motion; the watcher becomes at one with the spectacle. In classical music, the listener stops hearing the individual instruments and becomes accustomed to the symphony. With Pep's Bayern, one does not notice the rotations between players, whether Alaba chooses to step forward or Robben comes infield. They appear to play harmoniously through the thirds creating classical football. It is hypnotising; fans watch in a state of opium enjoyment.

There are wooden sheds at the side of the pitch for the groundsmen to keep their tools in. Mostly, in these sheds, they listen to the wireless and relax between sessions. When Pep was coaching, though, they came out to watch. As the ball clapped from the boots of the players on the wet surface the fans stood mesmerised. Even the mascot stopped to watch. 'Bravo! Bravo!' shouted Pep, as Thiago let the ball run through his legs, fooling a young player who went beyond the ball. At the end of the practice Pep talked to the lad for almost ten minutes. It was Joshua Kimmich, who would later become more famous for being broiled by Pep in front of 81,000 people, following a draw with Dortmund. 'I love him,' Guardiola later said. 'I love working with these players, who want to learn and improve.'

Afterwards, the players gathered in the centre circle to do stretches. Xabi Alonso and Ribéry tried to hit the crossbar with a pass, but both accidently scored top-corner goals. Guardiola, who had finished with Kimmich, was further out than both players but called for a ball. Instead of demanding focus on the stretches, he took a touch and hit the crossbar. The fans finally became excited. Some began to shout Pep's name, most clapped. In Thomas Carlyle's 'Great Man' theory, individuals like Napoleon, Gandhi, Alexander, Lincoln and Caesar decide history through their intelligence, drive and charisma. Guardiola is football's Great Man. 'If Pep decided to be a musician, he would be a good musician. If he wanted to be a psychologist, he would be a good psychologist,' disciple Xavi once said. [xlix]

In a previous era, Claudio Pizarro had to convince younger players to acknowledge the fans, forcing them to sign autographs. Nowadays, it is decided what players are going to sign autographs before training begins. On this day, it was Javi Martínez and Philipp Lahm. Xabi Alonso stayed out after every player had gone in, letting his young son take shots at him. He had the aura of a man enjoying the latter stages of his career. Once considered a style rival to Xavi Hernandez of Barcelona, Alonso adapted his game in response to Guardiola's demands.

Conditioning

Suitably impressed with the day's entertainment, Nico and I found an empty room in the offices of Säbener Straße to talk. Bayern took him on as a strength and conditioning coach after university due to his history working in the game's codified cousin, American football. Andreas Kornmayer (the man who hired him, more recently of Liverpool FC) had a background in judo and valued the dynamic movements that other sports use to assist in injury prevention. Soccer is a heavily specialised sport that places continuous pressure on the same muscles: 'Always hamstring, always groin, always hip flexors, always lower back,' Nico bemoaned. 'Because they are just doing the same thing day in day out since they were nine years of age. Players may just be weaker there, or may have an awkward movement pattern.'

He works with academy ages focusing on regeneration, strength emphasis, co-ordination, movement patterns and game preparation. 'I have implemented a lot of American football stuff and might do small-sided games which have characteristics of both soccer and American football, where they can pick up the ball, pass it, throw it and tackle each other, and still have an end-zone or a goal to score in. This brings in a chaos approach to sports so they are using everything; they are not just always using the movements that soccer players have.' On other days, he commands his players to do boxing sparring drills. It is fun for the players and takes strain off their 'football' muscles.

A multi-sport approach is not universal to all clubs in the modern game, however. It is something that Nico has freedom to implement at Bayern, but he feels that the future game should incorporate varied sessions inspired by other sports. Quite simply, using different muscles means fewer injuries as a consequence of less strain. 'That is the idea behind athletic training itself, to give them an all-round athletic muscular corset and a wider movement capacity. We will never make good basketball players out of them, but there is a transfer you see when you shoot hoops every once in a while. It opens up the motoric system and separates one movement from another which makes both movements better.' Sometimes at Bayern, Nico will set up a square and let his players have a judo fight, in which they try to pull each other out of the square. The watching players bet on who they think the winner will be. The loser and his supporters are made to do push-ups. It is competitive, enjoyable, and promotes flexibility.

Nico views multi-sport approaches as an obvious evolution in the game to come. He feels many things are done incorrectly in soccer. To improve, staff must look at what experts in other sports are doing. 'Let's say you need to improve players' running speed. Don't dribble around cones. The ball will limit your frequency, intensity, and step length. Do what track and field guys do, because they know where you lose that last part of a second. For cutting, look what rugby players do, they are really technically sound at it. I did not learn my lifting techniques from normal guys, but from the German national team powerlifter Sebastian Kaindl, because he knew the real technique of how to get the last 10%.' Ibrahimović's incredible flexibility came from taekwondo. Ryan Giggs played until he was 40 thanks to yoga. Perhaps to cope with the quick changes in transition in football, players should be coached basketball-styled fitness sessions. Kammann, when questioned on tactical periodisation and the belief in Spain and Portugal that sessions should always be based around real football, concedes that such multi-sport exercises apply mostly to youth ages, but stresses that even at first-team level variety should be offered to reduce strain on key muscles.

Build

In the modern game, with less space between the lines, a greater physical profile is needed in players. Kammann informed me that at some clubs, players can bench their own body weight from 14 years of age. 'If a coach is not open to sport science, then he won't get success in the long term. Certain injury patterns follow managers wherever they go, especially as they refuse to bring in the right people.' Kammann is one of the right people. 'The more successful a coach was as a player in an era before strength and conditioning, the more close-minded he is. Arsenal brought a guy in five years ago from a rugby background. They realised that they weren't getting the athletic results that they could have with their financial opportunities. So they went and got Des Ryan from the Irish Rugby Federation. If I remember correctly, they haven't had a single ACL injury at their academy in the last two years. It is an investment and if you think from an academy perspective, if your players are injured less, they have more time to train and develop.'

There are examples of footballers whose careers suffered from serious injuries. Michael Owen and Robbie Fowler at Liverpool peaked early in their careers, but rued injuries later on. 'This may have been down to repeated stress on the same parts of their bodies, or they may not have built up a good athletic programme in their youth,' (there is also no winter break for recovery time in Britain – another reason why England struggle at tournaments). But despite having multiple injuries, Nico reiterates what Dr Orhant said in Lyon: there is no such thing as a naturally injury-prone footballer; all injuries are preventable.

Owen and Fowler were part of a generation of footballers who grew up without nutrition programmes. At Sporting Lisbon, as discussed, every player has a dietary programme from an early age. 'Someone just has to educate your players on what to put into their bodies,' Nico says. 'A friend of mine works with the New York Giants, New York Red Bulls and AS Monaco. She tries to get the families and girlfriends of players involved. By that you create a certain flow that makes it easier for the player. And it's easier to fight misconceptions. You need glucose in your body, you need dairy products because they're an easy protein source. One nutritionist told a player not to eat eggplant. When did vegetables become bad!? There are so many wrong ideas about nutrition, athletic training, regeneration and other stuff out there, that you always have to be able to defend your position via legit science and data.'

Soccer, though, is not like American football in terms of variations in body type. Most positions in football are similar enough to ensure that conditioning training can be universal: 'Of course if a player lacks fitness, he needs to do extra shifts. If I were a coach with the first team I might give the players on the wing different jumps to do than the centre-backs, but not so much because of their position, but because of their size and their levels of movement capacity. The only guys I would rethink the training for is for goalkeepers.' Nico works alongside Bayern's reserve goalkeeper Tom Starke, who combines playing with coaching at the academy. Earlier, Starke joined in the *rondos* with the rest of the team to improve his footwork. He bridges the first team philosophy with the academy. The younger ages try to play a similar positional game model to that of the first team, building up in triangles in a 4-1-4-1 formation. Which ties in to the reason as to why Germany always win. The transition from academy playing style to that of the first team is mostly similar.

*

Starke Mentalität

The German ability of grinding out wins with a single-minded ruthlessness is a craft. Yet despite their obvious mental strength and perfect use of game-management, the Germans, like the Spanish before them, also have a clear pathway for young players from academy to national team that means, when they pull on their famous white and black jerseys for the first time, the transition has been seamless. Following their dismal Euro 2000 performance, the DFB (German association) and the Bundesliga worked together to draw up a plan. A talent development programme was produced that trained more coaches and players than before. 'Post-Euro 2000 was about changing philosophies as well as employing more full-time coaches and upgrading facilities. The DFB wanted to move away from playing in straight lines and relying on "the German mentality" to win matches,' wrote *The Guardian*. [1]

The pathway below is that of Bayern Munich, the core provider of players to the German national team, and mirrors the process that saw Barcelona assist Spain in their World Cup 2010 victory and Sporting Lisbon help Portugal in the 2016 European Championships.

1. A young boy joins the academy for the first time aged eight or nine.

2. He is taught a style of football that is synchronised from foundation up to older ages.

3. When he signs a professional contract aged 17 he is placed into a 'B' team, a stepping stone from youth to senior football with competitive demands.

4. From the B team, he joins the first team squad. The first team play the same style as the B team and academy, making his transition easier.

5. The first team style of football is the same as that of the national team.

6. He joins the national team and is fully aware of his roles and requirements in the formation and has mastered his position on the pitch.

7. The national team is typically made up of players he has played alongside at club level for many years. They understand how each other play through non-verbal communication. [41]

---

41. Ruesch, J. and Kees, W., 1982. *Nonverbal communication (Vol. 139)*. University of California Press.

Take Andrés Iniesta. In his first training session for Barça as a 16-year-old he walked 100 yards from La Masia to where the first team met. At the security gates, he was greeted by Luis Enrique and introduced to the captain Pep Guardiola: teammates who would become his coaches. He was able to progress so easily because the style was synchronised. With other boys who shared his lodgings – Gerard Piqué, Cesc Fàbregas, Víctor Valdés and Pepe Reina – he won the World Cup.

In Britain, academies have different ideas in regards to the type of players they wish to recruit, as well as their approach towards developing those players. The various FAs deliver courses and inspect academies, but they are autonomous bodies that can create their own programme of development. Germany's DFB, though, as the 'North Rhine-Westphalia' chapter will later explain, blanket over every young footballer in the country.

It was discussed with Nico how, following on from academy football in Britain, there is no obvious stepping stone from youth to senior football for a player, apart from a loan spell in an unfamiliar environment that can potentially stifle progression. If a youth player does, fortunately, make it into the first team, rarely does that team play the same style as the academy, such is the survivalist short-term mentality of managers in Britain; they are more reactive than proactive. And if perhaps the styles of the academy and the first team are the same, it is not enough to benefit the national team, as no Premier League squad, for example, is truly home-grown. At national level, there are no two Premier League teams that play the exact same style of football (some teams are similar, but not exact), culminating in a mismatch of progression. All in all, when a youth player reaches the national team, he is a stranger to his teammates and the style. Rinus Michels explained 'team-building' to be more than social cohesion, but a process of developing a clear methodology or game model. In Britain, because of various agendas, a flowing methodology is not always evident.

To get a lightbulb to turn on using an electric circuit all of the switches must be 'open', ensuring the path is unbroken. To have a successful national team, the difficult path youth players navigate must be open. Sadly, domestically, at most corners from academy to the national team, it is 'closed' and the British game remains dark. By way of contrast, German and Spanish associations work alongside their clubs. 'We have a "fidelity strategy" that ensured 77% of La Liga players are able to play for the national team,' said league president Jose Luis Astiazaran of their ten-year plan. [li]

They play a similar style of football in their domestic leagues – high pressing with quick shifts of possession – that is reflected in their national style of play. Alongside this, the pathway that young players take, be it at Valencia or Schalke, is 'open' and is mostly similar to that of domestic rivals. Seven graduates of Barcelona's La Masia academy featured in the 2010 World Cup final, whilst seven Bayern Munich players (including the departing Toni Kroos) featured for Germany in 2014; most notably the home-grown trio of Lahm, Müller and Schweinsteiger. In that German winning squad, six players (Neuer, Höwedes, Boateng, Hummels, Khedira and Özil) had previously played together at the 2009 European Under-21 Championships, beating England 4–0 in the final (only James Milner from the England squad would go to Brazil five years later). Germany's squad had five years of playing together, perfecting on-field relationships and rehearsing positional play, whilst England persisted in taking strangers to strange lands.

*

As we stepped outside, the waiting crowds had all dispersed. Sprinklers wet the pitches as dusk settled. It looked like most other complexes, but felt different. What is special about Bayern, what makes them unique in both Europe and Germany, more than their pioneering fitness work and open pathway for youngsters, is their impeccably high standards. Nico did not romanticise the question when asked about uniqueness, and is straightforwardly German in his answer: 'The biggest thing that is unique here is that every day I walk out past the first team and I see how hard they work when Müller, Lahm and the team are out there. In one of their first practices after the World Cup the players trained at 100%. When one player made a bad pass, he was screamed at by the other players because it was not the standard that we have here.' The greatest teams in history, from Ajax in the 1970s to Milan in the 80s and Manchester United in the 90s, all shared the common thread of having exemplary standards. That, despite all the study in the world, cannot be learnt. It has to be lived.

Nico has since progressed to a more senior role at Bayern's Bavarian neighbours, Augsburg.

THIRTEEN

WINGS OF CHANGE:
RED BULL SALZBURG

'How I hate Salzburg,' Mozart wrote from Paris to a friend in 1778. 'There is nothing going on, musically; there is no theatre, no opera!' The great irony now is that Salzburg loves him dearly. Some 480,556 tourists visited the home of his birth in 2014. His music ghosts between the ancient cobbles of Altstadt, the old town, where his face looks out from every gift shop. Mozart yearned to leave the city and used it only as a foundation he could return to upon travelling the continent in his youth. His father, Leopold, took the boy wonder to imperial courts in Prague, Vienna, London, Bavaria, France and Italy, presenting his talents to nobility in the hope of gaining commission. Salzburg for Mozart would be but a stepping stone on the path to greatness.

But that was then. The city now is wondrous. Its beauty is natural; a green flat land enclosed by the Alps. The journey there from Munich offered several hours of postcard snapshots. At the start, in Bavaria, high black trees gathered around large wooden houses, and even though they were secluded from everyday society, they still boasted FC Bayern flags on huge poles. Trains from Munich to Salzburg run every hour of the day. There are street signs to each respective city, such is their closeness. From the outskirts of Bavaria, the Alps can be seen in the distance, almost unreal, like a painting you can never reach. You do, however, eventually pass them by, taking in lakes, forestland, and distant castles on the way. Fairy tale settings.

City resident Dietrich Mateschitz's story is a fairy tale of sorts. At 38 he was director of a small German toothpaste company. By 60 he was the richest man in Austria and beyond. His company, Red Bull, grew to be seen everywhere, as the face of extreme sports and racing, both on land and in the air – they even sponsored local boy Felix Baumgartner's jump from space. Mateschitz works from his company base 'Hangar-7' (a collection of bars and restaurants surrounded by historic aeroplanes) on the outskirts of Salzburg. From there, Red Bull orchestrate the direction of their football clubs across the world.

History

Mateschitz is reserved: 'Society events are the most senseless use of time.' One simply cannot imagine him partaking in the trivialities of Salzburg's scene. Yet with one friend, the German superstar Franz Beckenbauer, a fellow resident, he spoke often about the power of football as both a spectacle and commercial venture. Mateschitz over time convinced Beckenbauer to help his company invest in football clubs and in 2005 Red Bull purchased SV Austria Salzburg.

'This has nothing to do with passion, playfulness or a profiling neurosis,' Mateschitz rationalised. 'In everything we do, we must distinguish between the activities of the brand, and me as a person.' It was not, he explained, a personal indulgence to enter football, but an idea to grow Red Bull. His friend Beckenbauer pitched to the German press how 'Salzburg is a sleeping giant' and used his links to convince Bayern Munich favourites Giovanni Trapattoni and Lothar Matthäus to manage the newly rebranded 'Red Bull Salzburg'. [42]

The takeover differed from that witnessed at Chelsea, Manchester City and PSG in that there was no indulgent spending initially, but instead a more thoughtful business plan was implemented. 'It would be wrong to buy a team of mercenaries,' Mateschitz said. 'Time and natural growth of the club is more important than an astronomical budget and dazzling names.' [liii] They did not entice new fans to their brand by overloading Salzburg with past-it celebrity footballers (like Indian Premier League

---

42. They purchased clubs in New York (2006), São Paulo (2007), Leipzig (2007) and Sogakope (2008).

clubs did in 2014 when David Trezeguet, Roberto Carlos, Nicolas Anelka and Lúcio arrived), but instead made calculated purchases of little-known talents. [43]

Former sporting director Ralf Rangnick told an audience of suits at a conference in Zurich how Red Bull approach transfers organically: 'The difference between us and other clubs is that in the first place when we sign or scout players we are fishing in a small pond, as we are only interested in players aged between 17 and 23. Our transfer policy is to sign players who are only on to maybe their second contract in their lives and they want to develop their career step by step, and if you get the right offer you have to let them go and have other players in the pipeline.' [44]

Name	From	For	To	For
Alan	Desp. Brasil	£2,980,000	Guangzhou	£9,440,000
Kevin Kampl	Aalen	£2,550,000	Dortmund	£10,200,000
Sadio Mané	Metz	£3,400,000	Southampton	£12,750,000
Peter Galusci	Liverpool	£0	RB Leipzig	£2,550,000
Stefan Ilsanker	Mattersburg	£0	RB Leipzig	£2,550,000
Bernardo	RB Brasil	£0	RB Leipzig	£5,100,000
M. Hinteregger	Academy	£0	Augsburg	£5,950,000
Naby Keïta	Istres	£1,280,000	RB Leipzig	£12,750,000
	Total	**£10,210,000**	*Total*	**£61,290,000**

It became a long-term strategy aligning with the patience of the city. Through football, Mateschitz felt he could add to the profile of Salzburg whilst ensuring Red Bull benefited mutually. (The RB Leipzig sales above, whilst allowing fans to understand the value of their players, are not especially telling, as Red Bull own both clubs and most likely see transfers between them as a way of depositing finances.)

---

43. A deal of controversy surrounded the takeover and subsequent changing of SV Austria Salzburg's identity (name, crest and colours). They reformed that year as a phoenix club, starting in Austria's seventh division. At the time of my visit, hostility had diminished as the two enterprises came to acknowledge their predicaments. SV Austria Salzburg are fan-owned and use their position as a force for good, campaigning and volunteering for initiatives in Gambia and elsewhere. When the 2015 refugee crisis was at its most difficult, the club opened its doors and gave food, water and other essential items to passing immigrants. As a fan-owned institution, supporters take assurance that the future is in their hands, similar to FC United and AFC Wimbledon, knowing they'll never again be commercially exploited. There is disdain for Red Bull, but not blind enmity. After all, 13,000 regular Salzburg fans chose to stay and support Red Bull Salzburg, satisfied with the direction of the club and the instant success delivered.
44. International Football Arena conference, 2014.

The Approach

Perhaps, because of its location in the shadow of the Alps – a place for a peaceful saunter – the mentality of Salzburg as a place young men progress from has remained since the days of Mozart. *What lies on the other side?* A stepping stone of sorts. Red Bull, instead of resisting futilely, go along with that mentality. 'We can give them the opportunity to play in a competitive league against grown-ups,' said the club's bright young head scout Christopher Vivell. Red Bull study the transfer market, invest in players with potential, offer them a platform and sell them on. 'Players can adapt and reach the next step.'

Do you scout less reputable leagues? 'Yes of course, we have a big scouting department. We try to know every market, which is interesting for us. We try to use all different possibilities of scouting,' online, statistical, video and live analysis, like at Juventus. 'Nowadays, there are videos in almost every professional division, and all kinds of statistics. So, we want to be prepared before we travel.' Like Juve, Salzburg know it is expensive to travel for live sensations when scouting and try their best to build up an understanding of a player before they commit to watching him in the flesh. They then entice players to the club with their state-of-the-art facilities and regular European competition (as well as the possibility of skiing on weekends – as previously determined, the modern footballer prefers to ply his trade in more cosmopolitan surroundings than before).[45]

The term 'Moneyball' is often used in recruitment. Do you use statistics when you are signing a player? 'Always, we try to do everything. We want to be more prepared and to be faster than our rivals. We have to know the young players all over the world. You always have to be active when scouting.' Statistics analysed include successful forward passes, final third entries, aerial duels won, scoring percentages and a variety of other core position-specific stats that identify striving talents.

The book *Moneyball* by Michael Lewis tells of how general manager Billy

---

45. It therefore won't be long until cultured players hold ambitions to play here. The city has museums, castles, cathedrals, bars and nightlife, all within its small confines (it is 65 kilometres square). 'It's a good opportunity to learn a different culture,' said Andre Wisdom of his time at Red Bull Salzburg, he being an anomalous Englishman abroad. The buildings in the old city are fine tributes to the architectural art form. They've been carefully considered, baroque in style with marble halls. There's a long-termism to them, to the city and now indeed to its football club.

Beane transformed the Oakland A's from a poor, below-average baseball side to winners through a revolutionary recruitment policy. They identified and enrolled players based on their underlying key statistics, such as batting and base averages, rather than adhering to the traditional diplomatic 'watch and discuss' approach.

Many of their recruitments were obscure; even Scott Hatteberg, the veteran catcher whose stats identified him as an ideal replacement for departing MVP Jason Giambi, couldn't believe the A's were so much as interested in him. His statistics pointed out that he could potentially become a good first baseman, so he was retained and converted, later justifying the acquisition with 49 home runs. Scouting went from old men around a table to Harvard students at computers. There was of course an instant bitterness, one that accompanies most forms of change. Traditional scouts persecuted the 'nerds' in a similar vein to the Church and Galileo. New is scary and therefore must be wrong. But sport evolved in line with technological advancements in society. The *Moneyball* idea would come to be deemed transferable to a myriad of sports, including football, and generated a wider interest in analytics.

But its association with football is ambiguous. A number of journalists referenced it when describing players purchased at a cut price. Others did so when discussing the use of statistics in athlete recruitment. Both examples are mostly accurate. But there are several myths attached to *Moneyball*'s relationship with football. Firstly, baseball recruitment involves player trades, not transfer fees. There is no cut-price £5m baseball purchase made below an expected value. Secondly, the quantification of football players was not conceived with the release of *Moneyball*. At several clubs, long-term paradigms were already in place that were consulted when purchasing players, years before the book was written. In other words, its effect was not as influential in football as in other sports. Despite that, its popularity birthed a greater interest in statistical analysis in football. The idea behind *Moneyball* isn't about using stats to identify players; rather it is about using stats to find a Hatteberg. A player undervalued in the market who is not being used effectively.

For Red Bull Salzburg, the Catalan striker Jonathan Soriano – stagnating in Barcelona's B team – would prove to be their Hatteberg, turning heads on the continent for his performances during the 2013/14 Europa League campaign. Interest peaked following Red Bull Salzburg's 6–1 aggregate victory over Ajax. Their high pressing was so structured that Ajax's Daley Blind and Mike van der Hoorn, confident ball players, were allowed to keep possession, but once they passed centrally or to either full-back, Salzburg forced them into a pressing trap. Ajax grew frustrated and lost their composure, trying to overcompensate in other areas. For Salzburg's third goal, Soriano lobbed the future Barcelona goalkeeper Jasper Cillessen from the halfway line.

It was a defining season of awareness for Red Bull Salzburg made possible by the philosophy of Ralf Rangnick (now of RB Leipzig): hired by Red Bull in 2012 to create a clear playing identity for each Red Bull club. When Mateschitz called him, RB Salzburg had an average squad age of 29. Rangnick told the owner the company slogan 'Red Bull Gives You Wings' is aimed at young people, but they cannot identify with older players. 'I told him how I would develop [the club] by signing young unknown talented players, and [by playing] high attacking transitional football which suits the Red Bull brand.'

'Our whole club philosophy is part of a Red Bull one and is based on that of our former sport director Ralf Rangnick. We still continue that idea which is based on fast, aggressive play close together, with team spirit and quick regains of the ball,' Vivell confirmed in retrospect. 'We defend collectively with fast switches of play. It is a clear mentality that was formed by Rangnick.' Players signed are carefully considered and must have both the right mental aptitude and technical capabilities to play within Rangnick's guidelines. 'If he has no character for pressing, then he will not be signed. But we do not always get to see the potential of the player in his environment – perhaps his coach is telling him to relax when out of possession – so we need to use our imagination,' said Vivell.

Ralf and Rene

In his native Germany, Ralf Rangnick is considered a pioneer in tactical development. 'He was on TV in the late 90s – probably 1999 – and was on there with a tactics board explaining how they work,' recalled Tobias Escher of the tactics website spielverlagerung.de. 'It was a big scandal; people were offended by it because they believed football was an easy sport that did not need complicating.' In Salzburg, Rangnick found a home. People here have an appreciation of tactical nous and cleverness in general. Grown men play chess in *Kapitelplatz* square on a giant board every day as tourists photograph the battle.

North of the square, beside the picturesque River Salzach, is the Red Bull *Akademie*. It is, without question, the most impressive academy facility in Austria – 200 metres long and made with local timber. For club owner Mateschitz it is the central hub of a long-term strategy, one that was developed by Rangnick: 'The team will rejuvenate naturally, by producing talented graduates from our academy.' [liv] Vivell concurred: 'We want to give young players the perfect development. Not only in football, but in their skills for life. This is very important for Red Bull. We have the perfect academy, one of the best in Europe. It is very new.' Hockey and football stars of the future share a boarding school and are encouraged to inspire each other with gentle competitiveness.

Rene Maric works for Red Bull Salzburg as a youth coach and explained the model running through the facility: 'It's about high pressing with ball-oriented movement*, high compactness, defending forward not backwards**, with a big focus on both transition phases and how to exploit them. It's implemented in every single academy team, just in ways. This means that every coach can adapt to the circumstances – player age, etc. – in some ways, such as the player roles and specific patterns, but the principles always stay the same.'

Rene, in his early 20s, is another member of a young generation of football coaches who enjoy dissecting the game. He works with the U18s and U19s (known also as the UEFA Youth League squad – who in 2017 illuminated the tournament, defeating PSG 5–0) and was hired on account of his tactical understanding. The game model that flows through the club was not just a product of Ralf Rangnick, though, as Maric stresses, but of Helmut Groß and Ernst Tanner, too. 'There is a ton of detail in it which is shared within the academy. It really belongs to Red Bull and there are

---

* Ball-oriented movement means for the player and team to readjust in accordance to the position of the ball (and its movement) when out of possession.
**Defending forward means pressing ahead of the ball both forwards and diagonally in every defensive action. Doing so avoids having to make recovery runs.

many thinkers/coaches behind it with every coach adding his own small details.'

A coach Rangnick admired and helped recruit for the club, Roger Schmidt, added to the model, whilst Ernst Tanner, current head of youth development at the club, assisted with its production. Helmut Groß, the one-time construction engineer 'built bridges by day and coached amateur teams by night', according to Paul Campbell. It was Groß, he wrote, who introduced ball-orientated defending to German and Austrian football. 'In 1989, Groß took charge of VfB Stuttgart's youth set-up, laying the foundation for a system that has since unearthed such talents as Mario Gomez, Sami Khedira and Timo Hildebrand.' Campbell wrote that Groß befriended Ralf Rangnick and the two watched videos of Sacchi's Milan so often their video tape player wore out.[46] Groß advises Red Bull and, alongside Rangnick, Schmidt and Tanner, has helped develop the model that has given Salzburg fame beyond Mozart's cobbles.

46. Campbell, P (2015). *The Blizzard – The Football Quarterly.* Sunderland: Blizzard Media Ltd.

FOURTEEN

AN INTERMISSION READ: INVESTING IN POTENTIAL; EUROPEAN TRANSFERS

'The club will draw up a list of players to fit [a] remit in collaboration with the analytics department. In the old days, it would just be the head coach and the president compiling the list, but football is big business now and many considerations other than simply his performances on the pitch are taken into account, like his age and potential, sell-on value, commercial revenues and such things.'

Carlo Ancelotti in his biography *Quiet Leadership.*[47]

Generating revenue is the most all-determining aspect of football, which has been the case, arguably, since the erection of stadia by landowners in the 19th century. Transfers are the public face of revenue and therefore hold great relevance for both fans and clubs, especially in the context of methods in football, having been used to redefine the notion of success since the Bosman ruling.[48] *As Ancelotti highlights, directors on the continent have for many years considered the above factors when completing a transfer. Take Ralf Rangnick's words from the previous chapter. All clubs consider age, potential*

47. Ancelotti, C; Brady, C; Forde, M (2016). *Quiet Leadership: Winning Hearts, Minds and Matches*. Great Britain: Portfolio Penguin. 125.
48. Kranz, A (1998). *The Bosman Case: The Relationship between European Union Law and the Transfer System in European Football.*

and sell-on value, but there are several, like Red Bull Salzburg, who place a great emphasis on such factors, actively shaping their commercial identity around investing in potential. 'We are only interested in players aged between 17 and 23,' he told a conference in Zurich, 'and if you get the right offer you have to let them go and have other players in the pipeline.' This chapter will explore a similar band of self-aware clubs.

'Year after year they sell, they buy, they develop and they look for value in the market,' wrote *The Telegraph* of Southampton's transfer model in October 2016. It is, they would write, a refreshing approach. It is also one that has been played out by clubs on the continent since the Bosman ruling took effect in the 1990s, when they grew conscious of player value. As Sæbø and Hvattum found, 'To help assess investments, it helps [clubs] to know the market value of the players and to identify inefficiencies in the pricing of [them].' [49] In other words, they seek to find undervalued talent. The process they describe applies to notorious wily operators: Porto, Benfica, Sevilla and Udinese, to name but a few.

So common is this approach in football's market of hierarchal wealth (in which clubs understand their place) it is deserving of terminology. It has been described by numerous sources as Financial Investment in Potential Growth (FIPG) and is defined as 'a refusal to spend beyond ones means, whilst ensuring a profit can be made'. [lvi] It's a decent description of a 'selling club' and for ease will be used in this chapter.

There has been an increase in studies relating to transfers in recent years, specifically the importance of clubs getting them right. 'Transfer investments are shown to have a strongly significant and positive impact on league points per game,' [50] (Rohde & Breuer 2016); 'Rise of popular and financial interest in association football puts higher pressure on professional clubs to invest wisely in their core competence: football players,' (Sæbø & Hvattum 2015) with Rodrigues (2016) concluding, '[In Europe's big five leagues] demand for quality players is high and competition to get them

49. Sæbø, O. & Hvattum, L. (2015) *Evaluating the efficiency of the association football transfer market using regression-based player ratings.* Molde.
50. Rohde, M. & Breuer, C. (2016). 'Europe's Elite Football: Financial Growth, Sporting Success, Transfer Investment, and Private Majority Investors'. *Int. J. Financial Stud.* 16 (4), 12.

fierce.' [51] All of which is a direct contrast to the mentality of board members and stake holders in a previous era, when they believed losses would occur naturally, didn't sell at the right time, and relied on patrons to bail them out.

Nowadays club officials have developed a greater degree of self-awareness. German academics Sybille Frank and Silke Steets wrote in 2010 about the hierarchy of wealth and the migration of talent in a transnational industry. 'There are many clubs', they acknowledged, 'which rely on national players, mostly young aspiring talents who are supplemented by players from abroad, and for whom these clubs are often a springboard to a greater career.' It is, as they highlighted, a mutual arrangement between player and club that embraces a 'stepping-stone identity'. [52] French international Lassana Diarra confirmed that mentality when, aged 23, he signed for Portsmouth. His comments at his unveiling to the British press were:

- 'The people at Portsmouth know I will not spend my life at this club.'
- 'If I shine, if a really big club wants me, I know already that everything will go well.'
- 'I really want to think about myself, about those who appreciate me.'

He performed well, won the FA Cup and was signed by Real Madrid for £20m. [lvi] Unlike Portsmouth who were saddled with debt and entered administration, clubs elsewhere have lived organically by using the transfer market to invest in the trajectory of players like Diarra. Historically, the notion of buying a footballer with the focus on later selling him did not exist. Clubs, before the Bosman ruling, did not need to sell their players; they owned them and retained all value. Yet with the evolution of player power, clubs have been forced to cash in on footballers like stock market assets before their value decreases and they leave on a free. The notion of 'trust' is now questionable. It is only in an age of greater ebbing money that asset-driven capitalism has allowed for the idea of success to be questioned and redefined. A club can now be successful, healthy and prosperous

51. Rodrigues, P.M.M., (2016). 'Football players' transfer price determination based on performance in the Big 5 European leagues' (Doctoral dissertation, NOVA–School of Business and Economics).
52. Frank, S. & Steets, S (2010). Stadium Worlds: Football, Space and the Built Environment. Great Britain: Routledge.

without ever winning trophies. For fans that is contentious – they never see the money – but for clubs, profit represents triumph.

The following subcategories are on transfer types, specifically the notion of investing in talent. I will look to compare the mentality of clubs depending on their hierarchal position in a financially motivated football world. Either they seek to achieve success (silverware), or they seek profit (sales). Geurts (2016) sees the two ideas as a conflict of interests, between profit maximising and success maximising: 'The former relates to a football club whose objective function is dominated by profits, while the latter motivates that clubs can be driven by sporting success subject to a budget constraint of zero profits.' Nevertheless, over time, by acting astutely, clubs can eventually turn profits into silverware (see Sevilla). [53]

*

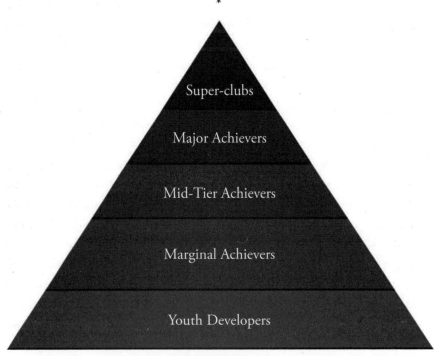

Figure 1: Heirarchy of Wealth pyramid.

53. Most research upholds the idea that clubs favour success maximisation and the inevitable loss of revenue as a consequence. It is therefore poignant to acknowledge how profit-seeking clubs (Atlético, Porto, Sevilla) manage to balance that agenda whilst achieving silverware.

All clubs are able to partake in the process of investing in potential (FIPG). Norbäck, Olsson and Persson (2016) explain the process as, 'The nursery club [making] a costly investment in talent scouting and development, which increases the probability of finding and delivering a star player. Nature then draws the talented player's true quality,' leading to a resale and profit. [54]

The nature phase is especially key in capitalising on potential. Take the ascendancy of Luis Suárez for example. A youth player at Nacional Montevideo (market value £16.8m) who was purchased by FC Groningen (MV £20.53m) for £680,000. At 20 years of age he joined Ajax (MV £102.9m) for £6m. Considering the economy of Dutch football, they retained maximum value when selling the 24-year-old Suárez to Liverpool (MV £329m) in 2011 for £22.7m. In a higher, more financial league, at a club with strong financial capabilities, Suárez's performances rose in the same trajectory as his value. By 2014 he had reached his summit and was purchased by Barcelona (MV £643m) for £69m. His career is a perfect example of Financial Investment in Potential Growth. As his performances on more valuable platforms increased (through the nature phase), so too did his value and fee, creating profit for all clubs.

1. Investing in Potential: Super-clubs

Clubs who quite consciously position themselves to achieve success in the transfer market are able to do so because at the top of the capitalistic food chain is always an owner willing to spend excessively, either to make a point or exercise ego. Roman Abramovich at Chelsea, Suleyman Kerimov at Anzhi, Florentino Pérez at Real Madrid, Nasser Al-Khelaifi at PSG and Sheikh Mansour at Manchester City have, since 2005, invested heavily. Chinese businessmen were encouraged by President Xi Jinping in 2015 to turn the country into a footballing powerhouse by acquiring assets at any cost. For such men, no fee is too much. They create waves below them for club owners elsewhere to ride.

---

54. Norbäck, P. Olsson, M. & Persson, L. (2016). *The Emergence of a Market for Football Stars: Talent Development and Competitive Balance in European Football*. Research Institute of Industrial Economics. 1126

Within this ecosystem of clubs and leagues of various incomes, it is important for an institution to find its level. At the top are the super-clubs whose duty it is to make expensive purchases and record debt in the pursuit of success. They are least likely to invest in potential and choose instead to purchase ready-made stars with actual and marketing talent. Real Madrid, as the topmost example of this tier, broke the world transfer record five times consecutively when buying Luís Figo, Zinedine Zidane, Kaká, Cristiano Ronaldo and Gareth Bale.

Simon Kuper and Stefan Szymanski found in *Soccernomics* that if Spain's two biggest clubs readjusted their priorities and stopped spending out on players, then it would negatively affect their league position: 'If Barcelona wanted to maximise profits, they would have to aim to finish 15th in the league, because they would need to slash their wages. A profit-driven Real Madrid should expect to finish a mere 17th.' A theme running throughout *Soccernomics* is that all clubs aspiring for sporting success run themselves a debt in doing so. Which they do, willingly. To remain competitive, they must spend, because if they do not then owners elsewhere will and they'll fall behind.[55] They are the 'success motivated' clubs, top of the capitalist pyramid.

Such super-clubs have a duty to purchase footballers at their summit value and retain them for their best years of form. Barcelona recorded a loss of €35m with Zlatan Ibrahimović in dealing with both Milan clubs. They hardly blinked. Their loss was consolidated by prize money and commercial income, having won the Champions League in both seasons before and after the deal (€15m prize money plus commercial sponsorship deals, estimated to be worth €244m by Deloitte). They could afford to get the deal wrong. Real Madrid blessed football with the first *Galácticos* team that won the 2002 Champions League. Financially, they grew as a global brand during that era, but in signing players at their summit they ran a loss in the transfer market. (Despite commercial profits subsidising, such an approach may be unlikely in the future with the introduction of Financial Fair Play.)

---

55. Kuper, S. and Szymanski, S. (2012). The Worst Businesses in the World. In: *Soccernomics*. 3rd ed. Great Britain: Harper Sport. 74–5.

Here are some examples of their losses in that era:

Name	From	For	To	For
Luís Figo	Barcelona	£37,000,000	Inter Milan	£7,000,000
Zinedine Zidane	Juventus	£62,480,000	retired	£0
David Beckham	Manchester Utd	£31,800,000	LA Galaxy	£0
Walter Samuel	AS Roma	£19,550,000	Inter Milan	£15,300,000
Ronaldo	Inter Milan	£38,250,000	AC Milan	£6,380,000
	Total	**£189,080,000**	*Total*	**£28,680,000**
		Loss of £160,400,000		

Table 1 - other than Walter Samuel, all players were retained for their best years of form.

2. FIPG: Major Achievers – Spanish Examples

Next are the clubs sandwiched between tiers in the pyramid. For them, the job is to invest in players who have consistently shown levels of improvement and who have a natural potential to reach super-club level. They purchase such players (from less valuable leagues) for the purpose of developing their status as a club, but are in a strong bargaining position to sell them on to super-clubs (or willing spenders) due to their financial stability if offers arrive. Enrique Cerezo, Atlético Madrid president, said of the matter: 'Atlético is a club that buys … There are teams that pay [players] a lot more and they leave … It's not an issue that worries me. Players of similar characteristics will arrive and they could do an even better job.' [lvii]

Atléti sit on the threshold of becoming a super-club as the seventh-most-valuable club in the world in 2016 (Deloitte). Before Fernando Torres made his debut, however, they were languishing in the Spanish second division. El Niño, the boy, became captain at 19 and was the focal point of their return to La Liga. Following his 2007 sale to Liverpool, club president Enrique Cerezo was able to implement a strategy of investing in potentially valuable attacking players:

Name	From	For	To	For
Fernando Torres	*Academy*	£0	Liverpool	£26,000,000
Sergio Agüero	Independiente	£18,500,000	Manchester City	£34,000,000
Radamel Falcao	Porto	£34,000,000	AS Monaco	£37,000,000
Diego Costa	Braga	£1,280,000	Chelsea	£32,300,000
A. Griezmann	Real Sociedad	£25,500,000	*	*
Mario Mandžukić	Bayern Munich	£18,700,000	Juventus	£16,150,000
Jackson Martínez	Porto	£31,150,000	Guangzhou	£35,700,000
Fernando Torres	AC Milan	£0	*	*

The process culminated in Atlético almost winning the Champions League, twice, but for the greater wealth of their more commercial, more expense-driven neighbours Real Madrid. Coherently, it is unlikely nowadays that the tournament will be won by a Red Star Belgrade, an outsider, like it was in 1991 when they bypassed predetermined paradigms like 'having less money means you can't win'. Following that Yugoslav triumph, it became true that rich clubs are generally more geared for success than poorer clubs. However, FIPG allows poorer clubs to become wealthy over time and therefore more likely to triumph. Sevilla are an example of this and are another Spanish rags-to-riches story, having gone from an Andalusian dockers' club in the shadow of neighbours Real Betis to becoming the most frequent winners of the Europa League and the first club to win a European trophy three years in a row since Beckenbauer's Bayern Munich of 1974–76.

The architect of Sevilla's golden era was not a single manager or player, but rather a director. Monchi took over the role in 2000 as the club flirted with debt and relegation. He explained his process: 'Sixteen people cover a series of leagues. For the first five months, we watch a lot of football but with no particular aim: we're just accumulating data. Every month we produce an ideal XI for each league. Then, in December, we start watching players who appeared regularly in different contexts – home, away, international – to build the broadest possible profile.' Monchi builds a database of over 200 potential targets each season. 'If a player says, "Chelsea want me," I say: "What are you talking to me for, then?" But if Swansea or Spurs want you, let's talk.' He's fully aware of Sevilla's hierarchal level. Some of their most profitable dealings are listed below:

Name	From	For	To	For
Christian Poulsen	Schalke	£0	Juventus	£8,290,000
Seydou Keita	Lens	£3,400,000	Barcelona	£11,900,000
Dani Alves	Bahia	£468,000	Barcelona	£30,180,000
Adriano	Coritiba	£1,790,000	Barcelona	£8,080,000
Gary Medel	U. Católica	£2,550,000	Cardiff	£11,050,000
G. Kondogbia	Lens	£3,400,000	AS Monaco	£17,000,000
Jesús Navas	Academy	£0	Manchester City	£17,000,000
Álvaro Negredo	Real Madrid	£12,750,000	Manchester City	£21,250,000
Federico Fazio	Ferro	£680,000	Tottenham	£8,500,000
Ivan Rakitić	Schalke	£2,130,000	Barcelona	£15,300,000

Name	From	For	To	For
Alberto Moreno	Academy	£0	Liverpool	£15,300,000
Aleix Vidal	Almería	£2,550,000	Barcelona	£14,450,000
Carlos Bacca	Club Brugge	£5,950,000	AC Milan	£25,500,000
Kévin Gameiro	PSG	£6,380,000	Atlético	£27,200,000
G. Krychowiak	Stade de Reims	£4,600,000	PSG	£28,560,000
	Total	**£46,648,000**	**Total**	**£259,560,000**

Signing a player who is unable to adapt is a problem attached to any transfer. Clever clubs, like Barcelona, identify targets from an environment that plays the same style as they do, namely Sevilla: Keita, Alves, Adriano, Rakitić and Vidal. Creating cohesion should be the aim for every purchase.

3. Sign Them Young

The most notorious exploiters of the transfer market are Porto and Benfica. Portugal is a welcome climate for players from the Americas looking to settle in Europe. Culturally it makes for a pleasant stepping stone with its hot weather and relaxed atmosphere, especially in Lisbon, and thanks to the almost non-existent regulation on work permits for foreign players, not found elsewhere, as well as the presence of third-party ownership deals at one time, Porto and Benfica have been able to sign players from all over the globe. Spanish clubs can only retain three non-EU players at a time. Italian clubs can only sign one per season. A Premier League outside the European Union is yet to be experienced, but work permits are expected. Yet in Portugal there are no such regulations. Once inside the country, South American players can apply for an EU passport in anticipation of their next move.

Example I: Porto

Seixo Alvo is a sleepy square where the pace of life is set by slow-moving cats. In the square is a bus stop, a bakery and a barber shop. It is also home to PortoGaia, the complex I visited in February. As church bells rang out in the distance for midday, the old men in the barbers turned toward the window and watched the big sports cars pass by. 'There goes Casillas,' one man pointed. 'No, that was Hector [Herrera, the Mexican]. You're blind!' Since PortoGaia opened up the road in 2002, the old men have seen many big cars pass through the square: Falcao's, Hulk's, James', Pepe's and Carvalho's to name but a few.

The front of the barber shop, and indeed the fronts of most casas and churches in Oporto, look like they are made from fine blue china, with thousands of tiles building their façade – an architectural idea that was exported from Brazil in the 19th century. This is the city where Portugal began. Its port was used by the king to explore the Americas. Oporto naturally has a strong history of recruiting from Brazil, mirrored contemporarily by its football club.

Through TP training regimes, players develop close to their full potential, before being sold on to wealthier markets. Porto director Antero Henrique explained several years ago that the club have over 300 scouts worldwide working at various hierarchal levels, who help to compile a 'shadow team' of players ready to be signed once a first team player is sold.

Tom Kundert of *World Soccer* magazine told me about FC Porto's fire-sale strategy, of building a squad to sell. 'They sign them from South America, young and talented, develop them into world-class players, get great service from them and sell them for a huge profit. They demand high fees because they've built up a reputation of having quality players, so the fee is there because you know you are buying the best in the market.' Author John le Carré once wrote that the more expensive a painting is, regardless of its quality, the less inclined a buyer is to doubt its authenticity. In other words, it must cost so much for a reason. The idea applies to football. Some clubs willingly spend excessively on Porto stars because they come with a supposed guarantee. But no player is a certain fit, and no painting offers certain resale profit.

Below is a table showing sales of over £10m since the Champions League triumph of 2004 (up to 2017). Almost half of the players sold were representatives of Jorge Mendes, the former nightclub owner, with seven of the first eight players sold Portuguese. As the game became more globalised the type of player bought and sold ceased to be Portuguese, with only three of the 16 players sold from 2009 being so. Most were brought from the Americas.

Name	Cost	From	To	Year	For	Age
Ricardo Carvalho	n/a	Porto B	Chelsea	2004	£22,500,000	26
Deco	£6,000,000	Benfica SLB	Barcelona	2004	£15,750,000	26
Paulo Ferreira	£1,500,000	Vitória	Chelsea	2004	£15,000,000	24
Maniche	£0	Benfica	Dinamo Moscow	2005	£12,000,000	26
Anderson	£3,750,000	Gremio	Manchester Utd	2007	£26,630,000	18
Pepe	£1,500,000	Marítimo	Real Madrid	2007	£22,500,000	23
Quaresma	£4,500,000	FC Barcelona	Internazionale	2008	£18,450,000	24

Name	Cost	From	To	Year	For	Age
Jose Bosingwa	£750,000	Boavista	Chelsea	2008	£15,380,000	25
Lisandro López	£1,730,000	Racing Club	Lyon	2009	£18,000,000	25
Lucho González	£7,700,000	River Plate	Marseille	2009	£14,250,000	27
Aly Cissokho	£225,000	Vitória	Lyon	2009	£12,150,000	21
Bruno Alves	£750,000	AEK Athens	Zenit	2010	£16,500,000	28
Raul Meireles	£0	Boavista	Liverpool	2010	£10,000,000	26
Falcao	£4,070,000	River Plate	Atlético	2011	£30,000,000	24
Hulk	£14,250,000	Tokyo Verdy	Zenit	2012	£41,100,000	26
James Rodriguez	£1,880,000	Banfield	Monaco	2013	£33,750,000	21
João Moutinho	£8,250,000	Sporting CP	Monaco	2013	£18,750,000	26
Eliaquim Mangala	£5,000,000	Standard	Manchester City	2014	£30,000,000	23
Fernando	£540,000	Vila Nova	Manchester City	2014	£11,250,000	26
Juan Iturbe	£3,000,000	Quilmes	Hellas Verona	2014	£11,250,000	20
Jackson Martínez	£6,670,000	Jaguares	Atlético	2015	£27,830,000	28
Danilo	£9,750,000	Santos	Real Madrid	2015	£23,650,000	23
Alex Sandro	£7,200,000	Maldonado	Juventus	2015	£19,500,000	24
Giannelli Imbula	£15,000,000	Marseille	Stoke City	2016	£18,190,000	23
Total	***£104,015,000***		**Total**		***£476,130,000***	

The mean average age of players when sold is 24.3 years. As players get older, they become less valuable, naturally. One reason as to why Porto achieve such high fees is because they have featured in the group stages of the past 22 Champions League tournaments consecutively – equalled only by Real Madrid and Barcelona (2017). However, their purchase of World Cup-winning 34-year-old goalkeeper Iker Casillas from Real Madrid, making him the best paid player in their history, signalled a deviation away from FIPG and undermined a decade of prosperity. Casillas' age and wage meant he had no resale potential – Porto were stuck with him. A year later they were flagged up by Financial Fair Play officials.

But president Jorge Nuno da Costa's investments firstly in José Mourinho from Leira, then André Villas-Boas from Académica, both of whom were former backroom staff members at Porto, is one of modern football's great stories. The PortoGaia complex is a landmark of his leadership as president. When he arrived at the club as director of football in 1976, local rivals Boavista were more attractive to players. Porto that year had only five league titles, their last one coming 17 years earlier in 1959. As director of football and later president he created a dynasty – between his arrival in 1976 and 2016 Porto amassed a further 27 league titles and two European Cups.

Example II: Benfica

The Glorious Eagles, as a club in the wilderness neither investing in purchases nor its academy, almost lost its identity after the millennium. In 2010, however, Benfica started to copy the Porto FIPG model, using the windfall generated to develop their facilities (described earlier). They later adopted an academy-led approach. President Luís Filipe Vieira explained their model to reduce debt: 'Of a paradigm giving opportunities to our young people to work and to grow with the main team.' After growth, they are sold for profit.

Name	From	For	To	For	Age
Ramires	Cruzeiro	£6,380,000	Chelsea	£18,700,000	23
David Luiz	Vitória	£425,000	Chelsea	£21,250,000	23
Ángel Di María	Rosario	£6,800,000	Real Madrid	£28,050,000	22
Fábio Coentrão	Rio Ave	£765,000	Real Madrid	£25,500,000	23
Javi García	Real Madrid	£5,950,000	Man City	£17,170,000	25
Axel Witsel	Standard	£7,650,000	Zenit	£34,000,000	23
Nemanja Matić	Chelsea	£4,250,000	Chelsea	£21,250,000	25
Bernardo Silva	Academy	£0	AS Monaco	£13,390,000	20
Jan Oblak	Olimpija	£1,450,000	Atlético	£13,600,000	21
Enzo Pérez	Estudiantes	£2,040,000	Valencia	£21,250,000	28
Lazar Marković	Partizan	£8,500,000	Liverpool	£21,250,000	20
João Cancelo	Academy	£0	Valencia	£12,250,000	20
Ivan Cavaleiro	Academy	£0	AS Monaco	£12,750,000	20
André Gomes	Academy	£0	Valencia	£17,000,000	21
Rodrigo	Real Madrid	£5,000,000	Valencia	£25,000,000	24
Nico Gaitán	Boca Juniors	£7,140,000	Atlético	£21,250,000	28
Renato Sanches	Academy	£0	Bayern	£29,750,000	18
Total		**£56,350,000**	**Total**	**£332,160,000**	

Benfica's mean average age of sale since 2010 was 22.5 years, further testimony to the value of youth.

4. Mid-Tier Achievers

A mid-tier selling club is aware of its position. It knows that there are less valuable clubs below it to sign from, and more valuable clubs to sell to. Udinese Calcio are the best example of that. They should be a small club, situated in a city near Ljubljana with only 100,000 residents. But under the ownership of the Pozzo family, Udinese built themselves up from minnows to European regulars. They did so through acute scouting and excellent selling. There are

50 scouts across the world on Udinese's payroll, mostly working in South America, Africa and eastern Europe: cheap environments. 'Our secret on the international transfer market is simple – or at least it sounds it when you say it: we have to get there before everyone else, or certainly before teams with more money and prestige,' chief scout Andrea Carnevale explained. [lix]

Udinese sign players young and retain them in two ways: either they loan them (they have more players out on loan than any other club in Italy) or sell them to their sister clubs. Harvard-educated Gino Pozzo owns both Granada in La Liga and Watford in the Premier League and is therefore able to triangulate players between clubs.

An FIPG approach has been essential for growth in Udine. Only 30% of television revenue is redistributed to Serie A clubs – Juventus take most of the rest of it – so other forms of income must be generated. Through sales, they made around £215m in a decade. Between 2006 and 2017, they purchased a mean average of 23.6 players each season. Once a player was sold, his fee was reinvested in the club. Pozzo spent £25m modernising Stadio Friuli for the 2015 season.

Below is every sale of over £5m (note the obscurity and versatility of clubs with which Udinese do business). '[They] built up a network of scouts around the world [who] focus especially on youngsters from second-tier nations.' (*Independent*, 2011).

Name	From	For	To	For
Sulley Muntari	Liberty Ghana	£0	Portsmouth	£8,500,000
Vincenzo Iaquinta	Castel di Sangro	£180,000	Juventus	£9,610,000
Asamoah Gyan	Liberty Ghana	£0	Rennes	£6,800,000
Andrea Dossena	Treviso	£340,000	Liverpool	£7,650,000
Fabio Quagliarella	Sampdoria	£6,210,000	Napoli	£15,300,000
A. Luković	Red Star	£2,300,000	Zenit	£5,950,000
Simone Pepe	Palermo	£2,130,000	Juventus	£6,380,000
Cristián Zapata	Deportivo Cali	£425,000	Villarreal	£7,650,000
Gokhan Inler	FC Zurich	£850,000	Napoli	£15,300,000
Alexis Sánchez	Cobreloa	£2,550,000	Barcelona	£22,100,000
Mauricio Isla	Universidad Católica	£446,000	Juventus	£11,820,000
Samir Handanović	Domzale	£0	Inter Milan	£12,750,000
Kwadwo Asamoah	Bellinzona	£850,000	Juventus	£12,750,000
Andrea Candreva	Ternana	£425,000	Lazio	£6,970,000
Mehdi Benatia	Clermont Foot	£0	Roma	£11,480,000
Juan Cuadrado	Medellín	£680,000	Fiorentina	£17,000,000

Name	From	For	To	For
Matěj Vydra	Banik Ostrava	£2,550,000	Watford	£7,140,000
Luis Muriel	Deportivo Cali	£1,280,000	Sampdoria	£8,930,000
A Peñaranda	Dep. La Guaira	£655,000	Watford	£9,000,000
Allan	Granada	£2,550,000	Napoli	£9,780,000
Roberto Pereyra	River Plate	£1,700,000	Juventus	£12,750,000
Nico López	Roma	£3,400,000	Internacional	£7,720,000
Piotr Zielinski	Lubin	£85,000	Napoli	£11,900,000
Total		**£29,606,000**	**Total**	**£245,230,000**

5. Marginal Achievers: The Dutch

Value is mostly determined by factors such as league strength, television revenue, club value, debt and contract length. [56] But regardless of constraints in stature, there are always profits to be had, no matter how large or insignificant a club is. Heerenveen is the smallest town to ever have had an Eredivisie team. There are only 30,000 people living there; mostly farmers with their own language. Sportingly and economically, Heerenveen SC are astronomical overachievers. Their transfer approach, along with that of their great Northern rivals FC Groningen (the Derby *van het Noorden*), has offered consistent marginal gains in the Eredivisie and has allowed for reinvestment into both facilities and better players. It is a long-term strategy that has taken many years, but has allowed for the market value of both clubs to rise. Profits from player sales have been invested into youth coaching, stadium expansion and, of course, a casino for Groningen at the Euroborg. Groningen's major sales of the past decade:

Name	From	For	To	For
Luis Suárez	Nacional	£680,000	Ajax	£6,380,000
Bruno Silva	Danubio	£170,000	Ajax	£3,190,000
Filip Kostic	Radnicki	£1,000,000	Stuttgart	£5,100,000
Virgil van Dijk	Willem II	£0	Celtic	£2,550,000
Dušan Tadić	Vojvodina	£935,000	FC Twente	£4,600,000
Tim Matavz	ND Gorica	£950,000	PSV	£5,950,000
Marcus Berg	Göteborg	£3,400,000	Hamburg	£8,500,000
Total		**£7,135,000**	**Total**	**£36,270,000**

---

56. Feess, E. and Muehlheusser, G., 2003. 'The impact of transfer fees on professional sports: an analysis of the new transfer system for European football'. *The Scandinavian Journal of Economics*, 105(1), pp.139–54.

And SC Heerenveen's major sales of the past decade:

Name	From	For	To	For
Alf Finnbogason	Lokeren	£425,000	Real Sociedad	£6,800,000
Daley Sinkgraven	Youth	£0	Ajax	£5,950,000
Filip Djuricic	Radnicki	£0	Benfica	£6,800,000
Bas Dost	Heracles	£2,340,000	Wolfsburg	£5,950,000
Danijel Pranjic	Dinamo Zagreb	£425,000	Bayern	£6,500,000
Miralem Sulejmani	Partizan	£221,000	Ajax	£13,810,000
Alfonso Alves	Malmö FF	£3,850,000	Middlesbrough	£14,450,000
Klaas Huntelaar	PSV	£765,000	Ajax	£7,600,000
Oussama Assaidi	De Graafschap	£1,020,000	Liverpool	£3,400,000
	Total	**£9,046,000**	**Total**	**£71,260,000**

The method of Marginal FIPG is to buy striving footballers from lesser clubs (both financially and competitively), offer them a platform and then sell them to wealthier clubs.

6. Academy Business

Eventually, if done correctly, FIPG profits can be reinvested into an academy, so a club can produce its own talents who align with their playing philosophy. Academies are also businesses, with an annual cost paid for by the board. That expenditure must be justified. Therefore, only the most outstanding talents who have the potential to impact the first team are retained. Everybody else is available for sale. If X academy costs £2m to run each season, then some player/players must be sold to the value of that sum to sustain the business.

Despite not being at the bottom of the pyramid as 'youth developers', Ajax are the most prominent example of a club using its academy to sustain economically. Their first-team structure and the pathway into the team is a conveyer belt that remains consistent. If, for example, a player is sold on, then an academy talent is able to emerge and fill his place. The collective is more important than any individual cog. Therefore, if Christian Eriksen leaves, Davy Klaassen steps up. They are green power. Around 30% of the Eredivisie comes from Ajax's academy.

Name	To	For
Viktor Fischer*	Middlesbrough	£4,250,000
Daley Blind	Manchester Utd	£14,880,000

Name	To	For
Siem de Jong	Newcastle	£7,400,000
Christian Eriksen*	Tottenham	£15,300,000
Toby Alderweireld	Atlético Madrid	£8,500,000
Jan Vertonghen	Tottenham	£12,750,000
Vurnon Anita	Newcastle	£5,100,000
G. van der Wiel	PSG	£7,650,000
M. Stekelenburg	AS Roma	£6,230,000
Thomas Vermaelen	Arsenal	£10,200,000
John Heitinga	Atlético Madrid	£8,500,000
Wesley Sneijder	Real Madrid	£22,950,000
Ryan Babel	Liverpool	£14,250,000
Total		***£206,140,000***

* Purchased by the academy.

Football Observatory's statistics found Ajax to be the most frequent producers of talent in Europe. They discovered that 77 footballers in the continent's top 30 leagues came through at the club. [lx] Sustaining that reputation does not come cheaply, but does have its long-term benefits. Wim Jonk, academy director in 2014, asked for an additional €1.8m to spend on elite coaches and facilities, but the board were only willing to offer €900,000. Independent financial specialists the Boston Consulting Group were then called in by the board to settle the dispute – few other clubs place such importance on academy affairs. 'Ajax youth has been regarded as the top academy for decades,' Jonk concluded. 'Many clubs have tried to copy what is happening here. In this regard, there are not many secrets. [It is] the details and the people [that] make the difference.' [lxii] Hence his valuation of coaches.

Several factors ensure Ajax are in the perfect position for youth to sustain them, as such an approach would not be viable elsewhere. Firstly, the league standard is less challenging than Europe's top five leagues and young players are within their depth. Secondly, Dutch society values youth, thinkers and innovators, and appreciates the inclusion of younger footballers. Other environments would be less tolerant to poor performances from academy players. Because of the demands of surviving in the Premier League (as of 2017 every PL side will be given around £100m in TV redistribution – Championship clubs in comparison earn around £3m), no board will allow for a manager to rely on youth. The Netherlands has a fertile climate for academies. In regards to the counter arguments – super-clubs Barcelona and Bayern Munich – while both clubs do include talented youngsters, they do not rely on them, and instead have B teams that allow for growth until the required standards are reached. They also fill vacant positions by signing the best players in the world.

*

There are no set rules for investing in potential, but more parameters that European clubs work within. They aspire to create an environment 'conducive to players succeeding and improving', according to Sevilla's Monchi. The examples mentioned highlight such boundaries, and show the methods through which clubs live organically at various levels. They:

• Avoid buying players over the age of 26. Younger talents hold a greater degree of potential and value (Porto and Benfica).
• Do not chase players in 'spotlight' form but instead identify obscure names (Udinese).
• Do not purchase players from the same league who command high wages (Heerenveen).
• Do not purchase players from higher leagues, unless they are unestablished and unwanted (Sevilla and Udinese).
• Identify the striving talents playing in less valuable leagues. No matter the level, there is always a league below.
• Alter the mindset and understanding of success, from winning trophies to making capital gains.

Despite the obvious benefits of investing in potential for sale, Monchi, once more, concludes that eventually profit maximisation should become success maximisation as a board gradually adjusts its agenda. 'No one takes a "what great economic results" banner to the stadium,' he said – and he should know.

FIFTEEN

TO DARE UPON THE DANUBE, PART I: VIENNA AND A LOVE OF PLACE

The Danube River ebbs and flows through boundaries without a care for whom they belong to. It rises in the Black Forest and soars, gushes and at times trickles through Austria, Slovakia, Hungary, Croatia, Serbia, Romania, Bulgaria, Moldova and Ukraine before emptying into the Black Sea. The width of the river was at one time used as a border between the Roman Empire and the Germanic tribes to the north – archaeologists to this day continue to search for fortifications along its banks. In its time, it has known both the ships of commerce and of war to sail along it.

On the 'Route of Emperors and Kings', passengers take delight in the historic palaces and residences of the Habsburg family that were built through the wealth of the Austro-Hungarian Empire. As well as tension and trade, the route has also known football. Years after dissolution, the living thread Otto von Habsburg, when informed of a match between Austria and Hungary, asked: 'And whom are we playing?' Austrian, Hungarian and Czech clubs competed annually in the 1897–1911 Challenge Cup; Wiener AC being most successful. Let us explore a charted course along the Route of Emperors and Kings, a present-day football one, beginning on a gangplank in Vienna and ending several days later in Budapest.

Vienna embraced football passionately in the 1920s. The sport was adopted by the working classes, as it had been in Britain, because of its simplicity and potential as a community spectacle, but it also attracted the middle classes who were fascinated by its tactical strategies. It was they who theorised and reconstructed a style of play that countered the tactics of the time.

The bourgeois Jewish communities and local coaches in both Austria and Hungary developed a *Danubian* style of football that was hypothesised in the local coffee houses. In *Inverting the Pyramid* Jonathan Wilson describes these cultural hubs of Vienna in which the football phenomenon grew:

> The coffee houses flourished towards the end of the Habsburg Empire, becoming a public salon, particularly noted for its artistic, bohemian aspect. People would read the newspapers there; play cards and chess. Political candidates used them as venues for meetings and debates, while intellectuals and their acolytes would discuss the great affairs of the day: art, literature, drama and, increasingly in the twenties, football. [57]

They were, in essence, forums for informal public discourse.[lxiii] In contemporary Britain, many public houses retain an identity and attract custom from that. In Vienna at that time, coffee houses attained varying identities, with some known for political chat, others for philosophy and some for music. The Ring Café, Schwarzenberg, was originally the centre for cricket discussion but also attracted football theorists. A major player in the social scene, Hugo Meisl, would come to coach the national team and incorporated a 2-3-5 formation born out of the coffee house climate, in which players showed 'ballet and grace . . . lovingly referred to by Viennese fans as the *Scheiberl* game.' [58] Victories against a proud Scotland team in 1931 (5–0) and then neighbours Germany (6–0) made Austria favourites for the 1934 World Cup, upholding their *Wunderteam* moniker.

57. Wilson, J (2008). *Inverting The Pyramid: The History Of Football Tactics*. Great Britain: Orion.
58. Hesse-Lichtenberger, U (2002). *Tor!: The Story of German Football*. London: WSC Books.

With the talismanic Matthias Sindelar, 'Viennese café society at last had a player and a game in their own image: cultured, intellectual, even cerebral, athletic but balletic at the same time,' David Goldblatt wrote. [59] Yet by 1938 both Meisl and Sindelar were dead. It was Austria's unwanted son, Adolf Hitler, who ended the country's glory years in both society and football. His hatred of Jews has been attributed to, amongst several other factors, his time as a 25-year-old homeless painter living in Vienna, fostering his belief that Jews controlled the dealership market and were thus responsible for his failure. Because of his artistic inadequacies and wider sociopathic issues, Hitler slaughtered Europe's Jewish communities. His delivery of war postponed football on the continent, hurting Austria the most in that sense. Jewish thinkers fled the country and Sindelar, who played for the bourgeois Jewish club Austria Vienna, had a Jewish girlfriend and openly opposed Nazism, mysteriously died in the night of 'suicide'.

Almost a century on I was allocated just a single day in the capital – a timeframe never enough to fully appreciate any city, especially not one as steeped in culture as Vienna. I contacted a club with contemporary significance – Sindelar's Austria Vienna – who'd much more recently identified and nurtured the outstanding talent David Alaba, then of Bayern Munich; a man so blessed in capacity he could eventually rival Sindelar as Austria's greatest player.

That morning at the training complex, a low bright sun briefly lit the silver morning dew, offering optimism, before grey clouds swallowed the moment and consigned the day to bleakness. Vienna, though, was anything but bleak. If the success of a football team was a reflection of the beauty of its surroundings then Austria Vienna would be one of the best teams in the world, contesting a 'beauty-league' with IFK Göteborg, Bologna, OGC Nice, Club Brugge, FC Thun, MVV Maastricht and a team of whatever part-time bakers-come-footballers San Marino could find to play.

The citizens of Vienna remain as impressive as always. They cling to the historic culture of the city with valour. Music is played from everywhere, inviting couples to waltz spontaneously (which happens more often than one would expect). Later, outside the Opera House, groups of people sat on chairs beneath warm blankets and the night sky, listening to the

59. Goldblatt, D (2007). *The Ball Is Round*. England: Penguin.

Philharmonic Orchestra who balanced brass, string and woodwind with the same effortlessness their colleagues of the 1800s would have shown. All of which is admirable; after all, a city is nothing but roads and buildings – it is the people who give it worth.

Positions

Ralf Muhr was at the gates welcoming me when I arrived. He is the academy director at Austria Vienna and created the philosophy that developed Alaba. To this day, coaches still talk about the Bayern Munich man's talent: 'He will make it, and if he doesn't then what hope does any other player have?' they would say to each other after practice. One of the most impressive things about him, more than his technical ability, is his understanding of the game. His intelligence is such that he's able to play in any position – defence, midfield, attack; left side, central, or right side – and appear as though he's a natural. 'David Alaba is our god. He has already played in almost all ten positions,' acclaimed Pep Guardiola of a player without weakness. [lxiv] Austria Vienna taught him, and indeed all other youth graduates, to play everywhere, including in goal: 'It is our philosophy to not create just one position,' Muhr said. 'With the little ones, we do not have goalkeepers; there has to be a soccer player in goal because it is important that this position can play football.'

Alaba played as an attacking midfielder in the youth teams but made his debut aged 16 as a left-back. 'This is now the role he has with Bayern Munich [as well as centre-back under Guardiola] because we try in our youth teams to create players who can play in most positions.' One theory suggests that by playing young footballers in different positions during their formative years, they are not able to become specialised in one singular position. At a conference in 2015, a Premier League head of academy told the audience about the time he killed a boy. Not literally (he's still alive and playing football) but figuratively – he killed his talent. So good was this striker the coaches spent hours pondering how they could improve him further. They decided to teach him how to play in a deeper position where he could get more touches of the ball, improving his repertoire of skills. He did so and became a decent number 10, but when he eventually returned to his original number 9 role he was not as outstanding. Within two years, he'd been released. Along with other factors, the speaker felt that they deprived him of hours specialising in his position and therefore curbed his growth.

Whilst that can sometimes be the case, the game nowadays is so fluid, with positions so interchangeable, that teaching various roles to youngsters helps their tactical understanding of the game as a whole, and therefore develops the susceptibility of the collective to learn tactics. 'A central defender should be able to play in central midfield and an outside player should learn to play off the defending and offensive line,' Muhr said. Arsène Wenger at Monaco converted a young Lilian Thuram from midfielder to defender and did the opposite to Emmanuel Petit – both players would win the World Cup in their new positions.

Theories of Competence

Positional changes are considered common practice in the modern European game. There are many examples, like Petit and Thuram, and indeed David Alaba, of footballers who readjusted to a new position and excelled there. One such player, Javier Mascherano, who had spent his entire career operating as a central midfielder, was placed at centre-back by Barcelona and won two Champions Leagues. Johan Cruyff wrote in *De Telegraaf* in 2014 that striker Dirk Kuyt was 'tactically blessed' to be operating as a left-sided wing-back in the World Cup. [lxv] And when the honest, hard-working full-back Philipp Lahm adapted well to central midfield, his manager Guardiola said, 'Philipp is perhaps the most intelligent player I have ever trained in my career. He is at another level.' [lxvi]

Several theories abound regarding positional changes and how moving a footballer from his natural position to an unfamiliar one allows him to perform well. What should be considered is that during a match a footballer's brain uses numerous complex mechanisms enabling him to perform. First of all, the player most often makes a decision based on what he has seen through his occipital lobe. His speed of thought when making fast decisions, considering spatial awareness and the environment around him, begins here. Secondly, the limbic system regulates emotional reactions to ensure that rational thinking is maintained. The cerebellum has a role in co-ordination and movement, and the temporal lobe opens the mind to language and memory which allows the player to receive tactical advice.

But the two mechanisms that most apply to a footballer adjusting to a new position are the frontal lobe and the dorsal/ventral streams. Movements and actions in a new position, such as overlapping as a wing-back, are organised within the frontal lobe. The dorsal stream is then the process of learning how to play, with the ventral stream being the mastering of a position. 'It has been shown that experts use different areas of their brain when making sporting judgements, regardless of whether the decision is in the sport in which they excel or in an unfamiliar sport,' wrote Dr Zoe Wimshurst in 2012. [60]

Combining those specific areas of the brain into a form of training is difficult to do. It is advised that players, especially younger ones, are allowed to taste and experience playing in various positions to open up their frontal lobe and stimulate their ventral stream. To support young footballers in what can be a challenging task, psychologist Chris Harwood theorised the 5 C's model, consisting of: Commitment, Communication, Concentration, Control and Confidence. Such behaviours are hallmarks of what Harwood describes as 'mentally tough, emotionally intelligent players'. But it is one 'C' in particular, 'Concentration', that relates to a youngster adapting to a new position. As a guided framework, by asking players at regular intervals in a training session or match what they were 'thinking, doing or about to do at that precise moment' reinforces concentration. [61] Austria Vienna do this throughout training exercises and, in matches with younger players, have regular 'time-outs' to ask a seven-year-old midfielder, for example, what he is thinking whilst playing in defence. They also rotate players throughout matches into different positions so they experience the game in its entirety. This prepares players for the future game. For example, by placing a young centre-back on the wing and asking him to dribble, he will be more confident to break the lines and carry the ball into midfield from defence as he gets older. After training and matches finish, analysts show youngsters footage of their positioning and question them on their thought processes.

60. Wimshurst, Z. (2012). Visual Skills in Elite Athletes. Available: http://epubs.surrey.ac.uk/791906/1/Wimshurst2012.pdf.
61. Harwood, C. *Integrating sport psychology into elite youth soccer: Player, coach and parent interventions.* Available: http://www.innovatefc.com/members/resources. Last accessed 31/12/2016.

David Alaba being made to develop his cognitive and motor understanding of football in new positions at Austria Vienna allowed him to acquire a full grasp of the game – so much so that when playing in new positions at Bayern, he performed well. 'I'll play wherever I can help the team,' he humbly told reporters, before his manager Guardiola gushed: 'He's just incredible, just wow ... he can play absolutely everywhere.' [lxvii] Muhr is of the belief that footballers are more well-rounded with a greater understanding of the game when being tested in various positions. It is at the discretion of a coach, however, if they wish to develop a versatile or specialised player.

Fighting the Tide

Alaba won 14 pieces of silverware, including five league titles and a European Cup, in his first six seasons at Bayern. The Press Agency named him the Austrian Player of the Year for five consecutive years, despite him being only 24 years of age. Nevertheless, for all of his phenomenal natural talent Alaba is a product of the environment he was developed in. As Muhr explained, he's intelligent; 'we have a mental coach and work closely with the school, where we have extra lessons for the kids in sport science and football related topics', has a great engine; 'we try to train with the younger ages on physical development', and is a boy taken from the city; 'we aim to bring players from our youth teams into the first team who are from Vienna. We have four or five players from other areas but the main group can live at home with their parents.' Austria Vienna want to be an academy for the people of the city. 'We have a lot of smaller clubs locally who develop players well and we look to bring in the best players from these clubs. It is a cycle as we later give players back to these clubs too.'

The academy director leans back in his chair and thoughtfully ponders the questions asked. In his office is a large whiteboard with fixtures and results of the U18s written on it. There are photos of Alaba everywhere. In some pictures he is wearing his playing kit, in others he is posing with silverware. 'I started here in 1994 as a youth coach. I was with the U8s and then I was here for four years before I became youth director. It is untypical of soccer for me to have been here for such a long time.' Like the great philosopher Rocky Balboa once slurred, 'If you stay in one place long enough, you become that place'. Muhr has become Austria Vienna. He kicks every ball and feels every tackle. It frustrates him to see this club struggle for marginal gains. 'It's very difficult [to retain players] because we lost a guy six months ago to Middlesbrough. This is normal as we have very good players who play in the national teams. While we are big in Austria, we are small in Europe.' Money on the continent and the lure of success is too great for Viennese youngsters to resist. 'Most of the top teams are good at developing players, including Middlesbrough, but it is very difficult to make it into the first team at these clubs. We tell [players] to develop here. We need youngsters playing in our first team and they will get that opportunity.'

In 2016 Vienna was at the apex of a socioeconomic study by Mercer into quality of life. According to the outcome, this is the greatest city in the world to live in, yet players still choose to leave for lesser places. Muhr concedes through gritted teeth that other clubs have better infrastructure and are therefore more desirable. The issues facing Austria Vienna are typical of the league as a whole – the best players want to leave – so he has steadied himself for the long game: 'The most important thing is the instillation of more academies. We started in 2000 to make youth development professional, with pro coaches and pro sports scientists, and this was the most important thing in developing better players.'

Austrian clubs are looking to the future. Their aim is to reinvest the money from youth sales into academies, to develop a better standard of player worth more money. 'All of the national team players now came through an academy here, not in Germany or England like in previous years. They developed here and I think it is very important for soccer here that we invest in our youth status more, so our Bundesliga becomes a league for developing young players in, to show bigger clubs that there are top players here to buy.'

Perhaps that is the deepest shame. Once the greatest empire in Europe, from which a worthy football team emerged, Austria may never again be a competitive power. Muhr and his nation of academies have to place their youngsters in a shop window of sorts and hope that a bidding war ensues. It is a far cry from the days of the *Wunderteam*, in an age when innovation could triumph. Now it is copied or bought out. The buildings inside the

Ringstraße – parliament, museums and the once buzzing coffee houses – are vacant pretty shells. Nothing but monuments to a forgotten time. But cracks of progress can be seen. Austria went 70 years between Sindelar and Alaba. In the latter, they found significance. Muhr takes optimism from the small improvements being made. Perhaps in 20 years another Alaba will emerge and will devote his career to improving the fortunes of his local club, a noble yet unlikely idea.

SIXTEEN

TO DARE UPON THE DANUBE, PART II: THE HISTORY OF HONVÉD

'The railways are the veins of the earth,
Culture and progress prosper where,
They cause pulsations of the air,
To nations greatness they give birth.'
Sándor Petőfi, Hungarian poet and liberal revolutionary, 1842

The enormity of the Austro-Hungarian Empire has somewhat been forgotten over time. Hungary counted Zagreb and Bratislava as its cities, as well as Budapest, while Austria included Vienna, Prague, Trieste and Kraków. Members of the aristocracy struggled to appease the many ethnicities within a region that stretched from Italy to Transylvania. Authorities tried to paper over the cracks of nationalist tensions, using railway development as a distraction, but political turmoil eventually led to the First World War. Hungary has had a tough existence since then. Wars, land loss, the Great Depression, the Holocaust, Stalinisation and total communism followed. On Petőfi's tracks I visited Budapest to find football: the only true constant. This is the second and final stop on the Route of Emperors and Kings.

To this day, Hungary is best known by many for its 'Golden Team' of the 1950s. While Austria never recovered from the decline of its *Wunderteam*,

Hungarian football thrived under communism; not due to state socialism, but rather as a reaction to it and the oppression of Hungarian nationalism. Coached by trade unionist Gusztáv Sebes, the Golden Team won 42 times between 1950 and 1956 playing a revolutionary 2-3-3-2 formation. They embarrassed England in the 'Game of the Century' in 1953 and lost only one match: the 1954 World Cup final to West Germany. Most of the squad were recruited by the state to play for Budapest Honvéd, the army team, where players became famous in their own right. Sebes was able to use Honvéd as a base to coach his team throughout the year, contributing to their success.

However, during the 1956 tour of Italy, Spain, Portugal and Brazil organised by Honvéd coach Béla Guttmann, students back home marched against Soviet rule. One was shot dead by state police and became a martyr to the cause. When word spread of his death, thousands organised militia groups and the Hungarian Revolution began. Members of the Golden Team refused to return to their home country. Honvéd's Sándor Kocsis and Zoltán Czibor moved to Spain to play for Barcelona, while their most famous talisman, Ferenc Puskás, signed for Real Madrid. Hungary and Honvéd fell heavily following the break-up of the team with neither club nor country returning to elite standards since.

It seems that the very same steel tracks revolutionist Sándor Petőfi wrote about are crumbling, yet still in use, in modern Hungary. Crossing the border from Austria, life travels back in time some 30 years. The paint on cars parked in overgrown gardens is rustic and flaking; houses are colourless; the men are moustached. It is all very 'post-communist', which is a shame for those living here. They are the helpless victims of poor decisions by their government. Regardless, they make the most of what they have. This is the Hungary unseen by tourists. Our train stopped at Győr station, which could have been the setting for an old spaghetti western, such was the eerie stillness of the platforms. As the passengers waited, several freight trains roared past towards the capital. Everything goes towards the capital.

Budapest has the densest population in Hungary. The country is gradually recovering from mismanaged communism under the steady leadership of Prime Minister Viktor Orbán. Following the fall of communism in 1989, people didn't know what to do. The first man to react to the potential of the situation was György Szabó, or George F. Hemingway as he later came to be known. Having studied in New York and Los Angeles for years, Hemingway understood how capitalism worked. Upon returning home he opened chains of Pizza Hut and KFC franchises and quickly became one of the richest men in the country (and probably the first self-made millionaire). His acquisition of Honvéd came in 2006 at a time when the club was suffering. Only three seasons earlier they had been relegated to the second division and went into liquidation the following year. The club owed tens of thousands and its Italian owners Pini considered merging with provincial side Dúnaujváros and relocating. But as history dictates, a saviour only comes in times of crisis. For the community of fans in Kispest, that's exactly what Hemingway proved to be. Following his buy-out, stability ensued.

*

Caught Between the Ages

Ábel Lorincz has worked for the club for two years. We met outside the hectic Keleti station through a bustling crowd of tourists and hailed a taxi to the neighbourhood of Kispest. The area is just outside Budapest and grew during the socialist era when legislation meant people needed a pass to enter the city; businessmen built factories here to avoid communist authorities. Nowadays, industry has centralised inside Budapest without the worry of encountering state authority, leaving Kispest behind. From our taxi, tower blocks swallowed what little daylight could be had, until we eventually turned a corner to reach Honvéd's brightly lit Bozsik stadium. 'The Club of Puskás' declared a sign at the entrance.

Ábel, an ambitious analyst, was to be my tour guide for the day and began by showing me the first team ground. Pieces of grass grew through cement steps on the fenced-in standing section of the stadium to the left, usually occupied by home ultras. Half-peeled faded stickers left by visiting groups adorned the rails inside the section: FK Vojvodina and Anzhi Makhachkala the most recent cases; memories of European nights long since gone. First team players slowly began arriving for that evening's fixture against Videoton – some of them carpooled – and parked on the clumped grass of the training pitch, much to the groundsman's annoyance. A five-a-side court sat to the left of the training pitch with a cemetery to the right of it. 'When a player kicks the ball over the wall to the graves he has to go and get it back,' Ábel explained, laughing. Over 100 youth players live inside the complex. Outside the windows of the club offices, clouds of factory smoke filled the afternoon air.

The corridors inside the stadium seemed worn out. Pieces of equipment, pipes and such, had been put down along the walls and left for somebody else to worry about. The furnishing was tired, stripped of colour. But despite that, the friendliness of the place made it seem humble, charming, and most definitely not drab. Upon reaching the owner's door Ábel knocked several times. No answer. Eventually a receptionist entered on our behalf and Mr Hemingway came to greet us. A burly gentleman, much larger than life and with a handshake like a bear, welcomed us into his office.

In great contrast to the corridors behind, Hemingway's office was Narnia. Oil paintings hung around his oak desk; a plump rug lay in the middle of the floor with plush red chairs for guests. The American-accented man offered us one and we settled down to talk. It was difficult not to immediately admire him. *What does an owner do?* I asked, turning on my dictaphone. 'I have to set a long-term vision for the club and approve all of the major financial decisions,' he replied frankly. 'I have to confirm the budget for the year and approve our sales and acquisitions. I don't get involved in the day-to-day running or putting the team together.' He has a managing director to deal with that. The football side is left for football people, or at least it should be.

At one time his director was an Italian, Fabio Cordella, who ran a wine partnership and counted Wesley Sneijder, Antonio Conte and Roberto Mancini as clients. Under Cordella, Honvéd became little-Italy as the club brought in Davide Lanzafame, Andrea Mancini (son of Roberto), Emanuele Testardi, Emiliano Bonazzoli and the former Arsenal teen protégé Arturo Lupoli. They were also close to signing Fabrizio Miccoli and Alessandro Del Piero, too, for whom they agreed to bring Puskás' number 10 shirt back out of retirement, until Sydney proved a greater draw. Cordella persuaded World Cup-winning defender Pietro Vierchowod to manage the club, but results didn't follow so they split. The most mysterious piece of business during the Italian era, though, was the appointment of unknown head coach Marco Rossi – sacked a year earlier by regional-level club Cavese after steering them to the bottom of the table. At the time of my visit, Rossi was back at the club in a second stint as manager; Cordella and the other Italians had all left.

Orion

The night sky is so vast and ever changing, stars tend to be misplaced. Farmers and poets gazed upon its dark blanket for a thousand years to see twinkling shapes emerge. Constellations do not actually exist, but are rather used as mnemonics by astronomers trying to pinpoint individual stars. Only by them aligning so perfectly can constellations be seen. Without an absolute alignment of stars, Orion would have no belt. For Hungary to shine, academies and first team squads must also align. That means the style of play from youth to senior football must follow the same line, at both club and national level, as discussed at Bayern. At Honvéd when I visited, it did not.

Marco Rossi was manager of the club playing a conservative Italian 5-3-2 with little build-up play from the back. His football philosophy was a direct contrast to that of the academy, where Dutchman Jasper de Muijnck taught players to build play from the goalkeeper in a dynamic 4-3-3. 'We brought in an academy director from Holland just to be sure that we are doing the same things that Ajax or PSV are doing,' said Hemingway in his office, though he may have been better off bringing in a director from Italy. 'We have the best football academy in eastern Europe. Sixteen of our 26-man squad came through our academy and it only started in 2007.' Sparta Prague and Dynamo Kiev would disagree, but Hemingway is right to be proud. Every year their youth team plays against Real Madrid in the 'Puskás Trophy' and usually wins it. The issue for Honvéd was that they had two contrasting styles at academy and senior level. The obvious contrast meant talented youngsters promoted to the first team were prone to stagnation.

The Issue

It was several years earlier that Jasper de Muijnck first encountered Honvéd. He'd been working with Louis van Gaal for the Dutch national team and came to Budapest to sample Hungarian football. When he arrived at the stadium, Jasper asked, 'How do I see MTK youth against Honvéd?' The receptionist drew him a map that involved going over some rail tracks, under a bridge and down a hill towards an overgrown football pitch. 'That's why

I have this romantic feeling about eastern European football. These were the two biggest academies in Hungary and they played on this little pitch,' he recalled. Jasper is a true football fan. Only a purist can find this face of the game as endearing as the flashing lights of elsewhere. When Honvéd sacked Pietro Vierchowod, Jasper became head coach for a month. 'It was incredible for me to walk out on the same steps as Puskás had done.' As academy director, he inspired his Honvéd players with stories of the man.

Since Cordella departed, though, there was no link from the academy to the first team. 'It's difficult because we don't have a sports director. The policy seems to be to just survive in the first league, but eventually we will drop out with that mentality,' Jasper said. Honvéd had more than 30 youth internationals at the academy that played an attacking, pressing game, but the first team played with old-school Italian conservatism. '[We have] two totally contrasting schools of thought. The owner hired me to make sure the academy went the Dutch way. You can't develop a kid to play in between the lines then in the first team he isn't allowed to. He will be 23 before he adapts to the first team – he should be able to do it when he is 17.'

Because of the differences in philosophy, Honvéd the first team and Honvéd the academy were run like two separate organisations. 'Living game by game is a big problem,' said Jasper. For him, it was as much of a success to form links with foreign academies who took an interest in his players. He had sent a player to Ajax and when the boy returned he was able to see the gulf in class and the dedication required to reach a higher level. Jasper remains forward-thinking in that sense. His understanding of the society around him led to his appointment as a part-time technical director for the Hungarian Football Association.

'Last year we had a tournament in Holland against all of the biggest academies in the world, the likes of PSV and Inter Milan and even the new Chinese academies. We got some good results against them all and reached fourth place, controlling every game and playing good football. The coaching level in Hungary is so low because coach education was so bad. Hungary has always had talented players but the exercises they did were without resistance and were not realistic and they could not adapt to real football.' Jasper believes this is to do with history and society: 'When communism came here they were not interested in being outstanding anymore; it was easier to stay in line and be normal, and all of the creative people left the country. I ask everybody, "What is the Hungarian style of play?" But nobody has the answer for me. They used to be outstanding playing transitions throughout the length of the field with interchanging positions but now they do not know what their style is. They are like all other small teams now and they sit deep and counter-attack.'

The same is true of Honvéd. According to Jasper, Rossi lives game by game with no interest in developing a game-model legacy. 'If you have two players who play the whole match and were born after 1996 then the government will give the club money because they want to develop young players.' Jasper said Rossi was given 13 talented youngsters from Jasper but he didn't want them. 'Living game by game is a big problem. I need to protect the young kids from going up to [Rossi] too early because we will lose them; they will stop developing.' If a player does enter the team too early the danger is, if he doesn't immediately perform, he won't get a second chance. He may lose his confidence and will stop trying the things that enabled him to get called up in the first place. This is an issue for all clubs on the continent.

The Watchman

A young analyst in his 20s, Ábel Lorincz travels the continent (out of his own purse) discovering the most pioneering methods in his field. Analysis is still only just taking off in Hungary; in fact, so dated is football here, Ábel hadn't watched a televised Hungarian league match in years. Why study an archaic approach? As we sat waiting for Hemingway earlier that day, Arsenal were playing Watford on a screen in the canteen. Ábel quickly explained the shapes of the teams and was in the process of praising the balance Alex Iwobi brought to Arsenal when, before he could finish, the youngster scored.

Ábel had been to visit Leicester City a few months earlier and was aware of the work being done at the club 'before they were famous'. He compared his role with that of their first team analyst: 'I learnt some new ideas about how to do post-match analysis when I visited. For example, Rob McKenzie was the recruitment analyst at Leicester and he talked about how important it is to get the players involved in the process. I am focused more on asking the players how they felt in situations and what could be improved upon –

what they think. The player might say that they have an idea how to do it better but they aren't sure. If they are involved, then they learn more than if it was a school setting where you just lecture and they fall asleep.'

If Leicester had a humble budget then Honvéd were poverty-stricken by comparison, but the financial impediments on the analysis department didn't worry Ábel. He believes that the quality of technology isn't what's important, more how it is used, and that '80 or 90% of analysis can be done with cheap technology', like cameras for creating highlights. 'What matters most is what you and the coaches know about football, not money.' At Honvéd, there seemed to be a split between the academy and first team that was not sustainable in the long term. They were two different clubs, something that was reflected at the lab: the academy had Ábel working tirelessly on the youngsters, but the first team had no performance analyst at all.

Unsurprisingly, Ábel could do both jobs, which became strikingly obvious as I quizzed him on the differences in analysis at both junior and senior level. 'Obviously the objectives are different because with the first team the result is the most important thing, whereas in the academy you can lose your games but if the players develop then you have achieved your aim.' There is more of an individual focus on the players in the academy, whereas in the first team work concentrates more on the pre-match analysis of the collective for the upcoming game, rather than the post-match analysis used to develop players. 'In the academy, we do more detail on post-match with less emphasis on who they are coming up against and how they should stop them playing.'

What Ábel emphasises to his players is how they are responsible for their own development. 'I speak about analysis and we encourage them to come to me to ask for situations from the game, or if they feel they are lacking in some department. The most talented players also get a development plan that lasts for three or four months. They have to decide what help they need from the coaches.' To fully understand how to help the players, Ábel embedded himself in the style of football the academy plays, to act as a mini-counsellor to reinforce the game model to them. 'The youth teams all play possession football. We want to control and dominate the game, and to get the ball back as soon as possible. It is very aggressive and we begin defending in the opponent's half.' In that sense, it couldn't be more Dutch.

Playing Politics

As a businessman, Hemingway is smart. He knows that the club is only one very good season away from success. Everything is primed for it apart from a few obvious factors, but he realises the potential of the project. 'In 2006, when we purchased the club after ten dead years, we did everything to build it back. We're building a new stadium next year and we want to be on the top of a rebirth in Hungarian football.' They're not the only club who are part of that rebirth. Ferencváros are equally prestigious (Honvéd boast Puskás but Ferencváros have Florian Albert) and have built a brand-new, state-of-the-art, 22,000-seater stadium: the Groupama Arena. Alongside Ferencváros and Honvéd, Debrecen have dominated Hungarian football since the millennium and have flown the flag in European competition.

But the team that are most likely to propel Hungary's rebirth were, at that point, still in the second division. Puskás Akadémia (the Puskás Academy) were not yet ten years old but already had the best youth facilities in the country. They were created by Prime Minister Viktor Orbán – an avid football fan – and are based in the village of Felcsút where he was born. Despite it only having 1,000 or so people living there, a contemporary 3,500-capacity stadium was built in the village in 2014. 'The Pancho Arena' (after Puskás' Real Madrid nickname) is one of sport's most interesting structures, resembling a Middle Earth edifice, with ten training pitches for Hungary's most talented young players to train on.

In typical eastern European fashion, its construction was controversial. With living standards of many falling, critics demanded to know why €13m of heavy state funding was spent on a personal dream for Orbán? 'President Hollande is not building a rugby pitch nor David Cameron a cricket field', the opposition pointed out.[lxviii] Alongside his Puskás Academy dream, Orbán was slated for introducing ID cards and hand-scanners to matches. 'Passion is not welcome anymore, they want us to clap politely and buy expensive drinks at half-time like we're at the theatre,' one Ferencváros ultra said.

Attendances fell as a result of both Orbán's modernisation and the standard of football on display. Nevertheless, the investments he made were well received by owners. Asked about the safety of his investment for the future, from his plush office Hemingway cited the work the prime minister has done as remunerative: 'I think that if this government stays a silver age of Hungarian football is coming. Not a golden age, that was in the 1950s. There are lots of young players; the national team have gone from 77th in the FIFA list to 18th in a couple of years. It is the first time we have been back in the top 20 for years. We want to be among the strong middle clubs of Europe, like the Dutch and Belgians.'

*

A couple of thousand people were in attendance that night. At half-time Hemingway walked on to the pitch to address the fans. It was Puskás' birthday; such is his legacy at the club every year they celebrate it. The owner made a ten-minute speech in tribute to the 'Galloping Major', praising his dedication to Honvéd. Earlier, I had asked him about the weight of history, and how the club are able to balance what has gone before with their vision for the future: 'There's no other Hungarian team who are as well known outside of the country as Honvéd.' Ferencváros and Debrecen are mostly famous inside Hungary he believes, but Honvéd's fame transcends the country. Perhaps he is right, which is why he changed the club's name back to Honvéd from Kispest FC.

Hemingway knows fame can only take the club so far. Modern football is decided by wealth. The super-rich Anzhi Makhachkala, a club from Dagestan with hardly any fans, history or fame, backed by billionaire Dagestani owner Suleyman Kerimov, visited in 2013 with superstar Samuel Eto'o and defeated Honvéd 4–0 in front of 5,000 fans. That for Hemingway was a moment of realisation. 'Our history is all-determining. Because of it, our style has been developed over the last ten years with an attacking idea,' yet the performance on the pitch said otherwise. Marco Rossi played a slow, protective style of football. If attacking football can be defined by brave off-the-ball movement, forward runs, cutting passes, combinations and final-third entries, Honvéd's approach was anything but. Afterwards, as I left the stadium and stepped into the dark Budapest night, Bill Shankly's quote about 'the Holy Trinity' at a football club came to mind. They all love Honvéd here, but do so differently.

Nine Months Later...

And then it clicked. I rang Ábel the following April having discovered that Honvéd were in a title-challenge with Videoton. 'What's going on?!' I asked, both confused and delighted. 'The turnout for matches is better than I've ever seen before,' he told me as I thought back to the moss-covered Bozsik József Stadion. Hemingway, riding the crest of Orbán's 'silver age' wave, had even submitted plans for a new 8,000-seater stadium. 'We also have Davide Lanzafame back, who is exceptional for this level,' Ábel continued. The Italian striker was once described as 'Bari's Cristiano Ronaldo' by his coach at the time, Antonio Conte, until a match-fixing scandal threatened to end his career. In Hungary, with solace, he was scoring with ease. 'And he can manage the game strategically. When to slow down, when to go for it, when to hide the ball and run down the clock. Nobody else knows this way of playing in our squad and we could never do it before,' said Ábel.

But their turnaround in fortune was not to be credited to one player. Hemingway had made a decision to align the club philosophy, to go with one school of thought. He chose to go Italian – Jasper was gone and a friend of Rossi's was hired as an analyst. According to their results, it was the correct decision. It does not matter whether the methodology is Italian, Dutch, Spanish or German, it has to match up, from the way U6s play up to the U23s. Hemingway could have chosen to go all Dutch and had same effect. Nevertheless, Honvéd's upturn in performances and the improvement of atmosphere within the camp is proof, if any was needed, that a coherent philosophy is crucial in the modern game.

We are only ever receptive to an institution (like a pub, restaurant or football club) through experiences had with people. Honvéd would be just another club visited were it not for the personalities of Hemingway and Jasper, and the helpfulness of Ábel. Because he had offered me a bottle of red wine and a Honvéd jersey as gifts; because of the aura of the Golden Team, the stories of Puskás and the feeling of history; because of the presence of amateurism and professionalism combined; because of all of that, I will always hold a bit of Honvéd in my heart. I hope that, for you the reader, such affections are shared.

SEVENTEEN

KNIGHTS OF THE YELLOW WALL: NORTH RHINE-WESTPHALIA

Budapest to Prague, then Nürnberg and Dortmund. Fields were replaced by factories. Football swells out of West Germany. There are 13 professional clubs, boasting a combination of 22 league titles, 18 cups and five European competition wins. They have been won by Bayer 04 Leverkusen, FC Schalke 04, 1. FC Köln, Fortuna Düsseldorf, Rot-Weiss Essen, Borussia Dortmund and Borussia Mönchengladbach. This chapter is a narrative of my train journey through the region, investigating how Germany became world champions. It begins in Köln and ends in Gelsenkirchen.

Getting Here

It was in North Rhine-Westphalia (NRW) that German football was assisted in its rebirth. Or at least partially. In 1998, the locally born head trainer of the national team, Berti Vogts, highlighted Germany's decline, specifically how the physical style of play that once powered them to victory was no longer applicable to this newer, more technical sport. He proposed a talent programme to create skilful youngsters, but it never saw the light of day. The man who would inspire Germany to create such a system was, inadvertently, Vogts' successor and fellow NRW native, Erich Ribbeck. His Germany squad at Euro 2000, slow and lumbering with an average age of 31.5 years, was eliminated in the group stages and inspired a period of national anger.

Kicker, Germany's more respected football magazine, dedicated 17 pages to the shortcomings of *Die Mannschaft*, the national XI, after Portugal sent them home. The DFB, Germany's FA, sat down with Bundesliga clubs to create a plan and, in 2001, came up with the 'Extended Talent Promotion Programme' (ETPP), which would be, essentially, a scheme to ensure the embarrassment of Euro 2000 never happened again.

ETPP required German clubs and associations to invest in their foundations, stating that unless the base was transformed, the top would remain the same. A rule was added into the contracts of all Bundesliga clubs by the DFB – if they wanted to be in the top division, they needed to build centres of excellence. 'The rule even specified how many players eligible for a German national youth team had to be in the squads [at these centres], how many coaches and physios the club had to employ, in which way the clubs had to interact with local schools and so on and on,' Uli Hesse explained. 'Failure to do this would result in a club's licence being withdrawn. Put simply, the clubs were told what to do, on pain of demotion to the amateur game.'

Most clubs were reluctant due to the cost of the project – €48 million per annum – but had little say in the matter. It was happening and they had to accept it. Advertisements went up on television screens nationwide later proclaiming the slogan, '*Unsere Amateure, Echte Profis*': Our Amateurs, Genuine Pros. In total, 54 'high performance' centres were built nationwide by clubs for the DFB that, as much as anything, became scouting bases to build a strong knowledge of the best youngsters in the nation. 'If the talent of the century happens to be born in a tiny village behind the mountains, we will find him,' prophesied ETPP director Jörg Daniel. Talented youngsters have since been required to play for their academy and train once a week for two hours at the nearest DFB base, or *Stützpunkte*. The very best boys selected to play for the nation are then picked from bases rather than academies.

As well as restructuring the top level of youth football with high performance bases, the DFB and Bundesliga decided that amateur youth football needed improving in every village and town through a process of education. 'DFB

Mobil' vans drive out to amateur clubs weekly to teach coaches various sessions, aligning them with the philosophy of what is required to create a technical 'German' player. Some 22,000 players are coached and later analysed by members of Köln's *Sporthochschule*; their performances reviewed throughout the year. All of which cumulated in Germany creating Mesut Özil, Toni Kroos and Mario Götze – skilful footballers who would play a central role in their 2014 World Cup victory. When DFB coaches arrive at one of 387 camps run each year, they tell youngsters: 'You're a member of the DFB, which means you are a world champion!' For them, every boy is a potential international star. This is the Germany I travelled through, a nation conscious of its players, fans and spectacle.

The Journey

On the morning of 7 April 2016, at around 9.30 a.m., a DB train from Köln's Hauptbahnhof station carried 300 football fans, some clad in red but most in yellow and black, to Dortmund's Hbf. There would be trains doing the same journey every 20 minutes that day. Borussia Dortmund were playing Liverpool in the Europa League quarter-final that night in what *BILD* had christened 'The Return of the King' (the monarch being Jürgen Klopp).

A football connoisseur would have found the journey to be most enjoyable. North Rhine-Westphalia is an interesting region. It is the most populated state in Germany, known locally as '*das Land von Kohle und Stahl*' (the Land of Coal and Steel). After the Second World War, NRW became the powerhouse region that rebuilt Germany from the ashes. Here, beneath the bleak billows of industry in a post-war age, clubs began to develop winning sides. It is a backdrop much like that in which Glasgow Celtic thrived in the 20th century: 'Them cold wet cobbles of success' as *The Herald* had described.

The area historically welcomed so many football clubs due to the heavy industrialisation of western Germany in the early 20th century. Sean Brown wrote, 'The history of the region is a history of continuous migration.'[62] With the emergence and expansion of industrial production came a great demand for workers. Migrants arrived from all over Europe, particularly

62. Brown, S (2013). *Football Fans Around the World: From Supporters to Fanatics*. New York: Routledge. 62.

from areas that had once been Prussia. The German word for Prussia, *Borussia*, would come to identify several clubs founded at the time in the region: Borussia Dortmund and Borussia Mönchengladbach being two well-known examples. Like in Britain years earlier, with the advent of greater free time, football offered itself as a community asset and would be adopted by working men in each city, town and suburb of NRW.

Football's popularity increased dramatically in Germany during the Third Reich. In 1936, NRW club Schalke (also known as S04) drew 75,000 fans when they played Nürnberg in Stuttgart. It is interesting that a club from the suburb of the steel city, Gelsenkirchen, culturally and economically behind Essen, Duisburg and Dortmund at the time, was able to attract so many fans from across Germany. They did so through their style of play, known as *Schalker Kreisel*, involving perfect link-up play, leading to the club becoming the base for the national team. Their popularity was also due to the political environment of the time. The Nazi Party had destroyed socialist and labour movements, and consequently both social forces lacked an organisational centre. 'In those circles a demonstration of sympathy for FC Schalke 04 meant a demonstration of sympathy for the no longer existing labour movement,' [63] Tomlinson and Young found, especially as Schalke were considered to be a workers' club.

9.32 a.m.

In present-day Köln, the Cathedral of Saint Peter is the city's most famous image. Large and ominous with dark twin spires, it is the most visited landmark in Germany with 20,000 people each day stepping beyond its threshold. In the 18th and 19th centuries, churches had to be the tallest buildings on land, their reaching height a tribute to God. But as society evolved, priorities changed. Nowadays, skyscrapers built for financial institutions are the tallest buildings, with sports arenas often second. Money and sport matter more than religion for many in the modern world. Köln's Cathedral of Saint Peter, however, blanketing trains underneath it in shadow as they pull away, is a looming contradiction. It stands at 516 feet, with the RheinEnergieStadion, home of the local club FC Köln, standing (only) 108 feet.

63. Tomlinson, A. & Young, C (2006). *German Football: History, Culture, Society*. New York: Routledge. 8.

Tenants FC Köln can be used as a tool to examine fan relations in Germany. Whereas in English football rivalry is the most obvious thread between clubs, in Germany clubs have friendships with teams inside their region and within their league. Borussia Dortmund, for example, are friendly with FC Köln and as a consequence Köln have taken on Dortmund's rivalry with Schalke 04. They also have a rivalry with Gladbach based on the two clubs competing for success in the late 1970s, and hold tensions with Fortuna Düsseldorf, as they are the two biggest cities in NRW with economic power. Bayer Leverkusen, as a well-backed club with money from the Bayer pharmaceutical company, are disliked by many fans in the region and beyond. But because of their close proximity to one another, Köln and Leverkusen dislike each other the most. For matches to be classified as a 'derby', though, as Ruud Hans Koning found, it has to be competitive. No club in the region retains strong dislike for Bochum or Paderborn, despite their locality, as they are not competitive forces.

9.40 a.m.

The train that morning, efficiently German, passed by stacked bricks and unused pallets, with coughing chimneys and grey skies commanding the background. It arrived in Leverkusen, home of Bayer 04, and the sky thickened. Founded by workers of the chemical company Bayer, whose logo (found on Aspirin packets) illuminates the city from a factory tower, the club languished in Germany's lower divisions until 1980. Having the company logo on their kit and its name in their title, Bayer Leverkusen were historically vilified. The ascendancy of village club Hoffenheim, backed by wealthy Dietmar Hopp, however, and the influence of Volkswagen over Wolfsburg, distracted many German supporters, who value economic and sporting fairness, from Leverkusen. With RB Leipzig in the Bundesliga from 2016, Bayer began to look traditional.

Their greatest recent point came in 2002 when, with Lúcio in defence and the self-confessed golden boy of his generation Michael Ballack in midfield, they reached the Champions League final, defeating both Liverpool and Manchester United en route. In the April of 2002, they were on course for the treble (Bundesliga title, DFB Cup and Champions League final), but ended May empty-handed. In what would be the most disappointing summer of his career, Ballack even lost the World Cup final to Brazil. Leverkusen were placed in a spiral of median performance for many years until 2014 when they appointed Roger Schmidt. The Leverkusen board, envious of the model created at Dortmund, decided that a strong identity of play was needed to expand the club. They watched how Red Bull Salzburg performed, most notably against Ajax in the Europa League, and hired Schmidt on the basis of his approach.

Schmidt implemented a 4-2-4 system, more for its high-octane pressing function than its traditional attacking purpose. In a league of Klopps and Guardiolas, he made Leverkusen the best club in transition in the league. In January 2017, they had scored more goals from counter-attacks (43) than any other side in Europe's top five leagues (a figure dating back to July 2012). 'They are one of the best, most intense teams in Germany,' Guardiola decided.

But on 5 March 2017 Schmidt was sacked (another victim of the Béla Guttmann rule [64]). 'I believe Roger Schmidt is an absolute top coach. But we have to act now if we are not going to lose touch with our targets,' sporting director Rudi Voller said. By then, however, Schmidt's style of play had become synonymous with all clubs in Germany, so *Spielverlagerung.de* writer Tobias Escher told me. 'The high structured press is a universal trend. They [clubs] all follow his model tactically. It is the way a lot of teams play, even the Red Bull clubs. When Guardiola came, the new idea of *Juego de Posición* was implemented and Thomas Tuchel adapted it at Dortmund, so there are two schools of thought battling it out now.' *But Klopp and Schmidt did not invent pressing, did they?* 'No. Every player has to work defensively and offensively together, that began in the 1930s with Otto Nerz and Sepp Herberger. You don't have to tell a German striker to counter-press, he knows he has to do that. Klopp and Schmidt just modified the style.'

In Germany, players are technically sound but tactically exceptional. *Is there something in youth education that is developing these players?* 'Yes, but we have to go back in time to the 2000s. We got complacent after 1990 when we won the World Cup, at a time when the youth system was changing. You had Sacchi's pressing and Cruyff's playing idea, and youth academies were

---

64. The great Austro-Hungarian coach once said: "The third year is fatal. If a manager stays at a club more than that his players tend to become bored or complacent and opponents start to work out counter-strategies." He would know. Guttmann managed 25 teams over a 40-year career, including: Porto, Benfica, Milan, Sao Paulo and Honvéd.

developing at this time. In Germany, though, this didn't happen. When we were knocked out in the group stage of Euro 2000 everything changed.' The DFB went to Holland, France and Spain to discover how they were developing talent and created the ETPP model. 'They pretty much founded youth academies and today you have the situation where there are strict regulations on them. If a club wants to get a licence in the Bundesliga, it needs to have a certain amount of training pitches for the youth team and even needs a certain lighting system. Every club then needs to have a certain number of players from their own academy in the first team, and we have a lot of coaches now who speak tactical language from U10 upwards. At this age, they develop a hunger to learn new ideas. This is a cultural change because in the 1990s tactics was not a topic at all, whereas players are now constantly confronted by it.'

10.03 a.m.

Twenty-three minutes later, at Düsseldorf station, 100 more fans aligned, most of them in red. This is the capital city of North Rhine-Westphalia and home to Germany's third busiest airport. It was here that Liverpool fans had flown to and stayed, bringing an atmosphere with them as they stepped on to the train – much to the conductor's annoyance.

A half-hour drive west of Düsseldorf, not on the train route but worth visiting nonetheless, is Mönchengladbach. With a population of 250,000, the town is little more than an overspill of elsewhere. The local club, Borussia, though, have a most fantastic history. Up until 1959 they had never competed higher than the Oberliga West, an amateur division, but in 1963 they began playing a talented 19-year-old local named Günter Netzer and started winning. In 1966, along with future rivals Bayern Munich, Gladbach were promoted to the Bundesliga. Whereas Munich was a region of great financial power, Mönchengladbach was not. The club had little to spend. Borussia, therefore, promoted players from the youth divisions, namely Berti Vogts and Jupp Heynckes.

Netzer was the star of the team. He became the symbol of Borussia in the same way Franz Beckenbauer became Bayern's. Both young men came to represent the socio-political upheaval in Germany's value system from 1968 onwards. They were born in simple homes in the year the war ended and played for clubs close to their towns. '[Netzer] became the darling of left-wing intellectuals who saw in him someone who broke with conservative traditions on and off the pitch,' wrote Tomlinson and Young.[65] The sports car-driving midfielder, before he signed for Real Madrid, had the same effect on Gladbach that a young Cruyff had on Ajax.

Their manager at that time, Hennes Weisweiler, now has the coaching academy where he taught (Sporthochschule) named after him. It is a finishing school in Köln (home of the analytics department of the DFB) for the best thinkers in Germany, including, quite recently, Roger Schmidt, who balanced ten months of study with roles as both a mechanical engineer and head coach of SC Preußen Münster; and Joachim Löw, where he devised the coaching philosophy that supported Germany in their 2014 World Cup triumph. History has a way of repeating itself. Fifty years earlier, Sepp Herberger, having recently won the World Cup for West Germany (with a team of amateur players), turned to the Sporthochschule to find a potential successor. Staff there were raving about Köln player Hennes Weisweiler as the best coach out of 80 on the course, and so, like Jürgen Klinsmann did with Löw, Herberger made him his assistant, training him up to be the next national team coach.

But Weisweiler was a home bird. He only wanted to work in the Rhineland, so in 1958, aged 38, he became head of the Sporthochschule. All of his talents were donated to teaching future generations of coaches, as well as powering local clubs, rather than the national team. He worked as coach of Köln and rivals Viktoria Köln, before being appointed Borussia Mönchengladbach head trainer in 1964. His style of play at the club, that has continued through the years with players like Igor Belanov and Marco Reus, was to attack and counter-attack. Many in Germany still call a goal scored on the counter a 'Gladbach'.

In Niederrhein, Weisweiler built a technical team which he described himself as 'strong on the counter with a result-oriented focus.'[66] The ideas he gathered as head of the Sporthochschule were innovative, the best in Germany, if not Europe (most other nations did not study coaching at the

---

65. Tomlinson, A. & Young, C (2006). *German Football: History, Culture, Society.* New York: Routledge.
66. Weisweiler, H. (1980). *Der Fussball. Taktik, Training und Mannschaft.* Schorndorf.

time), and he poured everything he learnt – psychology, training exercises and tactics – into little Gladbach. They won the league in 1970, '71, '75, '76 and '77 with Danish Ballon d'Or winner Allan Simonsen up front, as well as the UEFA Cup in '75 and '79.

But money talks. Or at least it got louder over the years. Gone went the era of 'may the best team win', replaced by an age of 'may the richest'. Gladbach's golden years ended quite naturally; the teenagers Berti Vogts and Jupp Heynckes became veterans, got their coaching qualifications and retired. They were replaced by new prodigies, specifically a boy called Lothar Matthäus, but he was from Bavaria, not NRW, so when FC Bayern made a record bid for him aged 23, he left. Football became too big for little towns and Gladbach fell behind.

Back in Köln, in 1983, 20,000 locals turned out for Weisweiler's funeral. The service was at St Peter's Cathedral – only two other men in history had received such an honour – with the subsequent renaming of the Sporthochschule after him an apt gesture. At the complex now, Bundesliga and DFB representatives come together to create a scheme of training for all coaches of the top four divisions. 'The German Football Association is currently convinced that an additional level of training is required in order to meet the requirements of trainers in the absolute top level,' the official website writes. 'The German Football League (DFL) is also of that opinion, which is why the football teacher's licence is now a prerequisite for being a Cheftrainerpost in the Bundesliga and the 3rd league.' Recognised as being more than UEFA-qualified coaches, higher than the Pro Licence, elite German coaches are able to become 'football teachers' at the school, like Hennes Weisweiler. [67]

10.21 a.m.

Eighteen minutes after leaving Düsseldorf the train arrived in Dortmund. 'Oh, when the Reds!' came shouts from the far end of the platform as BVB and LFC

---

67. The quality of coaching in Germany is supplemented by the quantity of potential Bundestrainers they have. According to UEFA, there are 28,400 B licence coaches in Germany, whilst only 1,759 in England. A counter-argument is that it is therefore more difficult for German coaches to reach the top level, hence Schmidt having to work in Austria before reaching Leverkusen, but as a competitive nation there is a trickle down of knowledge that ripens the quality from amateur to elite.

fans walked together in unison. It would prove to be a day of festivities, with friendships formed on both sides. The two clubs shared similarities beforehand, both of whom had a Kop stand – Dortmund's considerably bigger, Liverpool's more famous – with both serenading players with versions of 'You'll Never Walk Alone'. It was in 1996 that that local band Pur Harmony recorded their take of the song, played at Westfalenstadion before matches, but it was first introduced to German football in 1977 by Borussia Mönchengladbach fans, having duetted with Liverpudlians in bars and restaurants at the European Cup final in Rome. A friendship emerged that week in May and continued over the years, enticing many Gladbach fans to Dortmund to see old friends; their flags in amongst the red in Alte Market square.

The square was heaving. It was there that fans of both red and yellow had gathered to drink and sing. Banners hung from every tree and pole, some regular, most new. Many of the new banners were tailored for the event and combined imagery of Jürgen Klopp's face with the colours of Germany's tricolour flag: *Bundesdienstflagge*. Fifteen years earlier, when Liverpool were last in Dortmund for the UEFA Cup final, there were no black, red and yellow German flags in the crowd, despite the club having Christian Ziege, Markus Babbel and Didi Hamann playing back then. This modern Anglo appreciation of Germany, of German football and its culture, is a phenomenon fuelled by disillusionment. British fans travel out to Germany en masse each year to reacquaint themselves with the game they once knew: to stand, sing and drink beer quite harmlessly.

Chris Williams is familiar with both teams as a Liverpool fan and Bundesliga writer. He travels to Dortmund often and was in his element when we met in the square. Red and yellow intermingled as pyro smoke and footballs shared the air. *Why do Brits now seek German football?* I asked. 'It's so similar, a working-class game with similar passion,' he responded. 'I suppose I get a buzz from watching football in Germany that I don't get in England anymore. It isn't a 90-minute game; it starts the minute you wake up, and when you meet friends in the pub, then when you walk to the ground. That emotion carries into grounds in Germany but has sadly drifted out of English stadiums. Germany still has that love affair between fan and club, which hasn't been eroded by a quest for financial milking of fans. Clubs are still part of the community here.'

An appreciation of German football has blossomed in Britain due to (for want of a better word) the quintessential 'Britishness' of their game. This Liverpool–Dortmund love-in was also, more than a recognition of similar football teams, a showing of European society's progression. Four thousand people were killed in Liverpool during the Blitz – second only to London – at the hands of the German Luftwaffe. In return, the Allies destroyed 54% of Dortmund (as well as 64% of neighbours Düsseldorf and 61% of Köln). Horrifying loss of life occurred on both sides. But now, on this April morning, the cities of Liverpool and Dortmund mingled and drank together, singing each other's songs and wearing each other's colours. There was no xenophobia, no fear of each other, no thought or mention of the war. More than a sporting occasion, this was, quite wonderfully, a promotion of peace.

The token club of British affection, Borussia Dortmund, are more attractive to fans than any other side in Germany. Their colours, the fervent commitment of their supporters, the attractive style of play, the beer – they're 'cool' by definition. Some clubs possess a number of these traits – Ajax have style, Besiktas have atmosphere, Barcelona have players – but Dortmund are a fantastic concoction of all things cool. Facilitating their attractiveness is an added layer of mystery, that essential trait that Albert Einstein described as 'the source of all true art and all science'. Because of the mysteriousness of Dortmund, their difficult-to-analyse tactics and forgotten history of struggle, fans from Britain are drawn to them.

The Following Day

There is a grey football court on Olga Straße in Gelsenkirchen where the local migrant sons play. İlkay Gündoğan was one of them, so was Mesut Özil – both are typical of the city and its wider region. During North Rhine-Westphalia's industrial heyday migrants, or *gastarbeiters*, were invited to come from Turkey as 'guest workers'. But when the mines closed and industry departed, the guest workers stayed and integration became an issue. The social unifier, as is so often the case, was football. Small but clever, always playing against older boys, Özil represented neighbourhood clubs Teutonia, Falke and Rot-Weiss before local giants Schalke 04, as omnipresent as the looming chimneys, scouted him for their academy.

With its dystopian appearance – a white bubble surrounded by woodland trees and factories on the horizon – Schalke's Knappenshmiede academy, translated as 'miners' forge', looks like a setting from a Suzanne Collins novel. History overwhelms the complex. Schalke were the best club in Germany in the 1930s and 40s and they haven't forgotten it. There are standards here, a winning desire that makes Knappenshmiede one of Germany's best academies. Alongside Özil, when Germany won the 2014 World Cup they were assisted by Schalke graduates Manuel Neuer, the tournament Golden Glove winner, and Benedikt Höwedes who played every minute. All three players came through the ETPP model and had represented Germany together since they were boys.

S04 also embrace the sociological history of the region. The players' tunnel at Veltins-Arena that youngsters progress to is a corridor themed as a mine shaft, with dim lighting and coal walls on either side. When mining for talent, Schalke draw on that history to entice youngsters to join. Theirs is one of the toughest catchment areas in the world, with Dortmund, Gladbach and Leverkusen in every youth league. But the competition is good. It has helped them to develop Max Meyer, Joël Matip, Leroy Sané, Kaan Ayhan and Julien Draxler. Not having regular, tough competition can be a hindrance, as discovered in Turin with Juventus.

U19 trainer Norbert Elgert told the BBC World Service that there are five pillars upholding Knappenshmiede's philosophy, which they judge players on:

1. Technique, space and time for the player on the ball.
2. Game intelligence and tactics.
3. Athletic ability, especially speed of movement.
4. Mental strength and fortitude.
5. Capability/suitability to play in the first team.

With local industries failing, Knappenshmiede proves to be a contradiction in business terms. The European Club Association, with over 200 member clubs, sends delegates to Schalke every year to learn from them. One topic they discuss is: 'What are the successful mechanisms of co-operation between the first team and the academy?' It costs €3m every year to sustain the academy, so Schalke have to justify the expenditure through preparing youngsters for the first team who are either retainable or sellable. Leroy Sané's €40m transfer to Manchester City probably covered the cost of Knappenshmiede for a decade. The winger, once more, is a technically gifted footballer developed through ETPP. As a boy, he attended both Leverkusen's and Schalke's academies before settling on the latter. There, his family would drive him to training both at Knappenshmiede and the local DFB centre.

In 2015 he made his debut for the senior national squad, which was expected. Not because his father played alongside Joachim Löw at Freiburg – the national trainer is a close family friend – but because the DFB have a hold over all the best youngsters in the country and moulded Sané into a technical German-style player. Growing up, he trained under the same umbrella style as his future national squad teammates, making his transition seamless. 'We see tremendous potential in him,' said Löw before his debut, speaking on behalf of the collective DFB. Sané's story started in North Rhine-Westphalia, but the point of ETPP is that, if the setting was Brandenburg or Saxony, or even a small town in Mecklenburg-Vorpommern like where Toni Kroos is from, it would have had the same ending. No stone is left unturned.

EIGHTEEN

THE GOLDMINE EFFECT: FEYENOORD ROTTERDAM

From the very German-sounding station of Herzogenrath it takes 12 minutes to reach the very Dutch-sounding station of Heerlen. The journey across the border sees life change in no way whatsoever. The currency remains the same; people look the same and bizarrely, despite the language barrier, accents are similar. On a clear day in Holland one can see for miles around. Most of the Netherlands is below sea level, and would be prone to flooding were it not for a clever system of dykes and dams. A reader wishing to take a mammoth football tour of Europe similar to the one in this book should start with a miniature exploration of Holland. InterCity trains begin in Maastricht and stop off in Eindhoven, Breda, Rotterdam, The Hague, Amsterdam and Alkmaar. Clubs belonging to these cities are most welcoming and deliver seminars throughout the season on their methods. Along the way, tulips of every colour grow beside one another. Cows graze, rivers meander and countless windmills turn in the gentle breeze. Most common though are football pitches; they appear beside churches and farms in places they simply should not belong.

There are over 3,000 amateur football clubs in the Netherlands. Families belong to their local club and spend Saturdays watching father and son play before cycling home. Unlike amateur football in Britain, with cold stone changing rooms and macho spirit, Dutch clubs have comfy clubhouses and artificial pitches. The sport also differs. Dutch amateur players keep the ball on the floor and try to manipulate space. British amateur footballers rely on masculine tendencies, aggression and high clearances upfield, usually because the pitch is so boggy that the ball cannot be passed along it. In the Dutch version of the game, there are long, controlled periods of possession, whereas in Britain there are quick turnovers of the ball. In the next few chapters on Feyenoord and Ajax, you will discover great parallels of football development in Holland. Two contrasting ways of producing footballers that, for the good of the Dutch game, are being forced to work together. Both methodologies, depending on the season, can be replicated in Britain and elsewhere, too.

Intrinsic Motivation

Before his appointment as a director of football at Brentford, the Dane Rasmus Ankersen wrote *The Goldmine Effect*, a book on the secrets of high performance in sport. In short, Ankersen spent seven months travelling around the world visiting 'goldmines' where talent was developed. They included, amongst others: Bekoji, a village in Ethiopia where the world's best middle-distance runners are produced; MVP track and field club in Kingston, Jamaica, home to the best sprinters; Iten, a Kenyan village that develops outstanding long-distance runners; and Brazil, to the favelas where exceptional footballers emerge. In identifying and recognising poverty-stricken environments as goldmines where talent is not only developed but sustained, Ankersen countered the belief that elite talent needs elite facilities to reach the highest level. Instead, *The Goldmine Effect* discovered, amongst a wealth of other findings, that the internal desire of an athlete – his intrinsic motivation – matters more than the affluence of his surroundings.

Prior to Ankersen's book, it was thought Usain Bolt and Asafa Powell, and indeed Jamaica's other world-class sprinters, had the very best in contemporary athletic science, allowing them to perform at a high level. What Ankersen found in Kingston, however, was a hard, dry field, a jaded grass track and some rusty weights outside of a shed. One telling quote from the founder of the athletic club, Stephen Francis, to Ankersen explains the philosophy of goldmines: 'A performance environment should not be designed for comfort but for hard work. It has to show people that the road to success is long and uncomfortable.'[68]

---

68. Ankersen, R (2012). The Goldmine Effect. London: Icon Books Ltd.

The danger in offering athletes the very best in terms of facilities, sponsorship and praise is that they can come to rely on such extrinsic factors and can be lulled into a state of complacency: luxurious surroundings have the potential to diminish effort. Football is laden with stories of young players who got too much too soon. Ankersen's research found that anybody can produce a goldmine, provided it inspires belief in the athletes who attend. He wrote: 'It has more to do with your ability to capitalise on the talent that already exists. Goldmines are not going to be discovered. They are going to be uncovered.'

The first impression of Feyenoord's joint first team and academy sport complex in Rotterdam is of a worn-out goldmine. When visiting, the tram pulls up alongside De Kuip, the looming, intimidating, historic stadium, forged in corrugated iron and concrete. To the casual observer it is an eyesore, but for football fans it is beautiful. Dirk Kuyt's face smiles down from a billboard next to that of Giovanni van Bronckhorst – the Rotterdam-born manager. Past the stadium, over the road and through some trees is a collection of football pitches. Feyenoord's Varkenoord complex is so unceremonious it shares its gates with a car garage and a small littered stream. It's open to the public (and ducks) and has moss growing through paving slabs in places. Initially, Varkenoord appears to be a collection of Sunday league pitches, but for a scattering of Opel sponsorship boards. There are in fact 19 different training pitches of various size.

On one pitch, a group of teenagers in hoodies are having a kick-about until a lone security guard ushers them away. Equipment is kept inside rusty containers with faded Feyenoord badges painted on. 'Hand in hand' reads the message underneath. It's impossible not to be charmed by it all. The furthest pitch from the entrance, where the first team train, has five vertical lines painted on to it, creating sections so the players can see where numerical overloads are happening on the pitch. Yet even the first team pitch has to be reached by a mossy concrete path.

'When it rains, the path to the training session is flooded. I see dads coming from work in their best suits and shoes and they have to walk through mud. Yes, we laugh but it is what makes this club special,' explains Glenn van der Kraan, head of development phase and researcher on talent development. 'We haven't got a dome where we can train inside. We go to the beach and run in the rain with the wind in our faces. It develops them as people. Your life isn't a straight path where you can go where you want to go; you have to struggle.' Feyenoord believe Varkenoord develops character. 'Our fans don't want a striker for €30m, they want to see a player come through the academy. It's amazing!'

Indeed, he is right. They are a special club shaped by the people of the city. Rotterdam has a tough, working-class population. It is home to the biggest port in Europe that was bombed to the ground during World War Two. There is a strong civic pride here, an insularity built up over the years. While Amsterdam dreams Rotterdam works, the people say. It takes a strong, gritty type of footballer to play for Feyenoord so the coaches here create more than just technicians.

The message van der Kraan offers aligns perfectly with Ankersen's book: 'The rest of the world, and especially in England, people are doing everything to develop talent and if you look at the complexes there, it's crazy! We say to the kids that you have to make the step from here to the first team. We can't give you everything you want right now, it's up to you to do it. A lot of kids aged 15 and 16 get agents and sponsorship deals and in the end, it only matters that you get to the first team.' One of van der Kraan's favourite books is *The Social Animal* by David Brooks on social mobility and ambition; the theme of developing hunger in children particularly resonant. 'Much of life is about failure, whether we acknowledge it or not, and your destiny is profoundly shaped by how effectively you learn from and adapt to failure,' Brooks writes in it. Without realising, Feyenoord help shape more destinies with their waterlogged training ground than clubs elsewhere do.

We Before Me

Most academies tend to focus on developing the individual to strive to break into the first team (Ajax set the trend), but Feyenoord are not like other clubs. Here, the objective is to develop the team (for example the U15s) and not just the individual within that team. 'If you cannot play together then you aren't going to make it in the first team. Every club I visit talk about the four corners – physical, mental, technical and tactical – but nobody is ever talking about the ability to play together,' van der

Kraan began. 'If you take Luis Suárez for example, at Liverpool he was the individual and people doubted if he could do it at Barcelona but he has adapted himself to be a part of the team. That is what we do with our kids. We want the best kids in the group to play together. The kids know who they can play with and that is why our team mentality is important because, whilst it is essential to develop the technical skills, you have to, at the end of the day, be able to play in a team. You have to work hard for each other and that is the Feyenoord way.'

The head of their academy, Rotterdam-born Damien Hertog, agrees that this team focus is unique to Feyenoord's academy but insists it isn't at the negligence of the individual: 'It is a misunderstanding if people think we don't develop individuals too. We develop an individual who can play as part of a team, which is something different. But the person with the best possibility to make it into the team is the one who understands the value of being part of a team.'

In 1992, Manchester United had a group of young players who came through the academy together and entered the first team. David Beckham, Nicky Butt, Ryan Giggs, Gary Neville, Phil Neville and Paul Scholes became the fabric of the club. Ajax in 1995 won the Champions League with a similar group of academy players who also progressed from the same environment. Edwin van der Sar, Edgar Davids, Clarence Seedorf and Michael Reiziger knew each other's game inside out, while the rest of Europe did not. Football history is filled with academy triumphs, from the Lisbon Lions through to Barcelona 2010. However, the probability of young players coming through an academy system together is now unlikely due to the emphasis on developing the individual. Feyenoord could prove to be the exception: 'We want them to all have belief in the same dream. When they are training and they look to the left they can see the stadium, and they all know they can actually get a chance to be a Feyenoord player because so many other kids have already gone through the system,' says Glenn.

Inside a cinderblock building, all of the Feyenoord youth coaches sit around a large table and discuss the players in their group, even though it doesn't affect them. The U16 coach will know everything about the players in the U6 group and likewise. There is a unity, an 'us-against-the-world' spirit that brings the whole complex together. Fostering that spirit is crucial:

'Our slogan is "no words only actions", and that is what we want on the pitch. We want you to work your socks off to be a top-class player. You have to work hard so you don't let your teammates down. That is the foundation for us. It is why I think this is a family club; we are all doing this together,' Glenn explained.

The spirit he speaks of has been a constant for Feyenoord since their bankruptcy in 2007. Back then the board, manager and fans unanimously decided to focus on the academy rather than spending out on players from elsewhere. Feyenoord went on to produce Jordy Clasie, Stefan de Vrij, Bruno Martins Indi, Leroy Fer, Daryl Janmaat and Gini Wijnaldum. At the 2014 World Cup in Brazil they had developed more players at the tournament than any other academy in the world. Damien Hertog delivered the Rinus Michels award (given to the best academy in the Netherlands) to Feyenoord five years in a row. 'It is what our identity is. It is the people who make Feyenoord special, you can't describe it, it is just a feeling [you have] as soon as you get here. It starts at 8.30 a.m. with the first training session and it ends at 8.30 p.m. when the last training session has ended. If you ask van Persie or Jordy Clasie, they always felt warm here and that is what we want to offer the players,' Glenn explains, and it is true. The staff create a warmth that the facilities do not offer; there are no indoor pitches so when it rains or pellets of hail fall hard and cold, the youngsters remain outside. Grit is needed both on the ground and in the heart.

A Winning Mentality

Welcoming visitors into the corridor of the cinderblock building is a collection of framed photographs of academy graduates. Young first-teamers Sven van Beek and Tonny Vilhena are the nearest frames, with Royston Drenthe and Jonathan de Guzmán the farthest. Clad in a black hooded jumper, Damien Hertog discussed the winning mentality that Feyenoord youth teams have. 'It is about building up resilience throughout their time in our youth academy. During training sessions, we rarely whistle for a foul, we tell them not to moan and to just carry on. We play to win in competitions. In training sessions, it is all about rewards and forfeits. The type of forfeit is up to the coach, sometimes it could be funny or sometimes it can be push-ups or running. Sometimes they may have to clean up the dressing room or carry something.' That day, in the canteen, three boys who had lost in a training session were waiting on the rest of their team, serving up food and ensuring they were hydrated. The three boys hated it, so in the next session they were more determined not to lose.

At many British academies, parents are not allowed to talk. The young footballers play on lush pitches with a Crucible Theatre atmosphere. Perhaps that is the correct way for them to develop, without any exterior pressures, although socially to go from such serenity to a professional match in front of thousands of baying fans is a difficult evolution. The player naturally becomes nervous and may perform below his standard, inviting verbal abuse from fans and presenting his coach with the opportunity to drop him. In future, the coach may be less inclined to play him again.

Feyenoord know that their youngsters need to be gradually exposed to a degree of volatility so they can progressively learn to cope with it. Glenn explains, 'It is all about faults and behaviour. The behaviour of the kids comes from the inside. The emotions are a thought they have and they have to deal with their thoughts. If they have never been in situations where they have been exposed, for example, if we bring them in from an amateur club to go to a tournament against English clubs, they are shaking. That is why we never tell the parents they can't watch.' Parents are in fact encouraged to be a part of the experience. 'The kid needs to know that he is at the best football club in Holland playing under the guidance of the best coaches. On a Saturday, he has to be able to play his own game and not worry about people watching – he has to cope with situations that he's been exposed to.'

To promote a winning culture, the children start training in a two-versus-two or a three-versus-three practice with forfeits for the losing team. Feyenoord also understand that children learn from each other and have decided that, rather than educating them onsite like Juventus, Honvéd, Benfica and other academies do, they send their younger players to a school for elite athletes. 'They are in a class with swimmers who get out of bed at 4.45 a.m. and are in the swimming pool at 6.00 a.m. until 9.00 a.m. By the time our kids arrive they have already been working for three hours. They are getting their eyes opened to what others need to do to be the best that they can be,' Glenn says. As well as learning from children in different sports, the academy players learn from kids of other ages. Feyenoord have a buddy system allowing seven-, eight- and nine-year-olds to train with 11- and 12-year-olds. 'We will have a left-winger aged six or seven training with a kid in the U11s or U12s. The older players show leadership and the younger player is looking and seeing what it takes to reach that level.'

Effort

In May 1940, the Luftwaffe bombed Rotterdam as the German army invaded the Netherlands, forcing the Dutch to surrender. Thousands of innocent people died. For locals, the suffering continued when the Nazis took control of the port. Allied forces dedicated five years towards bombing it. Rotterdam was obliterated; a bed of flattened rubble. It was the survivors who rebuilt the city and fostered the tough mindset that has carried through subsequent generations. Modern Rotterdam is an architecturally diverse place, blessed with futuristic designs. Quirky metal buildings reflect the sun on to passing trams. In typical Dutch fashion cyclists keep pace with trams on a road dedicated just for them. In the middle is a canal accompanied by tulips of every colour. This is the council's way of making Rotterdam look like a traditionally Dutch city, like Den Haag or Utrecht, but beneath the surface is a grit born from adversity; a civic pride and feeling of difference. When Rotterdammers come together at De Kuip the atmosphere is without rival. Few places are as intimidating.

Feyenoord fan Mark Lievisse Adriaanse acknowledges, however, that the image of them as the gritty club of Rotterdam is a recent one. 'From the 1910s to the early 1960s, the club was nationally seen as a team of aesthetics, playing beautiful, advanced football. This changed during the '70s. The team identity became a working-class one that prioritised hard work over beauty.' He finds the more recent identity to be dangerous, in that fans popularise workhorses over elegant breeds, despite them not necessarily making the team stronger. 'Rotterdam itself is also rapidly changing. Buildings are as easily built as torn down, neighbourhoods change constantly. The harbours have moved from the inner city to the outskirts, and their jobs are automatised. The population is still primarily low-educated, but not working in the harbour anymore. Moreover, the city is gentrifying very, very quickly. This will for sure alter its identity.'

Rotterdammer Damien Hertog understands its contemporary social fabric. As club favourite Ernst Happel once said, 'A day without football is a day lost.' That quote applies wholly to the people here. Hertog knows what a Feyenoord player must be like, in both personality and mentality: 'Our spectators and the people who live in Rotterdam know what it means to work hard and get an income. If you work hard for 90 minutes and fight for every inch on the pitch, then the spectators appreciate that the most. If you don't, they won't accept you. The fans want to see a team fighting and playing for each other, not as individuals. We say "hand in hand" at the club – it is something that Feyenoord stands for. It is the culture of the club and we have to bring this culture in to our young players and then we talk about attributes that we have to develop, which is obviously the technical, mental, physical and tactical part.'

Ironically, the player who most represents those values is Dirk Kuyt, raised in the windy seaside town of Katwijk in South Holland, a world away from Rotterdam. Yet in Katwijk he grew up pure, dieting on fish and milk. He saw how hard the people worked and would have been a fisherman were it not for football: 'But when I was 11 my father said I should stay on the land and try to become a footballer,' he recalled. Kuyt knows the value of hard work and, because of that, finds himself as the captain of Feyenoord. Not only that, he is the current golden boy of Dutch football, a knight returned to save the game from slipping into ruin. That is most ironic, given his appearance and technique, but the Dutch love Kuyt. For the national team, he worked harder than anybody and always valued his place. Football is historically a masculine sport and players of Kuyt's ilk have always retained an appreciation from fans.

In a bygone era, Dutch footballers would leave to play abroad, often at Milan or Barcelona, but would always return to help bring a young generation of talent through. That was Dutch culture. Johan Cruyff did so for Ruud Gullit in 1983; Frank Rijkaard for Dennis Bergkamp in 1993; even Edgar Davids for Wesley Sneijder in 2006. Now, however, with the decline of the Eredivisie, Dutch internationals don't want to come home. Inspired by Gheorghe Hagi, Wesley Sneijder and his neighbour Robin van Persie moved to Turkey; Clarence Seedorf retired in Brazil having grown up in neighbouring Suriname and having married a Brazilian wife; and Rafael van der Vaart opted for Real Betis because of his Spanish family.

Kuyt came home and inspires everybody in the country. 'Dirk is 36 years of age and has played in two World Cups and one World Cup final. He has won a lot of trophies and has gained a lot of big achievements in his career. There is nobody who can explain to a young guy why he shouldn't work as hard in training as Kuyt – he is a really good role model,' Hertog says. At Feyenoord, the buddy system begins with Kuyt. Glenn van der Kraan recognises the lack of examples nationally: 'You need kids who are 18 coming through and getting advice from players who are 30 and have had great careers. It is something that has changed and is a big problem for us. Our youth are not so self-criticised anymore. They don't say after one bad match, "Okay, I need to step up my game" anymore; it is easy to blame the coach or other external factors. There are agents of kids who are 14 telling them how good they are. This generation wants positive attention all of the time.' Because of this, the purely raised professional Dirk Kuyt is invaluable to Feyenoord.

A Game Played Upstairs

Glenn van der Kraan was coaching for Anderlecht as a 19-year-old when, at a tournament in his native Netherlands, they were pitted against Feyenoord. Stanley Brard (former head of academy) and Gerard Rutjes (former head of development phase) heard him talking and began speaking to him after the match. When Glenn was asked to come to Feyenoord to work he was initially reluctant. His brother, James, was already employed as the head of youth scouting and the two had decided they wouldn't work together if the chance ever arose. But Brard was convincing and Glenn joined as an U10 coach. That was six years ago. Now he is head of ages U6 to U12 and has developed the club's Soccer Lab programme.

It is a data system that gathers information on youngsters from the coach's input – how they trained and played – from which Glenn can develop a training schedule. Most interesting is the research Glenn did with the University of Amsterdam and the University of Tilburg on talent development. 'I found that decision-making is really important for development. The best players were the quickest decision-makers. Everyone in the world knows that now, but what I wanted to do was to discover how we can improve that. Together with one of the finest professors in human movement science we made a test on how to find out what a guy is looking at when he is playing football. We discovered that our best players knew exactly where the ball was going to be two seconds before the pass was played. My aim was to get all of that data and find out what the kids do and how we can improve them. For example, what we do now is, when we play three versus three, we don't use bibs. We've got certain training sessions with lights where we train our players' perception. We start younger now with four-, five- or six-year-olds – that is what we are good at. My role is to try and find the right training methods for these youngest kids so they can work on these areas.'

Glenn's research on the prefrontal lobe discovered attributes that can be developed in five- and six-year-old children. 'What we found was that kids go to training sessions and then afterwards they just get a ball and play football again. You can see the winning mentality in that. We say to our scouts that it is all subjective – everything they do is subjective, but they should watch the kid play; watch what he is like before and after the training session, because then they will see what type of human being he is. In the end, he is not just a football player but a human being and you can see even at four or five if he has a winning mentality.'

Hours and the Street

When in Lyon I sat watching children of all ages play football on a dusty court beneath the Guillotière bridge. They were young urban artists, the Zidanes and Riquelmes of their neighbourhood. The Netherlands mirrors Britain, and indeed most of the West, in that its children are almost social recluses. Youngsters are not playing as much football as they used to, thus drying up the wells of talent that professional clubs once drew from. Feyenoord (Glenn, namely) researched the number of hours their children played football outside of training. The figure was just shy of nine hours per week. In South America that figure was double. What the club decided to do was offer children the opportunity to increase their number of unstructured hours playing football. If a training session begins at 5:00pm, the coaches decided to throw 50 footballs out at 4:00pm and tell the children to just play. 'So there are over 100 kids playing one hour, three times a week, with kids of different ages, unstructured. Those hours a week are 150 hours a year, which we hope will inspire kids to play football when they go home,' Glenn explained. In their new complex, Feyenoord want to build a football playground with different playing obstacles, allowing children to be creative and have fun. 'They can do two-versus-two or anything they want to do.' Unstructured play allows children to develop socially as well as technically. It is here that the leaders emerge and coaches can see who is showing sportsmanship and a degree of organisation. [69]

Hertog agrees that the decline in street football is an issue. 'It is not something new but it worries us as well. If you count training hours at home as well as here there is a big drop overall so a lot of academies will compensate those hours at the club. They want to bring kids to the club earlier where they will spend a whole day, or maybe their academy is like La Masia where they stay over.'

He believes players and their parents need to take a degree of ownership over their ambitions. He feels the need to openly communicate with players about the issue and hope they find the time to combat it: 'We encourage them to play more, to train for themselves and we explain that there isn't enough time here at the academy. You don't want to have to spend quality training time working on passing the ball with both feet – you should choose to do that at home, especially when you are 18 or 19. Training then should be on decision-making and finding spaces on the pitch, not passing the ball. If you still need that then you have to train in your own time if you really want to make it.'

Dutch legends like Johan Cruyff and Dennis Bergkamp treated the street as their best friend. They would play unstructured games with peers and, when they all went home, would kick a ball against the wall alone, judging the direction of it and learning how to manipulate it when it came to their feet at different speeds. But such a dedication toward spending hours alone with a football shouldn't stop when a player becomes professional.

Hertog asks me if I have seen the interview of Robin van Persie talking

---

69. Feyenoord differ from Ajax on the structuring of their sessions. Whereas Ajax play smaller-sized matches allowing kids to have many touches of the ball, Feyenoord play in larger areas, more replicative of a football match. Glenn explains: 'We want our kids to have a broad vision on the pitch and play bigger-sided games, so they have a better ability to play together and see the full depth of the pitch. It is a different idea but there is no set way of becoming a professional footballer.'

about Bergkamp. I had. In it van Persie describes the dedication Bergkamp put into his craft: 'I don't have enough words to describe him. I once finished my training early and was watching him from the jacuzzi. He had just come back from injury and was doing an exercise involving passing and shooting, with boards and mannequins. I sat and waited for him to make a mistake – but he never did. I got wrinkly hands from the bathtub. He did that exercise for over 45 minutes and he didn't make one single error. To me it was art.' [lxxiii]

Hertog smiles thinking about it. 'Why judge a player at 15 years if he is training at 70% of his capacity, because even van Persie only learnt later. There are players who want to work hard in every training session and there are also players who are laid-back and just like to have the ball, but they are really gifted and creative, just lacking work rate. Maybe he will realise when he sees Dirk Kuyt train, like van Persie saw Bergkamp.'

Timing

With so many factors to consider, how does Hertog know when a player is ready for the first team? 'You can never know for sure. You have expectations and you have your experience which you can compare things to, with former youth players like Clasie, de Vrij and Wijnaldum, so we rarely misread when a player is ready.' It is important for Hertog not to send a player up to the first team too early as there is a high risk of stunting his development. 'But you know his attributes and skills and you can tell when he is ready. The coaches talk about the players a lot and there are a lot of eyes watching them. We also have coaches at the academy who have played at the highest level in football so that helps when we are making decisions.'

At Feyenoord, Roy Makaay is one of those coaches. Ajax, similarly, have Bergkamp and Winston Bogarde training their attackers and defenders. If one visits PSV's quiet woodland retreat outside of Eindhoven, Bolo Zenden, Andre Ooijer and Mark van Bommel may be seen. This is a Dutch idea to improve not only the young players but the coaches, too, who are able to work alongside the retirees and learn from them. 'I think it is good to have diversity in your coaches at the academy,' Hertog explains. 'The importance of a coach who played at the highest level is that he knows what it takes to play there, so there are details that are seen in world-class football that he is able to tell our youth players. It is important to share that knowledge. But we have coaches who haven't even played professional football who are good socially with the players, who have patience and can stimulate their performance more. They are guys who have worked for years and trained as teachers so they know how to communicate with children. It takes more than a knowledge of the top of the game to be a good coach.'

NINETEEN

UNDERSTANDING AJAX OF AMSTERDAM: LITERATURE

The way most teams play in the modern era can be traced back to Ajax. Arrigo Sacchi, having spent his early 20s selling shoes, would watch old videotapes of Ajax in the 1970s and formulated a system of play that transformed Italian football. 'There has been only one real tactical revolution and it happened when football shifted from an individual to a collective game,' he said. 'It happened with Ajax.' [lxxiv] *Sacchi's Milan, Guardiola's Barça, Klopp's Dortmund – modern football's pioneers were all influenced by Ajax.*

Amsterdam is one of the world's creative hubs and is fertile ground for football development. Ajax, its club, are the eternal innovators; their methods often leeched upon and copied by teams in a televised age. Because of that, they constantly have to reinvent themselves, creating a new way of developing talented footballers every couple of years. Somehow, they manage to stay ahead of the pack. It is in their DNA to pioneer; it is in their culture to play attractively. Within their guidelines is an artistic appreciation: it must be 4-3-3, it must include exceptional youngsters, it must dominate the ball. However, such is the passion for the club from its ex-players and directors, and so powerful is its worth as a national institution, disagreements on the direction of the club are as common in Holland as yellow tulips. Ajax have been through a lot in recent years. In order to appreciate the methods they use now, we must trace their beginnings.

Rotterdam works, Amsterdam dreams. Though one must be careful not to dream too much when visiting the city. The canals and cafes, bicycles and shoebox houses; after a while they all look the same in the hazy air. Amsterdam is the cultural capital of the Netherlands, even if Den Haag represents the political capital. Sixty years ago the city differed greatly from the buzzing partying-yet-intellectual Amsterdam of today. In a black and white age, men stood for years watching the same rain fall on the same canals. That black water now glows in shades of iniquity; a tinge somewhere between liberal and crude depending on perception. Nevertheless, alongside the tawdry tourism there still beats a deep philosophical heart. The quieter streets away from Centraal Station hold greater sophistication. Money given to the city government from marijuana tourism is donated to the museums, galleries, theatres and concert halls.

In the 1960s the Dutch began to form their modern identity. Shaking off the slumber of German occupation, a disenfranchised youth culture awoke. That post-war generation of hippies, saddened and tired by war, spread across the Western world in one of the first examples of a united global conscience. Students living in Amsterdam made the city a mecca for travelling hippies, beatniks and Provos. All the while, most of the nation remained conservative (and indeed continues to be so), despite its cultural epicentre progressively becoming a tolerant metropolis.

As so often tends to be the case, football mirrored society. AFC Ajax, one of the city's bigger teams, though not particularly successful, were to become an extension of that forward-thinking Amsterdam era. Englishman Vic Buckingham blended a traditional WM formation with his belief that the ball should be passed between teammates (pioneering at the time). 'Possession football is the thing,' he told David Winner in *Brilliant Orange*, 'not kick and rush.'[70] Before departing the then amateur Ajax, Buckingham presented a skinny Amsterdammer from the east of the city with his debut. Johan Cruyff's mother worked as a cleaner at De Meer stadium and he joined the club when he was ten. With his long hair, cocky demeanour and heavy smoking, Cruyff seemed like a Provo. He wasn't; he was a rebel, but he shared their belief that the world could be changed, and like them

70. Winner, D (2001). *Brilliant Orange: The Neurotic Genius of Dutch Football*. London: Bloomsbury.

he intended to change it. His fluid style of play, so unlike anything seen before, coupled with his outspoken nature, made Cruyff a symbol of his generation. But for all of his talent, the big bang for Ajax did not explode until school teacher Rinus Michels was appointed as manager. It was he, Cruyff and some other talented boys from the city's neighbourhoods (Piet Keizer, Ruud Krol and Sjaak Swart) who propelled AFC Ajax from semi-professional community club to European champions within a decade.

Michelsianism

The JC Amman school for the deaf in Amsterdam was one of the first of its kind when it opened in 1912. The vision of the school was to identify and educate deaf children as early as possible, with students as young as three years of age overcoming their difficulties there. Of the countless numbers of staff that passed through the school gates in the following century, none were as recognisable as Rinus Michels. During his tenure at the school, the future Ajax, Barcelona and Netherlands trainer learnt how to communicate effectively. He had to organise the children to focus solely on him as he gesticulated and demonstrated gymnastic techniques to the group. Later, as an international manager, Michels would stand right in the face of his players and deliver his instructions; partly attributing to his nickname 'The General'.

With Johan Cruyff an exception, a customary prerequisite for many successful managers has been a less than spectacular playing career (Mourinho, Wenger, Benitez).[71] Michels complied with that rule as a powerfully built but technically average number 9. His heading ability helped Ajax to win the title in 1947 and then ten years later in 1957. Injury forced him to retire early at 30 and therefore, in a pre-professional era, Michels began working at the school.

In 1965 he returned to Ajax as head coach. The club saw the modern work he was doing at amateur club JOS as a part-time coach and moved quickly to bring him back. When he arrived, Ajax were facing relegation, yet the next year they won the league. Training grew in intensity and a real tactical focus emerged. Michels' shift away from an old English WM formation

---

71. Perhaps this is changing once more, considering that many of the game's best managers – Simeone, Guardiola, Ancelotti, Zidane – had spectacular playing careers.

to a 4-2-4 suited Ajax, especially Johan Cruyff. The freedom granted to players was an extraordinarily innovative idea for the time. Compressing space and making the pitch seem small when Ajax did not have the ball, before dispersing and making the pitch as wide and long as possible when they did, were two principles of play – both of which remain part of the academy syllabus today.

By instructing his team to react when they won and lost the ball, Michels became one of the earliest coaches to consciously develop how his team approached transitions. 'To be able to raise performance in modern football, it is absolutely necessary to have fast transitions from defending to attacking and the other way around,' he wrote.[72] Ajax's starting XI were also free to interchange positions, provided a teammate filled the vacant space. In training, they would often throw and catch the ball within their shape, rather than passing with their feet, allowing them to identify the triggers to move. 'If you pass the ball to A, how will it get to B?' Michels taught his team to make 'dummy' passes into the wrong teammate, so he would be pressed and space would open up for the original intended target to receive. Nowadays it is called a 'springboard' and is often employed by a number 6 when receiving from his centre-backs to open up space in the centre of the pitch. Everybody at Ajax was a playmaker who thought three passes ahead of the game.

In David Winner's *Brilliant Orange* the versatile defender Ruud Krol explained the rationale behind Michels' *Totaalvoetbal* system that convinced him and his teammates to buy into it: 'We talked about space in a practical way. When we were defending, the gaps between us had to be very short. When we attacked, we spread out and used the wings. Our system was also a solution to a physical problem. Fitness has to be 100%, but how can you play for 90 minutes and remain strong? If I, as left-back, run 70 metres up the wing, it's not good if I immediately have to run back to my starting position. So if the left-midfield player takes my place then it shortens the distances.'[73]

---

72. Michels, R (2001). *Team-building: The Road to Success*. The Netherlands: Uitgeverij Eisma bv. 107.
73. Winner, D (2001). *Brilliant Orange – The Neurotic Genius of Dutch Football*. London: Bloomsbury.

Winner wrote that the Dutch analyse space more intently than other nations because the country has so little of it. It is a valued commodity; its use often considered and argued over by Dutch councils. Michels' team of the 1960s and early 70s incorporated not only the free mood of the era but also the Dutch appreciation of space. Like modern Feyenoord and Athletic Bilbao, they were shaped by the society around them.

Under Michels, Ajax developed the roots of their pressing style that remains today, which was 'independent from and simultaneous with the same process being enacted under Viktor Maslov at Dynamo Kyiv',[lxxv] Jonathan Wilson explained. Michels said of his version: 'When possession is lost, move up quickly and put immediate pressure on the player with the ball. Defensively this means that you quickly get the ball away from your own goal, and for the build-up it means that you create a counter-attack situation when the ball is regained.' He often stated that Totaalvoetbal was necessary, that he only employed it because of the deep defensive block of the opposition. Frequent changes in position between the lines would surprise the other team in an age when man-marking was common. Every Ajax player was able to participate in the attacking phase, as long as they selflessly felt responsible for the defensive phase, too.

In 2001, aged 72, Rinus Michels shared a lifetime of accumulated knowledge on football coaching in his book *Team-building: The Road to Success*. The opening pages feature a lovely analogy comparing the team-building process to classical music. He wrote:

In between my videotape collection of match analysis and successful games of Ajax, Barcelona and the Dutch national team stands a tape in which the approach of world-famous conductor Bernstein is described. It shows how Bernstein starts a rehearsal with a philharmonic orchestra from America. The conductor asks all members of the orchestra to play a piece from their musical arrangement. He listens with concentration, and only nods now and then. After a few minutes Bernstein analyses, using carefully chosen words, what he has heard. 'Individually you are all very accomplished, but as an orchestra you have to travel a long and difficult road. You think you have achieved the ultimate level, but perfection in an orchestra can be taken from 95 to 100 per cent.'

It is not only the task of the conductor to ensure every one of the individual musicians is able to contribute, he must also ensure that the result is harmonic.

What Michels created at Ajax was harmonic; their style bordering on artistry. They could score a goal whenever they wished, but that would be too obvious. Instead, they passed the ball, moved the opposition and created spaces. A goal would come eventually, but the passages of play beforehand contained as much beauty as the rippling of the net. It was aesthetically brilliant and the Dutch loved it. His years of team-building culminated with a 1971 European Cup triumph against Ferenc Puskás' Panathinaikos, and thanks to his foundations Ajax would win the next two European Cups without him. They were the first club side to dominate the trophy since Real Madrid in the 1950s. By then, Michels was in Barcelona with Johan Cruyff ending their 14-year wait for La Liga. In 1974, they took the Dutch to the World Cup final together. From an unspectacular beginning as a semi-pro club where Michels sold magazines on the weekend for income, the Ajax he left were befitting of their Greek god namesake: a towering warrior of great strength and stature.

Contemporary Ajax still uphold a 'Michelsian' view of how football should be played. In Dennis Bergkamp's thoughtful biography *Stillness and Speed* (written by David Winner once more), he speaks often about coaching Ajax's youth team players. The Total Football appreciation of space, distances and timing of movement become a theme within the book, as he describes how Ajax deliver those messages to youngsters. Written in 2013, Bergkamp explained: 'It is about measuring. Cruyff talks about that with the youth at Ajax now. Measuring offensively, but defensively as well. It's all about distances. I know where the gap is, I know the speed of Patrick [Vieira, a recipient of one of Bergkamp's passes]. So I know where the space will be in two or three seconds.'[74] Michels taught Cruyff to find beauty in the assist, who then taught Bergkamp, who, when I visited the club, was mentoring future generations of Ajax names still unknown.

Michels would take pride in knowing that the threads he sewed still bind

---

74. Bergkamp, D. & Winner, D (2013). *Stillness and Speed: My Story.* Great Britain: Simon & Schuster.

his club. He once declared: 'I am especially happy with the fact I have been able to help make the Dutch way of playing famous all over the world.' He would be ecstatic then to know that his style of play now defines the modern spectacle.

Cruyffianism

Convention is a mindset that can be defied. A true Amsterdammer knows this. Cruyff taught him so.[75] As a manager, his squads shared the same fluid brilliance that defined him as a player. It was 'Michelsian' in nature, but with an added focus on maintaining possession. 'There is only one ball, so you need to have it,' was his message. In his autobiography, translated into English posthumously, Cruyff explained the positional play that characterised his squads:

'It isn't the man on the ball who decides where the ball goes, but the players without the ball. Their running actions determine the next pass. That's why I go crazy when I see players standing still on the pitch. To play like that for me is out of the question. In possession, 11 men have to be in motion. Busy fine-tuning distances. It's not a question of how much you run, but where you run to. Constantly creating triangles means that the ball circulation isn't interrupted.'[76]

In training, he would stop sessions and correct the positioning of players. 'Move one metre to the right and you have a much better angle for the pass.' In his mind, he played dot-to-dot from the goalie Menzo to van Basten up front. As a player, Cruyff would organise his teammates around him. He would point at empty spaces and move them about like pawns on a chess board. He already thought about the game at a deeper level than anybody else, so when he became manager his philosophy was pre-shaped. His Ajax

---

75. Cruyff was a gift from God. Some people are blessed with ideas but shy away from them in fear of vanity. Some people are blessed with natural skills, but so rare is their talent they do not understand it. Cruyff was neither of those people. His footballing ability was so fine, so beautiful, it made him the greatest player in the world. Not only that, he understood why he was. Only he grasped how to play like Cruyff. His turn – the touch he takes deeper towards his own goal to fake a cross before swivelling back in to the danger zone – though he would say otherwise, showed a degree of prior thought. He had a solution for every problem in the game. And after he finished playing, he continued to be a celebrated visionary as a coach. Neither Maradona, Puskás, Pele, di Stefano nor any of the other greats can boast such an influence. A local hero come good; a prodigy who surpassed his enormous potential. Johan was, for many, football's greatest.
76. Cruyff, J. (2016) *My Turn: The Autobiography*. Pan Macmillan. London.

team played a 3-4-3 with three defenders, four midfielders, two out-and-out wingers and a striker. 4-4-2 had grown in popularity on the continent as a formation that stretched the pitch vertically and horizontally, so Cruyff attempted to counter it. 'If you have four men defending two strikers, you only have six against eight in the middle of the field: there's no way you can win that battle. We had to put a defender further forward.' [lxxvi] Maintaining possession was central to Cruyff's version of Total Football of the late 80s. [77]

Johan had played with other Amsterdam natives in the 70s and valued the possibilities young academy players brought. An Ajax built in his vision would prize the academy over everything. Aron Winter was promoted to replace Ronald Koeman (who controversially signed for PSV and became a pillar of their European Cup-winning team), while other graduates included goalkeeper Stanley Menzo, teenage winger Dennis Bergkamp, Richard and Robbie Witschge, John Bosman and the talented duo of Frank Rijkaard and Marco van Basten, whose careers would entwine so successfully in Milan.

For the purpose of trivia, Cruyff's Ajax also had a young Scottish 'next big thing' named Ally Dick (who presently coaches the Stirling Albion schoolboys a Scottish version of *Totaalvoetbal*). Dick told *The Herald* many years later that Cruyff's training was beyond compare to what he had encountered in Britain: 'That was the big difference between British football and Dutch football at the time, they worked much harder. Pre-season we trained morning and afternoon and played a game every single evening for a week against local opposition.' He had been the fastest player in Scotland but, as he recalled, van Basten covered him in dust. [lxxvii]

'Cruyffian' football was a necessary evolution to Michels. Whereas original variations of *Totaalvoetbal* considered elements of fitness work – lots of running, overlaps and underlaps – Cruyff's version focused on positioning; on the timing of passes and movement, on creating overloads and making the right decision of who to pass to and when. 'You play football with your head, and your legs are there to help you,' Cruyff would tell players, reinforcing how their eyes were most important; 'they should see a situation and make it beautiful.' By creating one-versus-ones all over the

---

77. It needn't be said, but contemporary Ajax remain well versed in keeping the ball. Their average possession stat for the Eredivisie for the 2015/16 season was 61.2%. At the academy, I would watch as youngsters combined passes around mannequins, their movements seamless. 'What you see, Cruyff wanted this,' a youth coach would tell me.

field and winning them (through a pass or a dribble, or by being stood in a clever position already behind the man), Cruyff believed he was throwing the opposition into chaos.

The Ajax philosophy begins with coaching one-versus-one situations nowadays, with great emphasis on developing the individual. Cruyff's work revolutionising the Barcelona academy is often praised, but at Ajax his Midas touch was also felt. At the end of the 1987 season they won the European Cup Winners' Cup final against East German champions Lokomotive Leipzig. The following year, Cruyff returned to Barcelona as manager. Before his return (Gregorian calendars in Catalonia jokingly refer to 'BC' as 'Before Cruyff') Barcelona had only won three league titles in 30 years (one came with him there as a player). They had never won the European Cup. There were low attendances, crippling debts and poisonous backbiting. In total thanks to Cruyff's ideology, the club would win four consecutive league titles and fashion the *Barçajax* school of thought.

Van Gaalianism

A good reference for 'modern' Dutch football was offered by Simon Kuper in Paris. He grew up in the Netherlands and is emotionally invested in *De Oranje*. Along with the rest of the nation, he was hurt by their poor qualification campaign under Guus Hiddink that saw minnows Iceland go to the European Championships of 2016 in their place. When asked if Ajax or PSV would ever win another European Cup, Simon answered: 'No, because there are two separate issues now. The league cannot compete economically as they have a very small TV deal, which has been the case for 20 years. It did not stop us producing really good players, though. We had bad clubs but a good national team – think Robben, van Nistelrooy, Sneijder. Now we have bad clubs and a bad national team. That's the new problem, it has never happened before.' Under Louis van Gaal in 1995 though, before football was overly dependent on money, the Dutch had good players and good teams.

Like Michels and Cruyff, van Gaal grew up on the streets of Amsterdam playing football. As a teenager, he would go to De Meer and watch from the stands as Rinus trained Johan and his Ajax team. A few years later he was signed by them, but never played for the first team. Van Gaal was an attacking midfielder and they already had the best in Cruyff. In fact, van Gaal's entire career has been measured, perhaps inspired, by the shadow of Johan Cruyff. The open 1960s are said to have been wasted on the devout Catholic van Gaal. If Cruyff epitomised the era with his long hair and chain-smoking, the clean-living LvG was his antithesis. He combined teaching with a part-time role as an apparently arrogant, self-assured footballer. He would argue with his coaches who urged him to shoot more – he preferred to pass. Upon retiring, van Gaal was made youth co-ordinator at Ajax, armed with a plan to return the club to greatness. But Amsterdam was only ever supposed to be big enough for Johan Cruyff. The two men were like scientists bickering over the most specific details of research. So blinded were they by their own worth, they often failed to see that they shared a philosophical line; an interpretation of a mutual hero: Rinus Michels.

In that he is attentive, obsessive, confident and passionate about young players, Louis van Gaal is a typical Dutch coach. Cruyff and Michels liked to create confrontation to raise the effort of their players by giving free kicks in training that were not so. Van Gaal wanted only to create harmony. Everywhere Cruyff left, van Gaal turned up. Or could it have been the other way around? Van Gaalian football dominated possession to a greater degree than the teams of Michels or Cruyff, but was more robotic according to Cruyff, less fluid, too regimented and rehearsed. Like Michels, the ball was moved in front of a deep-lying block to open up space. If one man was pressed by two players, that meant there was a numerical advantage elsewhere on the field to be exploited.

André Villas-Boas, a second-generation student of van Gaal (the apprentice of José Mourinho), explained the Dutchman's approach: 'Louis van Gaal's idea is one of continuous circulation, one side to the other, until the moment that, when you change direction, a space opens up inside and you go through it. So, he provokes the opponent with horizontal circulation of the ball, until the moment that the opponent will start to pressure out of despair.'[lxxviii]

The danger in playing that style of football is, if players are not positioned correctly to receive (on a diagonal angle) and the pass goes horizontal then they are open to a counter-attack. The reason footballers receive on a diagonal angle is so they are between both vertical and horizontal lines, in an area where the opposition defenders do not know whose job it is to mark.

Cruyff valued freedom, but van Gaal favoured discipline. 'Soccer is a team sport, and the members of the team are therefore dependent on each other. If certain players do not carry out their tasks properly on the pitch, then their colleagues will suffer,' he told Kormelink and Seeverens.[78] Because he was a teacher, van Gaal knew when to offer advice and when to stay quiet. Every detail was worked on: shooting, passing, dribbling. He spoke a lot with younger pros and had a purpose for their inclusion: 'Players who have received their education at Ajax and are now established in the first team act as guardians of the Ajax style. Players who come from outside have to make adjustments.'[79] Van Gaal laid out his plan and the players bought into it.

From a tactical perspective, LvG shared many basic principles with Cruyff. Both men believed that the possession phase should build up from the goalkeeper and that Ajax were stronger when they had the ball. But whereas Cruyff allowed his teams to have flexibility, van Gaal trained every action and counter-action. For him, the system was paramount. He never worked on Plan B in training, only ever the system. If his players perfected the system, then there would be no need for an alternative. Bergkamp said of him: 'Louis is didactic. He gives his players instructions to make the system work. And the system is sacred. All players are equal to van Gaal, big names do not exist for him, and everyone is subordinate to the team and system, his system.'

Having arrived as youth co-ordinator, van Gaal became fascinated with the talents of Seedorf, Davids and Reiziger. He demanded they be promoted to the first team at the earliest opportunity. It is therefore a small irony that when he became the first team coach, it was a Finnish boy obsessed with football, and not a local Amsterdammer, that best represented his Ajax team of the 1990s. Scouted by Ton Pronk whilst playing for MyPa in Finland, Jari Litmanen was not long out of the army. His friends all called him 'Diego' because of his long, black, South American-looking hair and his Maradona-like ability. But van Gaal was not impressed with Litmanen at first. They still had Bergkamp in the number 10 role until 1993 when he transferred to Inter Milan. Van Gaal would not play two number 10s – that was not the Ajax way – so Litmanen had to wait.

78. Kormelink, H. &, Seeverens, T (1997). *The Coaching Philosophies of Louis van Gaal and the Ajax Coaches*. The Netherlands: Reedswain Inc.
79. Ibid.

With Bergkamp gone Litmanen thrived, winning the Eredivisie in 1994; he was voted Footballer of the Year with 26 goals. Van der Sar marvelled at the Finn's dedication. He would convince him, Overmars and Davids to stay behind after training and do additional exercises, while on the coach to matches Litmanen and the lanky goalkeeper held long intellectual conversations. That level of thought was overheard and valued by the manager. LvG spoke constantly with his players and looked to give them points from his notepad; he especially valued the dedication of the Finn. An academic environment would be fostered at Ajax.

In training, van Gaal promoted communication. He encouraged his players to question him and each other constantly. It culminated in one of football's greatest triumphs, the 1995 European Cup win over AC Milan. That victory in Vienna allowed Kormelink and Seeverens to review the tactical and team-building philosophy van Gaal installed at Ajax, which embraced aspects of Michels and Cruyff and still applies to many parts of the club's modern approach:

1. He created a game model and encouraged the players to invest in it.
2. He upheld high levels of discipline in training, as well as through personal standards.
3. The formation could be adapted depending on the opponent, but the style remained constant.
4. Every player had a role within the structure to follow.
5. The structure allowed for triangular passing combinations to be played so possession could be recycled.
6. They pressed high and fast to deny the opposition success in transition.
7. They were patient and waited for the right pass to present itself.
8. He valued the intangibles of young academy footballers.

The Velvet Revolution

Their decline was slow and painfully obvious. From 1995 to 2010, Ajax won only four league titles out of a possible 15. As football became increasingly reliant on wealth, Holland's Eredivisie was overlooked by sponsors and inevitably fell behind. Had Ajax matched the wages being offered elsewhere, they might have built on 1995's Champions League success to dominate Europe for years to come. As it happened, money was elsewhere and their young stars all left. Edgar Davids, Patrick Kluivert and Michael Reiziger (AC Milan), Clarence Seedorf (Sampdoria), Finidi George (Betis), Kanu (Inter), Marc Overmars (Arsenal), van der Sar (Juventus) and finally Litmanen, Frank and Ronald de Boer (Barcelona) had gone by the millennium – most of them on free transfers.

More damaging for Ajax was not the loss of personnel, but the loss of identity. Their style is paramount – Positional Play essential. Therefore, if any player leaves the club – as has happened in every single transfer window in recent years – a replacement is able to step up from the academy and take his place. They sell their players organically, to open spaces for new young academy graduates to fill. It is part of a succession plan. 'We want to have the best young team in Europe,' van der Sar later said as marketing director. For every position, Ajax have a list of youngsters ready to step up. Every player is graded and coaches judge when it's time for him to progress. Once an established first team player is sold, a portion of the revenue is reinvested into the academy, thus feeding a cycle for further talent to emerge. The shirt has a greater value than the man wearing it due to the waterfall approach they have of teaching every academy team the same system. Under Martin Jol, an outsider from The Hague appointed in 2009, that wasn't the case. Ajax became reliant on the individual wearing the shirt rather than the team and as a consequence lost their identity.

They stopped being organic and instead became a generic club performing at their financial capability. Cruyff grew frustrated. 'This is the worst Ajax I have ever seen,' he said from his Catalan home. [80] Disgusted at the number of people working for the club who simply did not understand Ajax, he organised a revolution. Frank de Boer would be head coach, Wim Jonk youth co-ordinator, Dennis Bergkamp the link between the academy and first team, Bryan Roy youth coach and, replacing the men in suits behind the scenes, van der Sar would become marketing director with Marc Overmars working as technical director. Jaap Stam and Ronald de Boer retuned later to coach at the academy. 'Cruyff will remain involved with the implementation of his football vision within the club,' came a club statement in April 2012. [lxxix]

---

80. Born, E (2014). *Blizzard: The Velvet Revolution*. 14th ed. Sunderland: Blizzard Media Ltd.

Cruyff's first lieutenant in the revolution, Dennis Bergkamp, described the Ajax academy he had entered at the time: 'If you look at the coaches we have now, they're so different. They all have their badges, and are all very sympathetic and know exactly how to play football and what kind of exercise you should do, and for how many minutes, and the distances between the goals, and where the cones should be. Maybe that's the problem. We never had that sort of attention [as youngsters], so we were more self-taught.' [81]

Bergkamp felt that the Ajax players in the first team had no solution when things went wrong; they would look to the bench and ask *what do we do now?* In the Cruyff-managed days, players had the personality to overcome difficulty. They were given more freedom by coaches at the academy but, being self-taught, were able to think for themselves. Van Gaal in a sense benefited from that with his '95 squad. In the civil war to come, Bergkamp would be one of Cruyff's closest allies. A result of Cruyff's revolution was that youngsters would learn specific details from retired players about resilience and technique. No longer would Ajax produce factory players who were all the same. His Ajax footballers would have a brain.

Cruyff knew Ajax could not compete with the financial oligarchs of modern football, so there was no use trying to beat them at their own game. As he once quipped, 'I've never seen a bag of money score a goal.' It was his belief that Ajax had to approach things differently, in a way that suited them rather than their capitalist rivals. He decided that the academy should stop producing robots, but players with personality like himself. Ajax especially should stop buying outsiders without an Ajax heart, something van Gaal would probably have agreed with, too. Unlike typical political revolutions, this one worked. Ajax under Frank de Boer won four consecutive league titles from 2010/11 to 2013/14, reforming their identity in the process and creating a trickle down in the academy ages that aligned with the first team.

But behind every silver lining lurks a cloud. The Dutch have a word for things falling apart when they are going well: *plankenkoorts*. At one time it applied to the theatre, when the actor forgot his lines in front of an audience. Now it's mostly used when discussing football. PSV won the two league titles as the revolution began to weaken. Wim Jonk's relationship

---

81. Bergkamp, D. & Winner, D (2013). *Stillness and Speed: My Story*. Great Britain: Simon & Schuster.

with the technical and management team broke down completely, so he left. Cruyff reacted angrily and stepped away from his advisory position. It looked like his coup would be dismantled. But following his sad passing in 2016, a city-wide realisation of his genius swept Amsterdam and many at Ajax decided, quite wilfully, to uphold his teachings. 'The way we work here is all part of Johan's legacy,' youth coach Peter van der Veen confirmed during my visit. Cruyff's spirit of innovation will forever remain interlaced with Ajax of Amsterdam.

TWENTY

THE COCA-COLA RECIPE

The Ajax methodology is a result of three evolutions: Rinus Michels' creative freedom, Johan Cruyff's positional play and Louis van Gaal's possession focus. Such is the process of evolution, successful traits are retained and everything else is gradually developed or replaced. Here, Ajax have invented and reinvented their development model over the course of 40 years to maintain an identity as pioneers. So successful are they at developing youngsters, they're the benchmark other clubs aspire to (and often plagiarise). This, fittingly, as the epicentre of football thought, was the perfect end to my journey.

Damien Hertog lets out a stunned laugh at the question. We're on a golf course beside De Toekomst, Ajax's world-famous academy facility, continuing our football chat. Hertog is here to watch Feyenoord's U17 team who, in a couple of hours, will overcome Ajax's U17s. 'What was Peter's answer?' he deflects, his eyes still smiling. He means Peter van der Veen, one of Ajax's most familiar youth coaches and a very good friend of his – they played together for Excelsior Rotterdam in the 90s. [82] I tell Damien that I'm meeting Peter the next day, so he is the first to answer the question of what

---

82. Peter, like so many charecters in this book, had moved on to a new role by the time of its publication; this time working with the KNVB's U16 side.

football will look like in the future. 'The challenge for us is to be creative and to do something where we surprise the rest of the world,' he says. 'Of course, I can easily say it looks like this – that it is more compact with less space and everybody is physically stronger – but we all know it will be like that. In Holland, we have always been creative and in the future, we will be creative to find opportunities to be better than the rest.'

Feyenoord develop the cognitive functions of their youngsters to make optimal decisions. Hertog is inspired by the speed of thought of players like Andrés Iniesta and Toni Kroos. 'I love the small, intelligent, decision-making players. Not only because they are small, I like the tall ones too! You can be physically strong but the mind is always faster, so I think it will go in that direction, more players who are making decisions faster.'

The following day Ajax's Peter van der Veen answered the question from a youth development point of view, rather than pondering the spectacle in general. 'Well you see, at the top of European football they play 60 games a season. The sparks are gone and the fire dies a bit. So physically it is going to be really interesting in the future. We think here that top talents never get injured,' he says, citing old boys Luis Suárez and Ibrahimović as examples. 'He must have a big chance to make it in the first team if he is never injured, because then he is able to develop. But it is a different step to make it to the top of the European game. Why are Messi and Ronaldo so good? Internal motivation is the answer. Ronaldo has a bike in his pool at home to stay in peak condition; players have to ask themselves, "Am I more driven than other people?" That is the most important thing. We have a few players in our academy whose drive is unbelievable. And in tactical terms? We [coaches at the academy] have to follow the game and predict what it will look like in five years.'

The Future

Peter was coaching three residential boys in a shooting exercise when I arrived. It consisted of a timed pass around a mannequin on the edge of the box and a cross in to the striker. The little number 9 must have had 20 shots on goal while I was there, from various deliveries. This is part of Cruyff's legacy; he was determined to improve the individual in isolated exercises, to ingrain technique as muscle memory through repetition. Peter was vocal throughout, encouraging the players and celebrating every goal.

De Toekomst translates as 'the future'. A bridge separates the academy and the Amsterdam ArenA, Ajax's 53,000-seater stadium. [83] The structure can be viewed as a metaphor for the journey from youth to senior football; *You're only a bridge away from your dreams*. Manchester City's Abu Dhabi group liked that idea and chose to build their state-of-the-art youth facilities next to a bridge near the Etihad. On matchdays, both City and Ajax walk their youngsters over their bridges to work as ball boys. They believe hearing the roar of the fans helps youngsters understand the significance of the club.

While Peter worked, I explored the complex. Like at Feyenoord, a narrow stream runs through De Toekomst, giving a feel of tranquillity. As I strolled about, a coachful of blond Scandinavian boys and fathers arrived for a fixture, all of whom appeared to be Ajax fans. They spotted club captain Davy Klaassen walking into reception and hounded him for selfies (paternal love forgotten, it was the fathers at the front of the queue).

The U18 squad was training on a far pitch. By the time I crossed a collection of small bridges to reach them, they had finished up, eager to get in out of the cold. Jaap Stam collared a young defender at the end of the practice and spent ten minutes demonstrating defensive movement to him. The teen stood in the drizzly rain nodding, both of them seemingly oblivious to the fact they were the only two people left on the field. Hertog had described the bits of knowledge that world-class footballers acquire as invaluable. Stam crouched, gesticulated, moved about and pointed, explaining to the boy how to shepherd great attackers, like he had done with Ronaldo and Vieri. A few months later he entered management with Reading FC.

Inspired by the environment, back indoors, I asked Peter van der Veen what it is like to work alongside names like Stam and Bergkamp. He recognised the knowledge they share with players but also points to the expertise they pass on to other coaches. 'I watched Stam do a defending masterclass and afterwards I was able to ask him what he meant by some of the points.' On top of that, Ajax care for their coaches and value education: 'We get the opportunity to gain a Masters in Coaching degree at the Johan Cruyff Institute. Everybody

---

83. Powerful, huge tapestries depicting significant moments in Johan Cruyff's career hung on every quarter of the stadium's exterior. Sad Amsterdammers stood beneath them silently gazing. No pictures taken, just mourning.

here has been put through university and every Friday we go to the institute and attend lectures on things like media training.' As a consequence, Ajax retain knowledge amongst their body of staff, with De Toekomst acting as football's 'Agora' – a place of philosophic discussion.

The Ajax Secret

Some places have an aura; a feeling of substance and credibility. De Toekomst is one such place. The standards attached to Ajax's academy are amongst the highest in the world. Van Basten, Rijkaard, Seedorf, Bergkamp. The names fall on every pitch, sprinkling players in motivation. They take confidence in knowing they belong to the club of Holland's finest. For the coaches here, there is a pressure to uphold the traditions and history of the club. 'I have fun,' said Peter van der Veen. 'I see beautiful things of a morning with the skills they are doing. When you work here you come into situations all over the world that wouldn't occur if you didn't work for this name. I was at St George's Park three years ago when we played a tournament there. The other coaches watching were asked to pick something tactical up out of the game and I had to present and explain it to them.' Such is the regard Ajax is held in by peers (and rivals) that their every method is studied and dissected.

Over many years that philosophy of development has evolved. For Ajax, like at Feyenoord, an innate drive naturally born within each individual is essential, scouted and harnessed, allowing coaches to create an infectious winning environment. 'It is a mixture of everything. The most important thing is the intrinsic motivation. If a player does not have that drive, then we can't do anything. They need to have fire within themselves, but you can also create an environment in training sessions that assists it. Today in the session you saw the two boys who were scoring most – well, the winner would get a drink from me. I kept the scores and it was 12-8. In team sessions, the loser always has to do something like a sprint and the winner gets to rest and drink, you know?' Peter goes on to say that winning is not offensive, but is a crucial part of player development. By nurturing a love of competition in the youth teams they will eventually reach the first team with the sort of desire required to succeed in football. In all sports, even chess, there is a winner and a loser.

Developing players like Ajax do is a secret recipe. Yet like all brilliant ideas there is no great mystery to it. It entails preparing the youngster for first team football from his first session in the junior squad; like constellations aligning. The system here is a 1-4-3-3. Ajax include the '1' because the goalkeeper is the first attacker who builds up play. Cruyff, when working as Barcelona manager, wanted his goalkeeper to be an outfield player – that way they would field 11 footballers. The goalkeeper role has advanced to a ball-playing one which, at Ajax, has seen young keepers participating in passing exercises with outfield teammates for many years.

For Peter, the secret to creating an Ajax player begins with teaching the child how to win his one-versus-one battle. For example, the left-midfielder taking on the right-back. Then youngsters work on two v twos and three v threes in small spaces where they get plenty of touches of the ball. The principles of the 1-4-3-3 formation grow in complexity as the child gets older. Peter explains how his intermediate ages (U13–U16) develop: 'How we build up to 11-a-side with our U13s – because they do not play 11 versus 11 at this age but need to understand the tactical principles of it – is by playing with a goalkeeper and a defence to build up. At U14 we get the midfielders to work together with the last three offensive players. And then with U16s it is about the team and its movement. If you train it, then at U14 it is more about everybody, so we train with three lines. At U13 it is two lines, so there is more focus on the individual in that age group.'

With the U13s, they develop build-up play from their base positions (goalkeeper and defence) and allow the attackers to work instinctively. 'We create the session and show them what the opportunities are. Of course, we let them find out for themselves but we ask them questions, like "Why do you think you have to go there?" And you feel it in the game, everything is related. From the first team down to the youth team, everybody plays the same way with the same characteristics. That is our Coca-Cola recipe.'

But how do Ajax stay innovative when everybody wants to copy your recipe? Logical thinking, Peter says: 'We see what the very top teams may want to implement in five years and try to be the first to do that. We have to be creative and try new things. If we think it is better for us then we will try it, we do not sit still. We want to be the first, to be special. That is what we have at this club more than any other team in Holland.' And potentially the world. As Peter takes a sip of water Edwin van der Sar walks past our table with a group of clients. Dennis Bergkamp is sitting two tables across from us. I regret not bringing an autograph book.

Any examples of your innovativeness? 'Well, if you see how the left-back and the left-winger play at Bayern Munich [Alaba occupies what is known as a "half-space" ahead of the back two defenders, in a channel just wide of his centre-midfielders. Douglas Costa stays out wide and stretches the pitch horizontally], we do it at U13.' Later, I will see the Ajax right-back drive infield with the ball vertically through the 'half-space' and central position, while the right-winger stays wide and engages the defenders with his positioning. 'We know it is the new thing and we are implementing it. We see it helps and the players come into spaces that we never used to think about. The opponents think, "What's happening?" so they are under pressure. We did a seven-versus-seven practice in certain spaces with squares outlined, and the right-back and the right-winger could not be on the same vertical line. I just say to the players when I am on the bench, "Winger!" and they do it. Sometimes they do it at the right moment and they say "Oh, I have space", which is satisfying for me as a coach to see.'

Sectioning the pitch off for exercises like Peter describes is testimony to the theory that football is more chess-like than ever before. Consider the chessboard and how pawns can only take the opponent diagonally; players are thinking about their lateral and longitudinal position more. Football has taken aspects of the *Totaalvoetbal* system of Michels, that appreciation of space manipulation, and developed it further into a quicker, more transitional sport. In Adam Wells' book *Football & Chess: Tactics, Strategy, Beauty,* he writes how the fundamental simplicity of both sports, because of the freedom given to make decisions by players, also makes them so paradoxically complex: 'Every movement or action affects everything else around it. One badly positioned piece or player can be ruinous.' [84] The best chess player in the world, Magnus Carlsen from Norway, is an Ajax fan who in the past has discussed football tactics with Ajax's centre-back, Joel Veltman. It is Dutch culture to analyse and consider problems before offering an intellectual solution.

---

84. Wells, A (2007). *Football & Chess: Tactics, Strategy, Beauty.* Devon: Hardinge Simpole. 7.

I Am Sterdam

Because the level of talent development in Holland is so high, wealthier clubs in Europe pick off the best players in the country at an increasingly younger age. But, in true Amsterdam spirit, there are no problems, only solutions. Ajax sought to work around this issue and decided to hone in on the emotional bonds that can be forged with younger players. Whereas Feyenoord have the buddy system with players, Ajax have mentorships. Peter explains: 'I work as a mentor for ten players. I try to give more attention to them than the other players in the team. There are three players in the U16 squad, two in the U15s, three in the U14s and two in the U13s. Every Friday we do a video analysis with our ten players and I will prepare clips. I then go to their schools and to their homes, just to create a bond with them, to push their development more than they would have at any other club. They get more attention, and every coach has got ten kids. We have been doing this for two or three years now.'

Ajax felt they had to develop stronger bonds with the children to convince them that De Toekomst was the best place for them to be. They visit the children at home, go into their rooms and play console games with them. The kids will show the coach their hobbies at home, subconsciously associating that Ajax coach with familiar home life (and a loving environment). Nobody ever fully leaves a loving home – it always remains close to their heart – so by forming a bond with the children under their mentorship, the Ajax coaches create a family atmosphere at the academy.

After lunch, a crowd of locals entered the mini stadium to watch the battle between Ajax's and Feyenoord's U17s. The coaches of both teams embraced like old brothers – they all know each other and meet regularly to discuss methods to improve Dutch football. Not qualifying for the 2016 European Championships accelerated dialogue, and the big clubs decided that, in order to improve the quality of talent development, they should play competitively more often. Now, this fixture between Ajax and Feyenoord will be played three times a season, as will fixtures against PSV and Twente.

'Talent develops talent, and the best young players need to be challenged,' Hertog had explained the previous day. 'We have a benefit in Holland that we are a small country with a lot of players; it's only a two-hour drive from one end to the other so you can always play. Competition is crucial and we discuss a lot with other teams how to improve our competition. Instead of playing in a league with 16 teams like we did last year, we have two divisions now with eight teams in each league. Our youth squads now play Ajax and PSV a lot,' Hertog said.

The match that afternoon was a demonstration of determined, passionate harrying from Feyenoord and dynamic quick passing from Ajax. Feyenoord's best player was a left-sided midfielder with hair like Ruud Gullit. He was fast, skilful and direct. I looked for his name on the programme: Tahith Chong, it read. Even the Ajax fans in the stands applauded him for his performance. Ajax's right-back was unable to stretch play vertically like he would normally do because of Chong's speed on the counter. The mini-Gullit provided four assists. Three months later he was signed by Manchester United. Equally as impressive for Ajax was their right-winger, who ensured that flank was a skill-school spectacle of attacking quality. Upon scoring, the Ajax winger waved at his father on the sideline: Patrick Kluivert. Justin Kluivert was the captain of the team and one of Ajax's best prospects. Two old men in flat caps in front of me nodded their approval, their message unspoken yet understood: Holland have an exciting future with players like these.

GLOSSARY

There are terms that appear throughout the course of this book that may not be familiar to all readers (but probably will be for many). For the purpose of flow, please refer to them here.

U8 (for example) – under-eights youth team. This goes up to U21.

Overload – a numerical advantage in one part of the pitch. For example, having three players in the left of the midfield area. The idea is often to draw in the opposition before switching play into space.

Underload – the reverse of the above; being outnumbered.

Deep – close to one's own goal.

High – or higher; near the opponent's goal.

Phase – a particular moment in the match. There are attacking and defending phases.

Transition – the moment in between phases. A transition to attack happens upon intercepting or tackling to win the ball back. A transition to defence happens once the ball has been won by the opponent.

Line/s – the horizontal line within a formation, such as a back or midfield four. Players try to find space 'between the lines' and are encouraged to 'break the lines'.

Wide – the length of a line horizontally.

Long – the length of a unit of players vertically.

Block – a collection of players in multiple lines. For example, a 'low block' is a deep collection of squad lines.

3-4-3 (or similar) – refers to ten outfield players in a formation.

Blind side – behind an opponent's press or line, where a player cannot be seen; '*To make a blind-side run.*' Defensively, a player can keep an opponent on his blind side to prevent him being passed to.

Superiority – to have a numerical advantage in a certain area of the pitch.

Press – to close down the space around either the ball or an opponent.

ACKNOWLEDGEMENTS

Without the time and assistance of so many people, *The European Game* would not be. First of all, I'm eternally grateful to Gareth Flitcroft, one of the most thoughtful men in football, for his support from the book's conception to completion. To Pete Burns at Arena Sports, thank you for taking a chance on me. I'm indebted to both of my proofreaders, Lee Baines, a fine teacher, and Will Veevers, my good friend. Sean Rainey, your graphics are absolutely fantastic. To the staff and pupils at Pontville School – particularly my Atlético lads – thank you for your belief; to you I say that regardless of life's challenges, if you aspire and persevere, you will ultimately succeed. And for inspiring and convincing a 25-year-old novice that such a task was achievable, I will always be thankful to my wonderful partner Hannah Hurlow.

Domestically: Liverpool FC academy, Sam McGuire. Sylvia, Paul, Edna, Rachel and Lily Fieldsend for their encouragement. Dr Joel Rookwood and Dr Liam O'Callaghan for channelling a passion.

France: Simon Kuper, Jonathan Johnson, Cedric Hascoet, Hugo Payet-Burin, Enzo Guagnano, Dr Emmanuel Orhant, Mehdi Joumaili.

Spain (and Catalonia and the Basque Country): Ekain Rojo, Iñaki Azkarraga, Jose Marí Amorrortu, Albert Juncà Pujol, Albert Rudé, Jordi Colome, Neil Moran, Kieran Smith.

Portugal: Tom Kundert, Sandro Carriço, Nuno Maurício, Vitór Matos, Ricardo Damas.

Italy: Filippo Galli, Luca Hodges-Ramon, Stefano Baldini, Roberto Brovarone, Pablo Longoria, Gianluca Di Marzio, Dario Vismara, George Rinaldi, Reza Ghaemi.

Austria and Hungary: Rene Maric, Christopher Vivell, George Hemingway, Ábel Lorincz, Jasper de Muijnck, Ralf Muhr, Gaby Kovacs, Dagmar Glaser, Richard Kitzbichler, Oliver Zesiger.

Germany: Chris Williams, Tobias Escher, Nicolai Kammann, Randall Hauk.

The Netherlands: Damien Hertog, Glenn van der Kraan, Peter van der Veen, Mark Lievisse Adriaanse, Steven Jones.

REFERENCES

i *The Guardian*. (2008) Fans' faux pas ensures that PSG lose even when they manage to win.

ii *QSI*. Who we are.

iii *ESPN*. (2016) The dominance of established 'superclubs' shows no sign of ending.

iv *The Guardian*. (2015) 1860 Munich, the city's other club.

v *Financial Times*. (2014) Can Paris Saint-Germain become the world's richest sports club?

vi *Le Monde*. (2016) En 1995, le PSG est passé à côté de David Trézéguet à cause d'une simple formalité.

vii *Ahram*. (2011) PSG hires Leonardo as new sporting director.

viii *Harvard Business Review*. (2014) Overcoming the Peter Principle.

ix *The Telegraph*. (2016) Crystal Palace's Yohan Cabaye: 'I left PSG for first-team football. Now I'm determined to win the FA Cup'.

x *The Guardian*. (2016) Carlo Ancelotti: the arch firefighter who always pays his way.

xi *BBC*. (2011) Qatari takeover heralds new dawn for Paris Saint-Germain.

xii *New York Times*. (2016) When Even Soccer Divides the French.

xiii *The Telegraph*. (2008) Karim Benzema keeps feet on the Lyon ground.

xiv *ESPN*. (2012) President delighted with Lyon cost-cutting.

xv *Ligue1*. (2015) Aulas: The Architect of Lyon's Success.

xvi *Building*. (2016) Grande Stade de Lyon: Stadium Franglais.

xvii *Ligue1*. (2015) Aulas: The Architect of Lyon's Success.

xviii *New York Times*. (2015) Using Only Local Talent, Athletic Bilbao Goes a Long Way.

xix *Euskalkultura*. (2013) Mariann Vaczi, anthropologist, Athletic goes against the tendencies of competition; they are the Asterix and Obelix of world soccer.

xx *Telegraph*. (2013) Catalonia and Basque Country reignite call for independent national football identities.

xxi *Inside Spanish Football*. (2014) Rubén Pardo extends contract with Real Sociedad until 2018.

xxii *Bleacher Report*. (2013) Sir Bobby Robson and His Gifts to Football.

xxiii *Sky Sports*. (2016) Eddie Jones admits his admiration for 'rugby fan' Pep Guardiola.

xxiv Marti Perarnau. (2012) Vitor Frade, el padre de la Periodización Táctica.

xxv Juan Luis Delgado-Bordonau. (Date unknown) Tactical Periodization: Mourinho's best-kept secret?

xxvi *International Business Times*. (2016) Andre Villas-Boas admits working with Jose Mourinho was the best time of his life.

xxvii *The Guardian*. (2014) Premier League clubs can learn from Portugal's profit centres.

xxviii *Mais Futebol*. (2016) Jesus, Vítor Pereira ou Mourinho: o legado de Cruijff em Portugal.

xxix *Give me Sport*. (2016) Cristiano Ronaldo hailed by Aurelio Pereira.

xxx *PortuGoal*. (2016) Portugal, united through adversity, aim to rewrite history.

xxxi *OBV*. (2014) Richard Williams: The Tenacity of a Black Father.

xxxii *La Region*. (2015) Hasta a Toshack le hubiese gustado.

xxxiii *FIFA*. (2008) Van Gaal: My football philosophy.

xxxiv *Spielverlagerung.de*. (2013) Juego de Posición under Pep Guardiola.

xxxv *FourFourTwo*. (2015) How Johan Cruyff reinvented modern football at Barcelona.

xxxvi *Mundo Deportivo*. (2013) Laureano Ruiz presenta 'El auténtico método Barça'.

xxxvii *The Telegraph*. (2016) An emotional return for Pep Guardiola?

xxxviii *Marca*. (2016) Barcelona's new model leaving La Masia behind.

xxxix *Independent*. (2010) The day Eric Cantona failed to bring down the French banks.

xl *The Set Pieces*. (2016) Transfer Window Myth-Busting.

xli *Juventus.com*. (2016) Mission.

xlii *The Guardian*. (2016) The secret behind Sevilla's success? Meet Monchi, the transfer wizard.

xliii *Italian Football Daily*. (2014) 'We fell in love with Vidal while Scouting Giuseppe Rossi'.

xliv *Independent*. (2015) Massimiliano Allegri interview: Juventus coach confident in his methods.

xlv *Corriere dello Sport*. (2016) Milan con 11 italiani giovani il sogno di Berlusconi.

xlvi *La Gazzetta Dello Sport*. (2016) Milan, casa Donnarumma: due giganti, le lasagne e un sogno rossonero.

xlvii *BBC*. (2013) German football model is a league apart.

xlviii *The Guardian*. (2016) Want to understand Pep Guardiola's football? Look at Joshua Kimmich.

xlix *The Guardian*. (2016) Pep Guardiola is a radical who will perfect his ideas at Manchester City.

l *The Guardian*. (2013) How Germany went from bust to boom on the talent production line.

li *The Telegraph*. (2010) Spanish reap rewards for 10-year investment in youth football.

lii *The Telegraph*. (2006) Salzburg goes wild for Wolfgang.

liii *Faz*. (2005) Zwischen mir und Abramowitsch liegen Lichtjahre.

liv *Profil*. (2015) Red-Bull-Chef Dietrich Mateschitz über Fußball und die Formel 1.

lv *LeftWingSoccer*. (2011) The Myth of Moneyball: Financial Investment in Potential Growth.

lvi *The Telegraph*. (2008) Portsmouth accept £20m Real Madrid offer for Lassana Diarra.

lvii *ESPN*. (2015) Atlético president Enrique Cerezo defends club's transfer policy.

lviii *Sapo de Sport*. (2015) Luís Filipe Vieira: 'O novo modelo é apostar nos jovens e reduzir endividamento'.

lix *Watford Observer*. (2014) The mastermind of the scouting network behind Udinese, Watford and Granada.

lx *The Guardian*. (2015) Ajax are the most prolific producers of talent as English clubs lag behind.

lxi *Consultancy.uk*. (2014) Ajax hires BCG to review its youth football academy.

lxii *Z News*. (2013) Ajax most productive academy in European football.

lxiii *Equaliser*. (2010) Crucibles and Coffee Houses.

lxiv *Squawka*. (2015) Guardiola: David Alaba is Bayern's 'God'.

lxv *De Telegraaf*. (2014) Johan Cruijff looft Dirk Kuyt.

lxvi *Goal*. (2013) Guardiola: Lahm cleverest I've coached.

lxvii *The Guardian*. (2016) David Alaba: 'I didn't know I could play as a central defender'.

lxviii *Cosmopublic*. (2014) Orbán builds Occupation Memorial – and his 'personal' Football Stadium.

lxix *Yahoo*. (2015) Hungary's Orban seeks football glory days again.

lxx *FourFourTwo*. (2014) Year Zero: How Germany restructured itself – and why it couldn't work elsewhere.

lxxi *ECA*. (2014) ECA visits FC Schalke 04 Youth Academy.

lxxii *The Daily Mail*. (2009) On almost shunning football for fishing, graft over glory, respect for Rafa.

lxxiii *The Mirror*. (2007) Van Persie reveals the bizarre moment he realised Dennis Bergkamp's genius.

lxxiv *World Soccer*. (2011) Interview with Arrigo Sacchi.

lxxv *The Guardian*. (2013) The great European Cup teams: Ajax 1971–73.

lxxvi *FourFourTwo*. (2015) How Johan Cruyff reinvented modern football at Barcelona.

lxxvii *The Herald*. (2001) Scot who played with Ajax greats.

lxxviii *The Telegraph*. (2011) Chelsea manager Andre Villas-Boas's footballing philosophy.

lxxix *Independent*. (2012) Johan Cruyff set to implement 'technical revolution' at Ajax.